YOUTH QUESTIONS

Series Editors: PHILIP COHEN and ANGELA McROBBIE

This series sets out to question the ways in which youth has traditionally been defined by social scientists and policy-makers, by the caring professions and the mass media, as well as in 'common-sense' ideology. It explores some of the new directions in research and practice which are beginning to challenge existing patterns of knowledge and provision. Each book examines a particular aspect of the youth question in depth. All of them seek to connect their concerns to the major political and intellectual debates that are now taking place about the present crisis and future shape of our society. The series will be of interest to those who deal professionally with young people, especially those concerned with the development of socialist, feminist and anti-racist perspectives. But it is also aimed at students and general readers who want a lively and accessible introduction to some of the most awkward but important issues of our time.

Published

Forthcoming

Desmond Bell
ACTS OF UNION
Youth Culture and Sectarianism in Northern Ireland

Philip Cohen and Graham Murdock (eds)
THE MAKING OF THE YOUTH QUESTION

Robert G. Hollands
THE LONG TRANSITION
Class, Culture and Youth Training

Angela McRobbie
FEMINISM AND YOUTH CULTURE

Kevin Robins and Frank Webster
COMPUTERS, INDUSTRY AND EDUCATION

Multi-Racist Britain

Edited by
Philip Cohen and Harwant S. Bains

MACMILLAN
EDUCATION

1988

First published 1988

Published by
MACMILLAN EDUCATION LTD
Houndmills, Basingstoke, Hampshire RG21 2XS
and London
Companies and representatives
throughout the world

Typeset by Wessex Typesetters
(Division of The Eastern Press Ltd)
Frome, Somerset

Printed in Hong Kong

British Library Cataloguing in Publication Data
Multi-racist Britain—(Youth questions).
1. Racism—Great Britain
I. Cohen, Philip   II. Bains, Harwant S.
III. Series
305.8′00941   DA125.A1
ISBN 0–333–33249–0 (hardcover)
ISBN 0–333–33250–4 (paperback)

Contents

Introduction: Perspectives on the Present

Philip Cohen

At a first, cursory glance many people may be inclined to misread the title of this book. We are, after all, supposed to be living in a multi-racial society, to send our children to multi-ethnic schools, where they do multi-cultural studies and learn to respect, appreciate or at least tolerate each other's diversity. That is the official story-line, and it is one in which we would all like to believe. Current realities are very different, however, and so is our title.

The realities include: a black community struggling to achieve social justice and a better deal for its children at a time when Britain is increasingly divided into two nations; a police force actively eroding civil liberties which the law is supposed to uphold; a popular press which daily relays racist images and chauvinistic sentiments whilst orchestrating moral panics against 'ideological bias' in schools; mass youth unemployment, in which ethnic minorities are over-represented, disguised by government training schemes in which they are discriminated against. We could go on, but the point of this book is not to rehearse, yet again, the terms of the present conjuncture but to take a step back and to look at what has helped to shape these several 'front lines'. We have, therefore, set out to examine in turn the problematics, the policies and the practices which have played a crucial role in constructing issues of 'race' within education and the youth service, amongst socialists, trade unionists and feminists, and most importantly of all, amongst young people themselves.

In this way we have tried to set a series of contemporary debates – absolute or relative autonomy of 'race', multi-cultural

1

or anti-racist education, separatist or pluralist youth provision, moral or physical force against racism – within some kind of wider context of understanding.

In Part I we consider some of the theoretical maps which have informed policies and practices, particularly in the field of education. Taking issue with the dominant view of race, ethnicity and class, I argue for a multi-dimensional model of ideology which allows racist discourse to 'speak' at a number of different levels of meaning, whilst also pinpointing its different modes and codes as these are articulated within the wider framework of society. I use this model to look at some of the key historical and cultural processes which have shaped Britain into a multi-racist society. By locating the peculiarities of English racism in the internal contradictions of its social structure, I try to draw a map in which it is possible to make cross-references between the Jewish, Irish and Black experiences in Britain with greater precision. Finally, by looking at popular culture as a complex site of negotiation between gender and generation, ethnicity and class, I suggest a possible focus for work with young people. I argue that unless the inner workings of the racist imagination are properly understood, there is little chance of challenging its 'common sense'. As long as educational initiatives remain locked in a 'civilising mission' which is itself founded on a hidden curriculum of middle-class racism, they will continue to be resisted by the majority of working-class pupils.

In Part II we move on to consider the territories which make up the front lines of current struggles. All the contributors in this section were associated with the group at the Centre for Contemporary Cultural Studies in Birmingham who produced *The Empire Strikes Back*. This book broke new ground in locating the politics of 'race relations' within the crisis of hegemony in post-war Britain. Here, that analysis is developed and deepened.

Paul Gilroy and Errol Lawrence begin by looking at the dynamics of race, youth and class in the light of recent political events. They examine the interpretations of the 1981 riots offered by political commentators and the mass media, and argue that these representations indicate the centrality of 'race' to the strategy of crisis management adopted under Thatcherism. The authors go on to contrast the reading of the riots constructed from above with the very different systems of meaning mobilised by the youth themselves. They trace the development of black youth cultures and their impact both on the politics of the black community and on white youth. The chapter concludes by looking at the attempts of the Anti-Nazi League and Rock Against Racism to establish a popular cultural politics centred on 'two-tone music' as a means of drawing white and black youth into a common struggle against racism. In assessing the successes and failures of these campaigns the authors address some searching questions to the British Left and Labour movement regarding both its past policies and present practices. Their conclusions are particularly timely in the light of the renewed debate about the role of black sections in the Labour Party.

In the following chapter, John Solomos surveys the effect of both Labour and Conservative government policies in marginalising black youth in the educational system and the labour market. He traces the shift from assimilation to integration to 'multiculturalism' as the basis of State intervention; he shows how the cumulative impact of these policies has been to reinforce institutional processes of discrimination and cement popular definitions of black youth as 'the problem'. A test case, examined in detail here, is the development of special training provision for black school-leavers and unemployed youth. Far from improving their situation, these schemes confirm their marginal position in the secondary labour market while simultaneously deflecting attention away from the real issues of race and class. With the development of two-year Youth Training Schemes (YTS) and the proposals to abolish the right to social security benefit of those under eighteen years old, Solomos's analysis of the restructuring of youth transitions and its role in reproducing inequalities of race and class has been powerfully confirmed. It remains to be seen whether the processes of marginalisation he describes produce new sites and forms of struggle amongst black and white youth.

In Part Three we move on to the terrain of anti-racist practice itself, and focus on strategic initiatives in the recent past which have set out to transform the position of youth in the community. We begin with a chapter by Pratibha Parmar, entitled 'Gender, Race and Power', where she looks at the struggle to articulate new policies within the youth service in response to the emergent demands of black women and girls. Herself a pioneer in the field of anti-sexist and anti-racist youth work, she draws here on her experience of working with Asian girls to examine some of the structural and personal forms of discrimination which they face. She argues that the gender blindness of the race relations industry has been complemented by the race blindness of feminist critiques. Both construct a pathological model of the Asian family which renders women and girls invisible or deviant. Her chapter concludes by stressing the need for new initiatives to support the struggles through which Asian girls themselves are fighting back.

The next two chapters focus on the Southall Youth Movement (SYM). This has been hailed as the most successful example of autonomous black youth organisation to have emerged in the last ten years, but its development has been fraught with internal conflicts and controversy. Two contrasting points of view are presented here as a contribution to a continuing debate which has wide implications for the future. Tuku Mukherjee begins with a sympathetic portrait in which he locates the evolution of the SYM within his own personal experiences of white liberal racism, first as a teacher and then as a youth worker in Southall. He describes how these experiences led him on a journey back to his own community and to support for the emergence of a new and more militant political leadership amongst the youth. His account emphasises the continuities between the experience of first and second generation, elders and youth.

For Harwant Bains, however, it is the terms and conditions of that continuity which need to be considered. His account looks at the way differences of caste and family ideology are articulated to processes of class and race discrimination, and how this occurs concretely in the position of Asian pupils within state schools. The result, he argues, far from radicalising the majority of young people in Southall, has tended to align them with conservative forces in the community, identified with Sikh nationalism and business interests. The more economically marginal their situation, the more politically conservative Southall youth have become. The SYM, he argues, has only reinforced this tendency. Moreover, its rhetoric of militancy hides its growing dependency on state funding and its lack of popular support. Finally, in describing the growth of a SYM reform movement in which he played a part, the author shows how the 'community' has been constructed as a new site of state intervention in a way that introduces further divisions amongst the people of Southall, a process which he believes can and must be resisted.

The debate then moves on to the terrain of the state itself. Ansel Wong, in interview here with Bob Catterall, draws on his own experiences of working in the Youth Service to discuss the limits and conditions of developing forms of provision which are genuinely responsive to the needs of black youth:

In many quarters large sections of white working-class youth have been written off as irredeemably racist and sexist, as much bad news for socialists as they are for feminists or the black community. In the final contribution to this book, playwright Trevor Griffiths, himself an ex-teacher, takes issue with that view. Interviewed here by a fellow dramatist, Karim Alrawi (whose own play, *Migrations*, made a powerful statement about the black experience of racism) and Harwant S. Bains, Griffiths defends his decision to write about a rock band made up of skinheads, some of whom have pronounced racialist views. Produced at the height of the National Front/Skinhead alliance, the play was criticised in some quarters for 'giving the devil all the best tunes', whilst others thought it was an important and so far unique attempt to engage dramatically with the cultural perspectives of that 'other England' for whom racism retains a popular appeal. Griffiths makes a strong case for an open cultural politics within which the issue of popular racism is not only dramatised but also related to wider issues such as youth unemployment.

Karim Alrawi and Harwant Bains remain skeptical of this approach, dependent as it is on appeals to reason and morality, and argue that the only way to deal with the hard core of young racists is through physical force deployed as part of the black community's response to the failure of the police to provide adequate protection for its members. In this way the book concludes by returning to the central issue of anti-racist education raised in Part I.

The texts assembled here have all been written from positions of direct engagement with the raw materials of racism. It will not, however, escape the reader that contributors do not all speak with one voice! There are those who privilege the black experience as paradigmatic for understanding racism, and others who argue for a model which takes account of the Jewish and Irish experiences as providing equally strategic perspectives for understanding the specific character of the Anglo-Saxon variant. There are those who privilege the autonomous struggles of youth and community and those who insist on the central importance of state education in both combating racist ideologies and advancing the aspirations of ethnic minorities. These differences in priority reflect and emphasise actual contradictions which the anti-racist movement has to face, and face honestly, if it is to advance. It is in that belief that we have sought to represent a spectrum of opinion rather than a single, monolithic point of view. That too is in keeping with our title. For if there is no single, universal form of racism there is also no global anti-racist strategy which can be read off from it. The institutions and practices which make up multi-racist Britain have to be tackled at many different levels and through a variety of means. If this book can contribute towards a more differentiated and more co-ordinated approach to anti-racist work with young people it will have more than served its purpose.

The chapters which were commissioned for Parts II and III of this book were written several years ago. The delay in publication is entirely my responsibility and I would like to take this opportunity of apologizing to the other contributors for this situation. It is a testimony to the strength of their work, as well as to the entrenched character of multi-racist Britain, that these contributions have retained their topicality in terms of the issues which they raise, and that many of the analyses have been confirmed by subsequent events.

I would like to thank the contributors for their forbearance, and Steven Kennedy of Macmillan for persevering with the book. Also Harwant Bains for putting together the material in Part III; Angela McRobbie for her timely intervention and support; and Jean McNeil for standing by me when the going got rough.

Part I

Problematics

1

The Perversions of Inheritance: Studies in the Making of Multi-Racist Britain

Philip Cohen

Duck Soup – from assimilation to multi-culturalism

There is a scene in the Marx Brothers' film *Duck Soup* which never fails to leave a profound impression on the audience. The President of 'Freedonia', played by Groucho, is pursuing Harpo who is a foreign agent, and has succeeded in infiltrating the palace disguised as his double. Harpo is cornered beside an open doorway and is about to be captured when he decides to turn his disguise into a new means of escape. He goes into a routine in which he literally plays Groucho's double, copying every gesture in perfect synchrony to create the optical illusion that the doorway is a mirror, and the President is merely watching his own reflection in it. The silent dance continues for some time with Groucho trying to catch his double out of step, by freezing or making an unpredictable movement, until finally the illusion is shattered when each changes places with the other by stepping through the mirror, at which point the chase begins once more.

This little scene can no doubt be interpreted on many different levels but I want to suggest that one way in which it can be read is as a parable about race and ethnicity in the modern world, and one which has particular relevance to some of the issues I want to discuss in this chapter.[1]

The film is set in a world dominated by crackpot nationalism, and tiny, warring states run by demagogic dictators with delusions of grandeur, who can't afford the price of a second-hand tank.

9

The film effectively satirises patriotism, or at least some of its more jingoistic forms. The figure of Hitler is always in the wings. But the film also contains another, rather more coded, set of references, which are even more central to our theme.

The Marx Brothers belonged to that generation of Jewish immigrants who were caught up and absorbed into the mainstream of American society in a period when the tide of anti-Semitism was reaching its height in Europe. To many, at the time, it must have seemed as if the choice between America and Europe was not just between the New World and the Old, but between life and death itself. Nevertheless, the American way of life was to pose a threat to Jewish identity in a way that the Holocaust did not.

Groucho's famous dictum – that he would never want to belong to a club which would have him as a member – is a direct comment on, and refusal of, assimilation. Its paradox is the paradox of Jewish refugees invited to throw their historical individuality into the melting pot of Middle America, as the price of survival. But that is only one side of the story.

In Germany itself many Jews who had succeeded against the odds in establishing themselves in leading positions in economic, cultural and political life thought at first that they would be safe from persecution. The illusion did not last long; their very success made them special targets of racial resentment and envy. Other Jews, less assimilated, and less well-off, tried to escape by other means, by changing their name or appearance, by going underground or trying to pass as 'Aryans'. It was precisely these 'hidden Jews' who were the pretext for so many pre-emptive strikes and who were singled out for the most brutal treatment when caught. For in anti-Semitic eyes, if it is bad enough to be a Jew, it is an even greater crime to pretend not to be one.[2]

To deny one's origins, to make false claims about one's ancestry, to assume the identity of one's oppressor, is often portrayed as a supreme act of bad faith. It would be more accurate to say that racism drives some people to existential suicide. Yet it is often overlooked that to change ethnicity in order to 'save one's skin' is also implicitly to subvert the logic of racial ascription; it is to snap the imaginary links binding origins and destiny, to refuse to be defined as a biological entity, to affirm the right to become other than what one is considered to be in and by racist discourses. Yet these

remain so many individual acts, fugitive manoeuvres, which exploit
the openness of ethnicity to cultural negotiation while confirming
the fixations of racist codes. That is why, in fully racist regimes,
groups who attempt to evade persecution through strategies of
assimilation or dissimulation are treated in such an ambivalent
way. Their actions are secretly welcomed as bearing witness to the
desirability of belonging to the 'master race', but they are publicly
punished for crossing the racial divide, or blurring its boundaries,
and daring to step into their masters' shoes.[3]

Helping young people to establish an 'ethnic identity' which is
not implicated in such alienating ploys has become a major concern
amongst certain sections of the anti-racist movement at the present
time. But the formation of identity is not such a simple and
straightforward process as some of the advocates of cultural
affirmation would have us believe.

The Marx Brothers' routine can perhaps help shed some light
on these complexities. The suspense we feel in watching the mirror
sequence comes from the fact that we are waiting for Harpo to
make a false move, a 'mistake' which will reveal his true identity
as an impostor and interloper. In becoming Groucho's double he
ceases to be Other for the other, by becoming other than what he
is. But he is not playing a waiting game in an existentialist café.
He has simply found a clever way of ceasing to be regarded as an
alien, by literally embodying the American dream – to become
the President. Yet this rests on an optical illusion which is fragile
precisely because it has to be sustained through human interaction.
For the mirage of absolute identification is no sooner offered than
it is snatched away by the incitement of an irreducible difference,
an otherness not of the subject's own making but one produced
by the powers that be. In this mimetic dance Groucho is the one
who leads, and who retains the initiative in trying to wrong-foot
his 'reflection', whilst Harpo desperately tries to keep in step. A
perfect transcription of the assimilation game.

One of its more subtle cruelties is that in reality there is
absolutely no illusion. We, the spectators, are already in the know.
And we all know who the real President is, who is the true all-
American boy and who is not. It is as if we are concealed behind
a one-way mirror, watching the action, waiting for the suspect to
give himself away, and meanwhile enjoying the contortions as he
tries to conform his self-image to what he imagines the other wants

him to be. It is this *hidden power of surveillance* which enables the state to institutionalise racism as a silent routine of common-sense classification and control, turning open doorways into plate glass walls as soon as the 'wrong face' attempts to walk through, restricting entry at each and every point of access as a matter of bureaucratic course. Racism does not become unconscious because it is institutionalised. Rather it becomes institutionalised because it operates unconsciously 'behind the backs' of the subjects which it positions within these impersonal structures of power.[4]

Harpo's crime, and it perhaps links the Jewish experience of immigration with other histories, is to have arrested an official policy of exclusion by a subterfuge, by learning the correct 'passwords' to gain access to the corridors of power while still travelling without papers or other recognised credentials. Passports to success are by definition not issued, and those that are link origins (place and date of birth, nationality, distinguishing features) to quite other destinations. Racism forges all our identities by such means.

Under these circumstances many immigrants have had little choice but to 'ape' the manners of the 'masters', albeit often exaggerated in such a way as to leave no doubt as to who is closer to the animal concerned. Uncle Tom sends up Uncle Sam, as the pretender to the throne exposes the pretensions of power in this and many other Marx Brothers' movies.

Against all this fancy footwork of 'me and my shadow', the anti-racist movement increasingly argues for an open acknowledgement of difference and domination. In educational terms this position is not likely to be arrived at in a single or a sudden move; compromise solutions abound. Their paradigm is indicated here when Groucho and Harpo sidle past each other to take the other's place on the 'wrong' side of the imaginary mirror, without for a moment breaking the spell of their double act. The mirror phase of 'race relations' is here pushed to its limit, its mechanisms of mystification unveiled, while its phenomenology remains intact. Opening the door from the imaginary (and imitation) does not lead to any real contact, which could only mean renewed conflict. Instead a certain structure of make-believe in racial harmony is being conserved. What, in fact, is modelled in the move is the shift from the assimilation game to multiculturalism.

The multicultural illusion is that dominant and subordinate

can somehow swap places and learn how the other half lives, whilst leaving the structures of power intact. As if power relations could be magically suspended through the direct exchange of experience, and ideology dissolve into the thin air of face to face communication.[5]

Nevertheless, such a move points beyond itself towards the possibility of a more material engagement with the problem, to forms of positive action in which ethnic minorities lay claim to a separate but equal place in the body politic. It is when this point is reached that the apparatus of masquerade is most likely to give way to open violence. Groucho comes out in his true colours, arrests Harpo for impersonating a police officer, and beats him up just to prove 'who's who'. When the more silent routines of state racism are interrupted, heads get broken on the street, for then too resistance finds its voice. This, of course, is not in the script, either of Hollywood movies or race relations. Yet it is exactly when a space is opened up for it that the difficulties of constructing a properly anti-racist theory and practice begin to emerge.[6]

More than skin deep – anti-Semitism and colour prejudice

The first and largest problem is how to devise a framework, whether analytic or organisational, which both distinguishes clearly between different types of racism and recognises the historical individuality of those subjected to them. For example, the *Duck Soup* sequence may be an interesting parable about the problematics of Jewish identity, but what has it to say about the Black experience of racism? Surely there can be little common ground for the very reason that it is not possible for Black people to 'save their skins' by changing colour. It is sometimes argued that colour prejudice is the paradigmatic form of racist ideology, and that anti-Jewish or anti-Irish sentiment is either a special case or else has more to do with religion than race.

The politics of exceptionalism can be challenged on a number of counts. There are some clear parallels between the experience of the Jewish and Asian, or the Irish and Afro-Caribbean communities in terms of class trajectories and response to racism. But there are equally significant differences. A slightly stronger argument is that skin colour has never protected Black people from policies of assimilation. The plantation slaves who were brought over to England in the eighteenth and nineteenth century and introduced into 'Society' first as domestic servants and then as simulations of the English Gentleman, were only the first in a long line to be turned into 'coconuts': black on the outside, white within. Skin colour as a visible symbol of difference can render these splits *more* invisible than in the case of the 'hidden Jew'.[7]

And that is the point. Visibility is socially constructed and can change over time. For example, Irish immigrants were singled out by the authorities as a specially 'dangerous' class in the 1850s, whereas in the 1950s their arrival was officially hardly noticed, despite the fact that they outnumbered immigrants from the New Commonwealth. This does not mean that prejudice against them had disappeared in the meantime. Paddy jokes had never been more popular than in the 1950s. Landladies hung up their 'No Irish, No Coloureds, No Dogs' signs without a second thought – all were equally undesirable. Indeed Blacks and Irish were *interchangeable* as animal categories of racial abuse.[8] It is not so much through its exploitation of visible difference as in what it renders invisible or comparable that racist ideology produces its effects.

Finally, in pursuit of natural symbolisms of inferiority, racist discourses have never confined themselves just to body images. Names and modes of address, states of mind and living conditions, clothes and customs, every kind of social behaviour and cultural practice have been pressed into service to signify this or that racial essence. In selecting these materials, racist codes behave opportunistically according to an economy of means; they choose those signs which do the most ideological work in linking – and naturalising – difference and domination within a certain set of historical conditions of representation. To make the issues of in/visibility depend on physical appearance is to bracket out precisely these historical realities.[9]

There is no better example of this than the enterprise of some white writers painting their faces black in order to experience 'at first hand' the everyday realities of colour prejudice. Rather than getting inside the skin of black people the project tacitly underwrites the popular common-sense view that the effects of racism are only skin deep, something which can be rubbed off as easily as greasepaint. Instead of establishing the ineradicable basis of colour prejudice, these make-believe Blacks – who are not even genuine 'coconuts' – produce a brand of socially committed voyeurism which is perfectly adapted to the needs of the white liberal conscience.[10]

Under these conditions the search for authenticity is inevitably an act of bad faith; born of an impossible desire – to possess a Black identity – it ends by substituting itself for the Black voice. Such projective identifications with the oppressed, with their intricate compounds of guilt and envy, arc the very stuff of contemporary race relations. In this case they are literally acted out. Yet the effect is no less cosmetic, covering the real determinants of the Black experience with a practice of representation which seeks to disguise its own implication in a certain history of racism. For what these writers are actually doing – albeit unconsciously – is following in the footsteps of the vaudeville actors who used to 'black up' to lend the racist characterisation of Black people the necessary 'credibility' for White audiences – something which, it was felt, and not without reason, Black actors could not be trusted to do.

I am not, of course, suggesting that anti-Semitism and colour prejudice are the same thing. They are distinctive modalities of racism, with their own histories and structures of meaning. Yet in some circumstances they may mobilise similar strategies. For example, an anti-Semite may say to a Jew, 'That's funny, you don't look Jewish', adding under his or her breath, 'though with a name like Cohen you can't help being one'. But the same person might say to an Afro-Caribbean, 'you don't act Black' with the *sotto voce* aside 'even though your skin is'. These are two parallel ways of getting under the other's skin whilst disavowing any racist intent. In addressing each subject generically a different descriptor is invoked – here the name, there the body. This has nothing to do with any absolute or *inherent* differences between Jewish and Black people! Jews have bodies scarred by history; equally the descendants of African slaves bear that history in their names. The fact that the reference in one instance is to genealogy (the Jewish name), and in the other to phenotype (the black skin) has to do with an internal differentiation in the discursive strategies of popular racism; anti-Semitism draws much of its normative imagery from *religious* discourse (and hence biblical genealogy) whereas colour prejudice derives most of its rationale from *scientific* racism (and hence the languages of physical anthropology). The points at which these two discourses converge and borrow from one another is itself partly determined by their respective histories. We will look at each briefly in turn before considering how and where the iconographies of the Jew and the Black are made to combine their 'special effects'.

The figure of the wandering Jew, or the Jew as eternal migrant is one of the most powerful and enduring myths of anti-Semitism. It is linked to three refrains; first, the Jew as a kind of *vampire*, committing ritual murder on Christian children and consuming their blood during the Passover ceremony, in an obscene reversal of the Holy Communion rites; second, the Jew as a *hidden hand* secretly manipulating the course of history to visit death and destruction on the body politic; and third, the Jew as a *parasite* preying on the host society. These images, separately or together, have been used to justify all manner of attacks on Jewish communities in Europe. They relay a single message: the Jews are a pariah race, and the Diaspora is their just and eternal punishment for their original and chronically repeated crime of Christ's murder. The flight of Jewish populations from persecution is thus further used against them, as confirming their 'nomadic' status.[11]

Throughout the Middle Ages these images remained anchored within the discourse of biblical genealogy and its theodicy of Christian privilege. But, of course, the advent of capitalism posed a threat to the hegemony of the Church and threatened to destabilise many of its traditional forms. In this transitional period, anti-Judaism increasingly gave way to anti-Semitism proper; the three key images of the Jew were rearticulated within a new constellation of meaning; they now served as metaphors of the very economic changes which were disrupting the social and moral order on which the Church had come to depend.

History, as Karl Marx never tired of reminding us, proceeds by its bad side, and in the discourse of anti-Semitism, the Jew is made to represent the bad side of capitalism – that is, its dynamic and destructive side. Merchant capital, in particular, plays a key role in this process; by dissolving traditional feudal bonds and feeding off older modes it paves the way for the advent of properly capitalist relations of production. It is no surprise, then, to find the Jew associated with merchant capital, in its purely negative effect. The wandering Jew thus becomes a symbol of its free circulation, whose invisible and parasitic influence on traditional economic life find their perfect metaphor in the image of the vampire and the hidden hand.[12] So whatever their actual occupations, Jews are made to practice a form of *generic* usury, either transgressing the moral economy of capital's 'just price' or undermining that of labour. Equally, courtesy of anti-Semitism, Christianity is able to dissociate itself from the worst excesses of capitalism, whilst continuing to preach a work ethic which makes the profit motive a special calling, aspired to by all, but realised only by a chosen few.

With the age of reason and enlightenment this thematic is transposed into the cultural sphere. Now the wandering Jew comes to represent the free circulation of *ideas*, whose bad side consists in threatening traditional orthodoxies of religious and political belief. The Jew becomes a symbol of the alienation and rootlessness of the modern intellectual, and this in turn is used to justify his continued exclusion from the professions and from academic life. Moreover, as soon as wandering Jews begin to put down roots they become even more dangerous; like the creepers which have been named after them they are supposed to spread into every nook and cranny of England's 'green and pleasant land'. Now it is the very tenaciousness of Jewish culture which is the threat. Finally, in the global conspiracy theories of modern anti-Semitism, the economic and ideological dimensions are brought together: the Jew is portrayed as a cut-throat capitalist bleeding the workers to death *and* as a free-thinking socialist poisoning the hearts and minds of Young England.[13]

The Anglo-Saxon version of anti-Semitism has some distinctive features not found elsewhere (see later section entitled 'Between people, nation and the Norman yoke'), but it would be wrong to think that the strategies of exclusion and assimilation to which the Jewish community in Britain has been subjected are unique to them; neither do they necessarily constitute the paradigm for the treatment of other ethnic minorities or immigrants. Racist equations do not always 'add up' in such a straightforward way! For example, given the association of merchant capital with both Jews and the African slave trade, you might expect that anti-Semites would subsequently have had little difficulty in making capital – or 'common sense' out of the putative link. But the English plantocracy in the West Indies pre-empted such a move.

They were the first to elaborate a racial anthropology which justified the slave trade – and the Black diaspora – in terms of a special theory of Anglo-Saxon supremacy, and one which had no need for wandering Jews, as either scapegoats or accomplices.

This theory set out to replace, or transform, medieval imagery of racial difference with a new model adapted to the specific conditions of the colonial enterprise under capitalism.[14] The traditional genealogies had increasing difficulty in coping with the proliferation of human 'species' now reported. The notion of polygenesis made more sense, but went against the mainstream of theological reasoning which remained based on the myth of a single line of descent from Adam. Deviant instances (Jews, Blacks, etc.) had hitherto been easily accommodated within the pantheon of 'monstrous races' produced by the interaction between classical teratology and medieval demonology. But the old *mappae mundi* which located these races at the margins of the known world were in the process of being redrawn. It was no longer possible to place Black people alongside centaurs and cenocephali as 'fabulous creatures' to be simply wondered at. How could the 'burnt faces' (Aethiops) be still regarded as the bearers of God's curse, to be shunned at all costs, now that their enslavement brought them forcibly into daily contact with Europeans? What was needed was a new mythology of racial origins and destinies which conserved the monstrous status of Black people, but put it to work in justifying the central place which their exploitation now assumed in the growth of capitalism. In other words, their marginality had now to be constructed in *structural* rather than *topographic* terms. The problem was complicated by the fact that racial hierarchies could no longer be modelled so easily on the feudal social order, since its fixed, separate and unequal estates of man was rapidly giving way to a more dynamic and fluid system of class relations.[15]

The task assigned to the racial anthropologies of the eighteenth and nineteenth centuries was to find a single, comprehensive principle of explanation which would underpin a rational theodicy of racial privilege and anchor structural inequality within an organic image of the body politic. At the heart of this enterprise lay the conversion of the colonial 'adventure story' into a 'civilising mission'. The 'white man's burden' was not only to exemplify the innate superiority of a master race, but also to demonstrate to 'lesser breeds without the law' the advantage to be gained from becoming loyal, dependent subjects. However, the project was not without its contradictions.

If freedom under capitalism was the right to buy and sell labour *but not souls*, could slaves, whose labour was no longer their private property, have souls at all? Moreover, if they were to be 'manumitted' as serfs had been, then clearly what they were being freed for, was wage labour under capital. In other words, if Black people were to be equipped with souls to be saved, if they were to be recognised as human individuals, then their potential kinship with an indigenous working class had to be admitted. If, on the other hand, they were regarded as a wholly alien species, denied human status and rendered unregenerate, then neither slavery nor Empire could be justified as 'a civilising mission' even though it might prove easier to maintain a great evolutionary divide between Blacks in the colonies and 'wage slaves' at home.[16]

The answer to this conundrum was to ground the 'special' position of Blacks *in nature* in such a way as to leave the 'free born Englishman', *of whatever class*, as the sole legatee of *culture*. It was, therefore, through the discourses of the natural sciences that Anglo-Saxon racism first discovered that the 'civilised faculties' were an exclusively English inheritance and 'primitive mentalities' were the lot of all those less fortunately endowed.

It was left to phrenology and comparative anatomy to found a new materialistic science of monsters, where protomorphs, mongoliforms and erythiotes replaced the classical blemmyae, cenocephali, *et al.* Still located at the margins of Reason, these new monstrous races had the great advantage of being precisely constructed to make them available to its 'scientific' procedures of dissection and analysis; no longer visualised at its borderlands, they became the pivotal point of the new maps of European knowledge which were setting out to colonise the world.[17]

Black people were made to occupy a 'privileged' place as an object of this natural science of man. Here they were characterised in one of two ways: as akin to apes or wild men, driven by more or less brutal instincts which had to be subjugated by special disciplinary techniques, or as noble savages or children of nature, who were uncorrupted by civilisation and should as far as possible be preserved in their separate and primitive estate. It would be wrong to think that the idealised picture of the noble savage offered a more enlightened, or less racist, view than the derogatory image of the ape: these were two sides of the same coin; in both cases Black people were made to lack the faculties of reason, morality and law. These remained the sole prerogative of the English as a master race. What we have is a racist double standard; applied initially to discriminate between African (ape) and American Indian (noble savage) it was subsequently developed as a means of drawing the line between bad and good natives, providing a rationale for that peculiar mixture of repression and paternalism which became the distinguishing mark of British colonial rule. More recently a similar, if rather more sophisticated, set of distinctions has been applied to Black communities in Britain itself.

Whenever Black people threatened to break out of these positions and enter history on their own terms a further strategy of misrepresentation was mobilised to keep them in their place. This consisted in fixing them as a 'missing link' *between* the animal and human estates so that they constituted an anomalous category, and as such, an even more strategic site of 'normalising' intervention. The Black would then be no longer just the Other, but a *hybrid being*, the offspring of a dangerous liaison, in cognitive as well as physico-moral terms, between Nature and Culture which went against the laws of civilised society. The myths of origin which were elaborated around this monster took many forms. In early racial anthropology, Blacks were held to be the descendants of matings between Europeans and apes; conversely, apes themselves were the product of illicit intercourse between Whites and Blacks.[18] Subsequently, the 'special' position of black people in the evolutionary scheme has been subjected to more precise measurements – in the size and shape of their skulls, or through the indices of 'intelligence'.

But whatever the permutations, the effect is to bring together the two sides of the racist double standard to compose a single contradictory figure – half wild, half civilised, an animal with a human soul. In this way the Black image is conformed to the requirements of the civilising mission and its peculiar double bind. Blacks are simultaneously encouraged to evolve into 'coconuts', in other words *good* hybrids, whilst also being exploited as a support for popular fantasies about racial miscegenation and monstrous birth rates. Running like a hidden thread through all these perverse constructions is the Great Fear of the Bourgeoisie, that somehow the Black community will forge the missing link with the White working classes, and that this 'unnatural union' will propagate 'revolution' and overturn the organic basis of the social order.[19]

From this brief discussion we can see that the ideologies of anti-Semitism and colour prejudice have quite distinct patterns of historical development. Yet, in a structural sense, they could be regarded as complementary. Jews are made to symbolise the destructive economic forces unleashed by capitalism – the Jew stands for 'dirty money'; Blacks are made to represent the libidinal forces which the civilising mission represses in those whom it educated to carry the 'white man's burden' – Blacks stand for 'dirty sex'. Clearly, there are many contexts in which the two images interact to reinforce each other! This can result in some bizarre constructions. We have seen how medieval anti-Semitism was fixated on the theme of ritual murder – Jews being supposed to drink the blood of their victims or bake it into unleavened bread. At one level, we noted, this is a simple reversal of the symbolism of the Christian Host. But it also draws on a popular peasant custom proscribed by the Catholic Church – young men secretly obtaining the menstrual blood of virgin girls and baking it into special biscuits which were then consumed as an aphrodisiac. Through this chain of associations the Jewish Passover is not only travestied, but further transformed into a *Black Mass*, confirming the link between Black people and the Devil, and investing the Jewish Antichrist with their legendary powers of sexuality.

The opportunism of the racist imagination, the plasticity of its constructions as well as its constant search for ever more economic ways of saying the same thing, is well illustrated by a modern variant on the ritual slaughter theme mobilised in a recent campaign organised by the National Front. The ostensible aim was to denounce the ritual practices of kosher and halal butchers as an extreme form of cruelty to animals. Rabbis and mullahs were shown holding long knives dripping with blood and gloating over the death throes of the animals they had just slaughtered. The message is simple enough – the presence of such monsters should not be tolerated in a nation of animal lovers. In this way, the Jewish and Black communities are once again made partners in a diabolical crime, one which can be absolved only by their elimination from society.

The points at which the discourses of anti-Semitism and colour prejudice intersect are neither arbitrary nor governed by any purely formal compatibility. The principles of their articulation are inscribed in and by the wider social framework within which they both operate. A good example of this is the links which English race thinking has forged between the Jewish and Black diasporas. We suggested that in the eighteenth century, Jews could not be made the guiding hand behind the African slave trade, because the English plantocracy claimed that role quite openly and proudly themselves. It was not until the 1880s, with the advent of an enlarged Jewish presence, that the Jewish name could be 'blackened', in another way, by associating it with a *white slave trade*. One of the main complaints of Victorian anti-Semitism was that Jews were kidnapping young Christian girls and selling them into prostitution in the brothels of various 'heathen' countries. The precise location was always a matter of speculation – the Middle East, Latin America, and so on, but this was less important than the image of the English maiden forced to satisfy the 'lusts of Babylon' to make Jewish fortunes. More recently a reverse theme has been added – the Jew as the hidden hand behind the Black immigration from the colonies. Whether as exporter of English girls or importer of Black men, the Jew is made to play his traditional role as a merchant in flesh, yet in such a way as to reinforce negative stereotypes of Black sexuality: dirty money allied to dirty sex. In this way the Jew is associated with a *black market*, and the link between the immigrant and the criminal hardens into its familiar, and all too contemporary, shape.[20]

It is perhaps important to stress that these constructs do not directly reflect the actual pattern of Jewish/Black relations in Britain. The real historical link between the positions of the two communities lies not so much in their material experiences of discrimination – which are governed by quite different political and economic conjunctures – but in their ideological construction as parasites preying on a host community – a conjoint image which did not need to wait for the enlargement of the Black presence to become effective but was already 'in place' within English race thinking at the turn of the twentieth century, (see below, section entitled 'The Codes of Breeding').

The racist imagination is certainly all too material in its sources and outcomes. But if it draws selectively on real events and processes it is not in order to 'exaggerate the facts', but to invest them with a symbolic function which works on quite another level – to lend *realism* to its story lines, to make even the most fantastic plots seem credible. This is not to say that such webs of meaning are 'all in the mind'; they have played an all-too-tangible role in promoting practices of colour prejudice within the Jewish community, and fuelling Black anti-Semitism. What I do insist on challenging is the notion that racist imagery merely reflects, albeit in a 'distorted' form, certain observable ethnic attributes.[21] That is precisely the alibi which gives racism its claims on common sense. Against this kind of rationale it is necessary to demonstrate that racist constructs have an internal structure which cannot be deduced from, or reduced to, the empirical characteristics of the populations against which they are directed.

The anti-Semite no more defines the Jew than the Jew creates the anti-Semite. The historical individuality of black people is no more defined by skin colour than it is by the forms of prejudice which have been focused upon it. To talk about 'the Jewish question', the colour question, and so on is precisely to conflate these different levels of reality. But if we want to grasp the complex dialectical interaction between the history of racism in its many forms and the history of the ethnic groups who have been variously subjected to attack we would be well advised to stop thinking that race is just another term for ethnicity or that one can be substituted for the other at all innocently.

Race, ethnicity and class

At first sight it looks easy enough to distinguish between these three terms. Race is the object of racist discourse and has no meaning outside it; it is an ideological construct, not an empirical social category; as such it signifies a set of imaginary properties of inheritance which fix and legitimate real positions of social domination or subordination in terms of genealogies of generic difference.[22]

The notion of ethnicity, in contrast, lacks any connotation of innate characteristic whether of superiority or inferiority. It is a myth of origins which does not imply a congenital destiny; unlike race, it refers to a real process of historical individuation – namely the linguistic and cultural practices through which a sense of collective identity or 'roots' is produced and transmitted from generation to generation, *and is changed in the process*.[23] But that change is inseparable from class struggle. Social classes are collective historical agents defined by their antagonistic places in the social division of labour, quite independently of individual consciousness. Yet these class places are reproduced through a set of positions which cannot be reduced to immediate relations of production, but involve the sexual and generational division of labour in society as a whole. It is *these* dimensions of class reproduction which may well become articulated through ethnicity and race.[24]

The relations between these three terms are, therefore, often very complex. Let us take the couple race and ethnicity first. Ethnicity, we noted, does not necessarily connote race; it may just as easily function as a mode of class consciousness. Race, however, always implies a reference to ethnicity. Indeed the discourse of racism either completely subsumes ethnicity, reducing linguistic or cultural identity to a biological substrate or else naturalises this identity within a fixed hierarchy of 'social traits'. Ethnicity may be racialised in either biological or cultural terms.

The relationship between race and ethnicity, however, remains, asymmetrical. Why, then, are the two terms used almost interchangeably in current parlance e.g. multiracial/multi-ethnic education. This is not just laziness; it points to a confusion which has serious consequences. For where ethnicity is conflated with race, it tends to be reified into a set of essential defining traits – Jewishness, Irishness, Blackness, for example – so that they cease to be part of a concrete historical process and become instead the abstract expression of an eternal trans-historical identity.[25] While such notions of 'inherent ethnicity' may be successfully mobilised in anti-racist work (for example, in giving images of 'Blackness' a positive rather than a negative charge) this is only achieved by appealing to deterministic beliefs about self and society which ultimately rest on biological arguments. Moreover, it is precisely in this reified form that ethnicity has been exploited to define, and even further marginalise that 'other England' which is neither Anglo-Saxon not middle-class, effectively reducing its presence to that of an exotic silhouette.

Ethnicism can take many forms. In its militant tendency it leads to the inflation of ethnic credentials which, in the context of positive action in the labour market, can sometimes fuel internal rivalries between ethnic minority communities. Its liberal variant, as we have seen, produces a socially committed voyeurism amongst those who lack such credentials. In either case, images of ethnicity tend to be fetishised as natural symbols of resistance in a way which robs them of their actual contexts of meaning.

The racist appropriation of ethnicity cannot be countered by simply reversing its procedures and ethnicising race. Moreover, to argue that racism is an inherent aspect of European society, or an innate disposition of certain groups within it, is not only to ignore other cases (for example, the role of racism in the rise of Japanese Fascism), but also to fail to see that even in its most entrenched and institutionalised forms within, say, Britain, it is continually changing, being challenged, interrupted and reconstructed. To deny racism its history is to surrender to a kind of fatalism. To confront white people with their responsibility for colour prejudice, whilst simultaneously defining them as congenitally incapable of doing anything about it, is one of the more unproductive double binds which currently flourishes in certain of the more 'race-bound' approaches to anti-racist education.

But perhaps the most pernicious confusion is that between racism and ethnocentrism. It is being used both to suggest that Black separatism is intrinsically racist *and* that there is nothing racist about a 'British' way of life in which little or nothing of Black culture is officially recognised. Of course, ethnicity, by definition, involves certain exclusive repertoires of meaning. How else would a sense of historical individuality be expressed? Every language and culture, *in so far as it is able*, privileges its own practices, using them to define its own origins and defend its own boundaries. Every form of ethnicity *if it has the means*, is ethnocentric. The key word is *if*.

How, then, does a particular version of ethnocentrism come to be established as a norm for the whole of society? Clearly this is where we have to consider the function of class. Antonio Gramsci coined the term 'hegemony' to describe the process of structural and cultural negotiation whereby one class comes to exert moral leadership over the rest of society, so that its own ideology comes to be generally regarded as 'common sense'. This is a strategy for winning the active consent of the majority of the population to policies and practices which keep them in their subordinate place, by making alternative ideas 'unthinkable', while remaining within the framework of representative democracy, and without recourse to overt coercion. Understandably, Gramsci accorded education and the mass media a primary role in organising class hegemony. Ethnic hegemony involves a similar though distinct set of strategies whereby a particular power élite lays claim to represent an ethnic majority in such a way as to impose their own norms of language and culture on the rest of society as ideals or models to which all should aspire.[26]

In many cases class and ethnic hegemony are combined and work through each other to render both processes invisible. For example, I referred earlier to the 'civilising mission' through which the English governing class sought to conform both the native proletariat and its colonial subjects to its own highly racist models of 'culture'. In so far as this mission succeeded it worked less through the overt inculcation of 'values' or 'standards' than through a more hidden curriculum which taught the lower orders to channel their aspirations through an exclusive 'ethnicity' which reinforced – and indeed 'naturalised' – their marginality.

Strategies of ethnic hegemony are not the sole prerogative of the ruling class. Other, more localised, power élites may operate in similar ways; a labour aristocracy may organise itself through a trade union movement in such a way as to substantiate its claim to speak for all workers, in and through the very practices which discriminate against particular groups of immigrants. In this case racism will be given an economic rather than an ideological rationale; the appeal will be to defend jobs and living standards against cheap labour, rather than to protect the British way of life and moral standards against the 'barbarians at the gates'. Different racist discourses are thus mobilised according to the strategies of class and ethnic hegemony which are being promoted. What is often called institutionalised racism is nothing but the process of negotiation whereby a strategy of class *and* ethnic hegemony is co-ordinated and sustained, so that the racism of the dominant class becomes the dominant or common-sense form of racism in society as a whole. This is an arena of often intense political and ideological struggle; in the nineteenth century between aristocratic and bourgeois codes; more recently between state racism and the practices of popular prejudice.

Perhaps it still needs to be stressed that the class problematics of race and ethnicity cannot be read off from the social origins or positions of particular individuals or groups who are identified with them. For example, there have been plenty of lower-middle-class people who have adopted aristocratic notions of 'breeding' in order to voice their contempt for all those (White and Black) whom they regard as their social inferiors. They may imagine that this turns them into aristocrats, but it no more does this than it turns the code of breeding into a petty bourgeois ideology. The problematics of the code are rather to be found in its internal principles of articulation, and their function in promoting a particular version of class and ethnic hegemony. Equally there is no necessary or simple correspondence between the *distribution* of class positions, which may be skewed by patterns of racial prejudice and discrimination, and the *reproduction* of those positions in the overall social division of labour. The concentration of Jewish or Black people in certain occupations, their treatment as second-class citizens, their subjection to particular forms of harassment and abuse, is a conjunctural effect of specific relations of force. It does not constitute them for all time as a special 'people class' or even an 'underclass'. Such reifications must be resisted, not only because they merely provide a positive reading of negative stereotypes, but also because they simplify complex and contradictory realities, and falsify the historical processes which produce them.

If we are to avoid such jiggery-pokery we will need to keep the concepts of race, class and ethnicity analytically distinct whilst remaining sensitive to their interconnection, at the level of social reality. It then becomes possible to ask a whole series of important questions. Which version of ethnicity is mobilised in which myth of class origin? Which 'racial' characteristics are attributed to which social classes? How do particular kinds of class racism enter into the construction of specific images of ethnicity, and how are particular class fractions racialised in the process?

Such questions have become central to current debates on 'race' in Britain.[27] On one side are the increasingly vociferous champions of a 'silent' ethnic majority, who are busy reinforcing the cultural hegemony of a privileged élite in the name of freedom of speech, democracy and the British way of life. On the other are those who seek to transform ethnicity from a badge of marginality and minority status into a new source of cultural capital and political power. We shall look at each in turn, for it is on this ideological terrain, dominated as we will see by mythologies of the past, that the future relations of class, ethnicity and race are today being forged.

Between people, nation and the Norman yoke

Ethnic majorities and minorities are not just demographic facts. Even, and especially, when they function in this mode they are part of a political arithmetic, and serve as 'reference groups' which have a symbolic value quite independent of their numerical size.[28]

The construction of the ethnic majority in Britain has depended on the intervention of two key terms – people and nation. One of the peculiarities of the English is the way these terms have been coupled together as part of a tradition of democratic resistance to the governing class – whilst at the same time becoming actively racialised and being used to marginalise ethnic minorities within society.

Sometimes it is argued that there is a 'good' socialist tradition of national/popular ideology, stretching back as far as the Diggers and Levellers, as opposed to a nasty chauvanistic version which is the result of its appropriation by the bourgeoisie. Certainly, these terms have been struggled over, and as a result their meaning varies considerably according to the context of use. For example, the kind of ethnic populism associated with 'folk culture' has one reading in the context of industrial ballads and quite another in the 'Merrie England' of Rudyard Kipling and Lord Kitchener. But equally Little Englander nationalism even at its most jingoistic is quite different from Sir Oswald Mosley's Fascist vision of a 'reborn island race'. Similarly the image of the freeborn Englishman takes on one set of connotations when it is used by E. P. Thompson in defence of civil liberties, and quite another when it is invoked by Enoch Powell in his infamous 'rivers of blood' speech.[29]

It is tempting, then, to condemn one side of the equation, whilst asserting the positive value of associating the life of the nation with the will of the people where this takes a 'radical' turn.

Unfortunately, there is the somewhat uncomfortable fact that a whole tradition of English socialism has rooted itself in national/popular ideology, only to become actively implicated in the promotion of racist and imperialist ideas.[30]

However, this does not give us licence to go to the other extreme and ignore the very real differences which do exist between these instances; E. P. Thompson is not to be lumped in the same reactionary category as Enoch Powell! Instead, we have to confront a more complex and contradictory reality, where a popular nationalism constructed as a means of achieving class hegemony enters into negotiation with a popular racism which develops as a means of resisting it. At the centre of these negotiations is a struggle between rival articulations of ethnicity. As we will see, this is a struggle which has played an important role in the rise of Thatcherism, but there is nothing new about it. It is as old as the 'Norman yoke'.[31]

In the 1640s, at the height of the Puritan revolution, a great debate took place on whether the Jews should be readmitted into England. On one side were the radical sects who were all in favour, and on the other an anti-Semitic faction headed by a merchant, William Prynne. The importance of this debate was that it served to crystallise the images and boundaries of a new body politic whose name continues to reverberate in contemporary race relations – the Commonwealth. The Great Debate took place against the background of a popular uprising against feudal privileges which were enshrined in the power of a Catholic monarchy and a Norman landowning class. Puritan propaganda turned the aristocracy's own code of inheritance against them to assert the innate entitlement conferred by Anglo-Saxon origins and blood to overthrow the 'Norman yoke', here associated with the Royalist cause. The cornerstone of this edifice was an image of the freeborn Englishman, invoked as a link between a popular legacy of ancient liberties presumed to have existed before the Norman Conquest, and a birthright of popular freedoms based on private property and the law. The freeborn Englishman articulated nation and people into a Commonwealth.

But was he conceived in terms of ethnicity or race? The answer very much depended on the positions adopted towards the 'Jewish question'. In the Parliament of the Saints, the Diggers, Fifth

Monarchists and other radical sects supported readmittance because, in their eyes, the historical legacy of Judaism lent biblical legitimacy to their own sense of political destiny. As the original 'chosen people', the Jewish presence was to confirm the Puritans' own divine calling to lead the nation out of bondage and into a promised land. Some of the Saints went as far as to claim that the Anglo-Saxons were one of the lost tribes of Israel; others wanted to model Parliament on the Jewish Sanhedrin and bring in Mosaic Law. Jewish culture was to be exploited to provide the freeborn Englishman with an additional set of ethnic credentials whilst Jewish people themselves were to be assimilated and lose their separate identity.

The anti-admittance faction took a different line. They emphasised that the Civil War was a war of bloods, and tried to link popular feeling against the aristocracy with anti-Semitism by suggesting that the Jewish community had only flourished because of Norman protection and no 'true-born Anglo-Saxon king' would have let them in. Judaism is presented as an ally of Rome, the secret agent of a Papist conspiracy to overthrow the Commonwealth. The English, in contrast, are portrayed as a chosen people, by virtue not only of their true adherence to the Christian faith, but also in terms of their racial ancestry. Race is used as a genealogical principle linking nation and people in such a way as to exclude anyone who is not Anglo-Saxon born and bred from its privileged patrimony of freedom.

Pro- and anti-Semitic positions corresponded to different class articulations. The Diggers spoke on behalf of the poor and dispossessed: William Prynne spoke for an emergent bourgeoisie, whose notion of the promised land was decidedly more materialistic and included colonies abroad. Cromwell decided to have the best of both worlds, and adopted the Jews symbolically, in order to 'convert' his army into 'children of Israel' embarked on a holy mission – to conquer Ireland!

We can see here how different readings of nation/people might support opposed positions, but might also function as complementary terms within the same discourse. Finally, and most dangerously, they may be conflated in a single, contradictory assertion of a racialised ethnicity within the idioms of popular nationalism. This is what happened in the Victorian period, when the myth of the Norman yoke was rediscovered and used to extend the franchise of the freeborn Englishman to include an emergent working class.

From the early 1800s onwards, plebian language and culture

ceased to be valued and patronised by the gentry as part of the national heritage. Instead, and especially in its urbanised forms, it came to be seen as a mortal danger to the moral and political order. The task then was to reconstruct proletarian ethnicity, in a form which would neutralise its threat, by subsuming it within the discourse of Anglo-Saxon racism. Thus considerable effort went into discovering beneath the rude exterior of the urban masses the 'heart of gold' of the English peasant. The artisan and labourer were metaphorically dressed up as yeomen in overalls and given a walk-on part in the cast of 'Merrie England'. Once they were equipped with this ancient Anglo-Saxon pedigree, the Victorian proletariat might be safely admitted to the lower ranks of civilised society.[32]

To evoke the image of some once-upon-a-time golden age of civil liberties was, however, to play with fire. It resonated all too strongly with forms of resistance to the dark satanic mills of industrial capitalism. And in practice, the task of constructing a popular nationalism which would hitch the Norman yoke to the imperial bandwagon proved more difficult than at first seemed likely. Yet the resistance did not come so much from the residual influence of Chartism, but from a racialised form of ethnicity produced within working-class culture itself. As we will see, this both supported spontaneous local upsurges of hostility against Irish, and later Jewish, immigrants *and* prevented their political exploitation, or development, into any larger, more organised movement.

Why did the nationalism of Empire promoted from above, and popular racism emerging from below fail to create a new, mass political force? One reason, clearly, is that popular Toryism and Labourism provided adequate platforms from which to promote the values of 'little Englandism'. There was no need for a third force in British politics to make the connection between nation and race in other than class terms. That equation was not only common sense, it was integral to the discourse of the body politic. Yet another, less discussed reason was the contradictory modes through which that discourse addressed the working class, the divided response which it provoked. Mobilised within a strategy of *ethnic* hegemony, the discourse positions the people positively as members of a superior island race, and invites them to despise and distance themselves from all those 'others' who lack such credentials. But within the perspectives of *class* hegemony, the people are an entirely negative presence, their culture regarded as a symptom of racial degeneracy, and a threat to the national heritage. The People are thus at once the 'salt of the earth' and the 'backbone of the nation' but also a 'race apart' and 'the enemy within'.

These two positions were most clearly articulated in the Great Debate on the State of the Nation, which took place between Liberal and Social Imperialists at the turn of the century. The debate served to cement the link between the 'condition of the people' and the 'future of the race'. It was part of a wider hegemonic strategy to re-form working class culture into a separate and subordinate component of the British way of Life.[33] The effect of the two positions was, however, to blur the impact of the imperialist message on the masses. Why, after all, should 'the people' identify with the class racism of the English aristocracy, epitomised in Lord Milner's famous remark (on seeing some soldiers bathing in a river) that 'he never knew the working classes had such white skins'. But equally, why should they recognise their interests in the eugenic concerns of the 'liberal' bourgeoisie, whose campaigns for moral hygiene were so blatantly directed against their way of life?

Nevertheless, these conflicting interpellations left their mark on the cultural forms through which the working class negotiated its own separate and subordinate practices of prejudice and discrimination; in particular they helped to produce a 'rough' and a 'respectable' form of racism. In the first instance there developed a set of practices of ethnicity through which the working class asserted a sense of positive pride in being a 'race apart'. These were bound up with rules and rituals of territoriality, which staked out magical forms of ownership and control over key sites of proletarian combination outside the labour process itself. These rough and ready rituals were largely enacted through street cultures, and by young men putting their aggression to work in defining and defending 'their' areas, against real or imaginary attack.[34] Parallel to this there emerged a rather different practice of moral community, centred on protocols of public propriety. These rules of 'common decency', engendered by hardship, included respect for privacy as well as mutual aid; they enabled working-class people to assert a sense of pride in being the 'backbone of the nation' standing against the corrupting influence of the wider capitalist environment. Women and elders were the principal guardians and bearers of this form.[35]

This dual structure tended to polarise working-class attitudes around positions of gender and generation, as well as to mark the great 'moral divide' between rough and respectable. For example, from the standpoint of territoriality, the police (and other civilising missionaries) were ranked alongside rival gangs as the main enemy of masculinity's pride of place. But from the perspective of public propriety, it was these young males and their gangs who were undermining the kinships of class and bringing its solidarities into disrepute. At the same time, both structures combined to demarcate a distinctively proletarian public realm. In a sense, street battles between rival gangs were only a more overt and violent expression of the kind of local feelings which were elsewhere more decorously, though no less competitively, organised in displays of municipal socialist pride. Territoriality and public propriety worked together to produce a framework of intensely insular loyalties, a sectional class consciousness based on a 'nationalism of the neighbourhood' and popular sovereignties of place.[36]

There are three, linked, features of this structure, which are pertinent to considering its role as relay or resister of racism. First, it is centred on a quasi-biological construct of community, where destinies are fixed to origins, and the 'consanguinity' of labour power is anchored to strategic images of kith and kin. When people speak of being 'born and bred' an Eastender, or having coal 'in their bones', they are talking about an apprenticeship to this kind of inheritence. Second, this patrimony constructs places of origin as sites of special, quasi-magical forms of ownership and control. You become an 'Eastender' by demonstrating that the 'East End' belongs to you. Third, the assertion of this kind of proprietorial pride involves strategies of social closure which define all those who are held to lack such credentials as 'outsiders' and a potential threat. In this way and through the medium of what has been called the 'social imaginary', a distinctive body politic is constructed, one which allows working-class groups to exercise certain forms of local jurisdiction over and against each other and to invent themselves as a local 'ruling class' without either adopting bourgeois values or challenging their hegemony.[37]

It is easy to see how this structure can animate a whole host of local and regional rivalries; Hoxton Rules Hackney OK, or Liverpool shows Wolverhampton the way to go home when it comes to football or socialism. Working-class humour has always revolved around jokes told by Geordies and Scousers about the public improprieties committeed by Scousers and Geordies. In so far as ethnic minorities are assimilated within these forms of representation, they will be attacked because they are Geordies or Cockneys, or come from a particular housing estate, not because they are Irish or Black. Ethnicism here resists racism. Yet clearly the structure may all too easily *become* racialised. The question is, under what conditions?

The answer is, I think, that the working class 'goes racist' when and wherever the presence of immigrants or ethnic minorities threatens to expose the ideological structures which it has erected to protect itself from recognising its real conditions of subordination. It is not because immigrants are actually undermining their standard of living, but because their entry into and across the local labour or housing market signifies the fact that the working class does *not*, in fact, own or control either jobs or neighbourhoods, that the immigrant presence is found intolerable. What the immigrant unconsciously comes to represent is a real power of capital and state *which is disavowed*. Racist practices fuse imaginary positions of omnipotence with real powers of social combination to support the make-believe that '*we* rule round here, not "them".' Far from it being the case that working-class racism is the result of a 'ruling-class plot to divide and rule the masses', it is a popular ideology which forges a real division between two imaginary ruling classes.[38]

In this context the dual structure of the proletarian public realm plays a decisive role in shaping the pattern of response. There is a 'rough' racism centred on territorial rivalries and the perceived threat of Jewish/Irish/Blacks invading 'our' areas. This is largely a racism of male youth. There is also a respectable racism organised around moral panics concerning 'outrages to public propriety' supposedly committed by ethnic minority communities. This is predominantly a racism of women and elders. Within and across these two forms a range of positions are possible depending on the extent to which the 'ideological protection racket' is built into real power bases within the body politic of labour, or whether it has to rely solely on the 'social imaginary'. In the first case, organised labour can afford to adopt a *laissez faire* attitude; as long as immigrants 'keep themselves to themselves', stick to their own occupational and housing areas, they are 'no problem'. They have their territories and public proprieties and we have ours. But as soon as immigrants are seen to be beginning to break out of these confines, for example, by asserting their claim to social justice, there is a shift towards a much more aggressive racism, based on a rationale of *relative deprivation*. Now the theme is 'they' are taking over 'our' jobs, 'our' schools and youth clubs, 'our' neighbourhoods, and so on, and bettering themselves at our expense. In this position the immigrant is at least held within a framework of comparison, however invidious. But where its sole relays are those of myth, ritual or fantasy, racial resentment or envy tends to become organised in a much more subtle and dangerous way. There is a process of splitting whereby certain social or ethnic characteristics belonging to some immigrant communities are culturally appropriated and reworked whilst others are violently attacked. Indeed, members of ethnic minorities may be targeted precisely because they dare to possess certain properties which English workers have been made to feel they lack. In this racism of *radical disavowal*, with its alternation between identification and annihilation, we can see the contradictory effect of assuming a position of imaginary mastery, through a discourse which also, and elsewhere, locates the indigenous working class alongside immigrants as abjectly undesirable.

The field of positions which exists within working class racism as a function of its complex negotiations with the dominant mode is thus a highly complex and differentiated one. The actual distribution of positions, and the pattern of shifts between them, will depend on local conditions of context and conjuncture.[39] But whatever the empirical profile, the main consequence is that at the level of concrete social relations this kind of racism is always internally divided, highly particularistic and resists outside manipulation or control. At the same time there is a strongly developed and popular nationalism of the neighbourhood which is ethnicist rather than racist in orientation.

In so far as there is a link forged between these two elements, it works at the level of the social imaginary. Here, though, national/popular ideology intervenes to some racist effect, through the medium of the family. Through its constant refrain of 'every Englishman's home is his castle' and 'blood is thicker than water' it makes working-class people feel that at least they are 'masters in their own homes', and that racism is just another way of looking after kith and kin. But this, too, is something of an old fashioned story.[40]

The patrimony of the free-born Englishman was from the outset something from which women and children were excluded. In the very act of being coupled together as representing the 'future of the race' they are pushed to the margins of the body politic, where they are made to signify both its and their vulnerability to outside attack. The final and recurrent usage of the Norman yoke is to link images of sexual and military conquest into a vision of England's green and pleasant land perennially threatened by foreign rape, saved only by the courage and loyalty of its yeomanry. If Britannia had to rule the waves, it was only to ensure that *she* would never never never be a slave! This was a scenario, popularised through countless exposures in the media, with which the working-class family man and his 'apprentices' could, and did, identify.

For example, if the imperial adventure story in its various manifestations was so popular with boys in Edwardian England, it was partly because it enabled them to elaborate their own version of the family romance, in which they could not only identify with the heroes' exploits in making English womanhood safe from 'bestial' foreign types, but also invent for themselves a similarly protective role in imaginary dramas nearer home, where distant cousins and legendary uncles who 'had made their fortune overseas' could sometimes by mobilised to play a supporting role.

It was these intimate patriarchal dimensions which gave popular racism its strength as a behavioural norm, yet militated against its development as a political ideology or organisational force. It was precisely because the protectionist structures thrown up by the working-class community so closely mirrored the insular formats of the imperial adventure story, because *both* were mobilised against the perceived threat of invasion by 'foreign' populations and ideas, that the two could operate independently of one another, without requiring the intervention of any racialist political party to give programmatic expression to their principles of correspondence.[41]

This paradox was proven all too clearly after the First World War, when the first serious attempt was made to realign national/popular ideology with the forces of working-class anti-Semitism. Sir Oswald Mosley attempted to stake out this ground by linking a decadent ruling class with Jewish finance capital as a double 'Norman yoke'. Fortunately, the British road to Fascism was blocked by just this ideological route, something which Mosley himself failed to appreciate. His failure is aptly symbolised in the attempt of the British Union of Fascists to march through the East End of London in 1936. Fascist street tactics were maximally calculated to affront the protocols of both public propriety and territoriality. As a result, the Battle of Cable Street united the whole population, irrespective, and sometimes despite, their political beliefs, to protect 'their' area against what was seen as 'foreign invasion'. For the politically conscious minority this may have been an act of international solidarity with the victims of Fascism in Germany and Spain, but for the majority, 'they shall not pass' meant 'we rule around here, OK!' Just how complex and contradictory the response might be was summed up in the story of one notorious local anti-Semite, who, instead of joining the blackshirts, could be seen hurling slates and abuse at them from the roof of his house, and shouting, 'They may be Yids, but they're *our* bloody Yids'. The very same structures which divided and ruled popular racism, and made it a normative element within working-class culture, also ensured, in the context of political mobilisation, that the community would be for once united and that Fascism, like Communism, would continue to be regarded as a foreign ideology – alien to the British way of life.[42]

In the post-war period, with the end of Empire and accelerated industrial decline, there have, of course, been renewed attempts to make political capital out of popular hostility to immigrants, and in particular to harness the imaginative powers of working-class racism to wider political ends. Where these initiatives have connected with the residual forms of neighbourhood nationalism, they have sometimes met with local and temporary success. In certain inner city neighbourhoods and occupational groups racist constructions could appear to offer a magical retrieval of a lost or threatened inheritance associated with the apprenticeships of growing up working class. Especially in the case of boys, for whom such patrimonies were fast disappearing along with the collapse of the traditional transition routes from school, the call to defend local sovereignties of place against the 'black invasion' often struck a responsive chord; a few made themselves starring roles in a remake of Merrie England, in which they were still fighting for the rights of free-born English men (as an oppressed and beleagured minority!) but now dressed-up as Custer, making a heroic last stand against the Indians.[43]

Such scenarios might capture the popular imagination; they might even be acted out on the streets, but they never got translated into any wider political or even electoral force. The strength of local opposition was certainly a major factor but it was not the only one; the contradictions intrinsic to working-class racism played an equally significant part. The meteoric rise and fall of Powellism underlines this point. The appeal of a rhetoric of 'ancient liberties under threat' to communities whose livelihood and traditions were under attack was obvious enough. Yet the real danger, of course, came not from the 'alien threat' but from the very forces of free enterprise capitalism which Enoch Powell represented. This parliamentary patrician was no 'people's friend', as the dockers, who initially marched in his support, soon found out to their cost.[44] The National Front (NF) moved swiftly to fill the vacuum left by the Powellite demise, but their initiative foundered on what I have called the dual structure of popular racism: if they tried to win the respectable working- and lower-middle-class vote, they had to pose as a responsible political party who were staunch defenders of public propriety; but in that case they alienated the very youth whom they needed as their stormtroopers on the streets. If, instead, they organised on the football terraces and otherwise incited violence, they offended against the moral economies of 'community' and lost electoral support. The dilemma could not be resolved, and resulted in numerous splits within the movement.[45]

However, what really pulled the rug from under the NF's feet was the emergence of new cultural forms and practices which no longer depended on localised constituencies of support. Popular discussions of race, nation and people increasingly began to be relayed by other means. Moral panics about immigrants orchestrated by the *Sun* or *Daily Mail* newspapers, took the place of local networks of rumour and gossip as the principle vehicle for outraged public propriety. Moreover, once the material solidarities of working-class life and labour began to 'melt into air', they released a cloud of images which might 'condense' in any number of configurations. In particular, images of ethnicity were no longer tied to personal credentials of place; they were up for grabs, incorporated within the endless bricolage of style. Against this background, youth cultures emerged which no longer depended on rules and rituals of territoriality to promote their 'narcissisms of minor difference'.[46]

This shift certainly produced a reaction which lent racist myths of origin a new lease of life; but it also released new forces of resistance which the Anti-Nazi league with its 'two-tone' style of cultural populism for a time succeeded in capturing. Significantly, its *absence* of local roots was the key to the ANL's success *and* failure. It was able to construct a spectacle of mass opposition to racism, but not to hold the shifting and volatile constituencies of youth it had mobilised. Ironically, it was Thatcherism which capitalised most effectively on the situation, by mapping this new terrain in a way which also chimed with a popular desire to return to historical roots.[47]

Thatcher gave the free-born Englishman a new lease of life by turning him into a moral entrepreneur of people's capitalism. However, in so far as her policy has created two unequal nations, it poses problems for the co-ordination of both class and ethnic hegemony. In order to legitimise the use of troops or armed police on the streets of Brixton or Belfast it was necessary to actively *construct* a silent majority who would support such measures as a necessary defence of the British way of life. The danger was that this majority might not remain silent, might even begin to voice other and less welcome demands, centred on some residual notion of civil liberties and the British sense of fair play – demands which, however limited, would certainly impose constraints on any policy of organised repression. So, how to pre-empt such a turn?

One way of looking at the Falklands War is to see it as a brilliantly stage-managed television spectacle in which all the themes associated with the Norman yoke were refurbished and encoded with a single *mise-en-scène*: Fascism as foreign ideology – an attack on the ancient liberties of an island race (the Falklanders) – the nation united as a people up in arms against an alien tyranny – the expulsion of invaders from British soil – a yeomanry in uniform fighting to protect kith and kin – the superiority of 'British stock' – and the final triumphant anthem at Port Stanley of 'Britons never shall be slaves'.[48]

All those who did not join in the chorus – sections of the Black community, a small radical intelligentsia – had the finger pointed at them. This 'other England' formed the new 'enemy

within' who threatened to 'swamp the British way of life'. If it was
OK to 'bash the Argies' it was fine to have a go at this 'fifth column'
too. Here, finally, a popular nationalism orchestrated from above
found common cause with a grass-roots racism, both rough
and respectable. Not-so-merrie Little Englandism was wrenched
out of its historical fortress and put to work under a new regime
for making Britain Great. But this did not produce a new racism,
as is sometimes suggested, rather it adapted and realigned existing
discourses to meet new conditions for maintaining hegemony.[49]
The reconstruction of ethnicity was central to this strategy, as to
the new movements which emerged to resist it. For there proved
to be more than one way of going back to the past to remake the
present.

Roots radicalism

I have suggested that the association of ethnicity with minority
status has little to do with the findings of the population census,
and a lot to do with the construction of 'silent majorities' based
on 'nation and people'. Recently, however, the term has been
somewhat transformed in both meaning and function. Initially
written out of English history altogether, or else included as the
inert object of its civilising mission, ethnic minorities are currently
enjoying a multicultural boom. Every school history textbook now
makes an obligatory, if passing, reference to the 'large contribution'
which various communities have made to British society, citing
achievements in the field of the arts, sport, the professions, and
other areas of public life. Having done their statutory duty to
promote 'positive images', these texts do not feel it necessary to go
into any details about the collective struggles which have been
waged against racism in Britain. The reader's attention is carefully
diverted from any event or movement which challenges the still
dominant Whig interpretation of English history, according to
which it is all a story of progress from the barbarity of slavery to
the enlightenment of current race relations, courtesy of liberal
reformers and the British sense of 'fair play'![50]
   The question is, whether in advancing beyond multi-culturalism
to an anti-racist position we have to do more than create the
conditions for the expression of ethnocentrisms which have hitherto

been marginalised or suppressed. Is it enough to demonstrate that the so called 'white' majority can be decomposed into a mosaic of national minorities – Irish, Welsh, Scottish, Jewish, Italian, Polish, Turkish, Greek and so on, who all suffer various kinds of discrimination? Or does the reconstruction of the national/popular have to be undertaken in a rather less ethnicist fashion? It is in the light of such considerations that we have to approach the 'roots radical' literature which has been produced over the last ten years, and which has done so much to retrieve the histories of the Black, Irish and Jewish communities in Britain.

This is part of a much wider movement, embracing popular music, literature and the 'ethnic arts', which has emerged to contest the cultural politics of assimilation.[51] It has become a powerful ideological force for unifying these communities across their internal class divides, by mobilising populist or nationalist senti- ment. Historical research is central to this enterprise and it has helped to give it an educational focus. For the first time, teachers are now in possession of materials to demonstrate that in a very real and important sense, Britain has always been a multi-ethnic society; they are now able to pass on to the present generation of Black, Irish or Jewish youth a purely *indigenous* legacy of struggle against racism. In this respect, roots radicalism clearly has an important role to play in reshaping the curriculum, in particular by eliminating the 'exoticist' tendency and insist on the centrality of these histories for understanding the internal development of British society.[52]

But it is not without its problems. Some of these stem from the understandable tendency to stress the autonomy of these communities as active makers of their own history in a way which overemphasises the continuity of past struggles with the present, and reifies ethnicity as their guiding hand. Roots radical texts are by definition about a search for origins, tracing an unbroken line of descent from the first settlers to the contemporary generation. Inevitably, this genealogical approach tends to flatten out the notion of historical individuality, removing the contradictions and discontinuities which govern the distinctive formation of any culture or social group in favour of a unilinear chronicle of events narrated from a single ethnic perspective. It has been called 'tunnel history', in that the historian tunnels back into the past looking for Blacks, Irish or Jews, and stops only when and where they are found.

The result tends to read like the Whig interpretation turned upside down. We get a picture of an oppressed community growing in strength, pride and political consciousness as the years roll by and the tempo of struggle quickens, while racism deepens its hold over the rest of society. This teleology of the oppressed runs into difficulties when it comes to explaining why the 'onward march' is sometimes halted. Anti-racist conspiracy theories are waiting in the wings, with the 'hidden hands' of capital or state ever ready to do their work; but this only succeeds in turning history into a kind of morality tale, an epic struggle between 'goodies and baddies' with the 'cowboy' and 'Indian' roles reversed. This may be good propaganda, or good therapy; it is certainly a necessary moment in the process of cultural liberation, but it does not necessarily make for good history. For what we are left with is a series of disparate, equally ethnocentric accounts; these may enable us to extrapolate some common denominators of prejudice or discrimination, but contain no theoretical principles to help cross-reference between them in terms of an overall analysis of the peculiarities of British social structure. Adding these separate perspectives together does not, in fact, help us to arrive at a history of multi-ethnic Britain, for this will always need to be something more than the sum of its parts. Indeed, it could be argued that in so far as each community stakes the separate claim of its own history to be included within a revised 'national/popular' tradition without in any way problematising the issue of its contradictory class location, the whole project tacitly underwrites the hegemony of bourgeois historiography with its pluralist models of progress.[53] Certainly the pedagogic fate of many roots radical texts in the classroom is to be milked for their positive images, especially those which can be correlated with educational achievement, and for the rest of the material to be inserted into the most abstracted kinds of multi-culturalism.

A parallel set of issues arises over the treatment of racism itself. The history of racist ideology tends to be presented as always the same old story, the same slurs and slogans, compulsively repeated over the centuries. Racism, like the poor, is always with us, its effect being both continuous and cumulative. But to treat racism as a quasi-universal norm indifferent to both context and conjuncture is to abandon any pretence at historical analysis. Implicitly, the argument falls back on psychological models, applied not just to individuals or groups, but to whole societies. Scapegoating and the 'narcissism of minor difference' become an in-built tendency of 'ethnic relations'. Even Sigmund Freud, who was no historian, felt that such generalisations explained nothing. How, for example, to account for the wide historical fluctuations in the distribution and degree of prejudice shown towards the same ethnic minority within a particular social formation? To get round this problem, and to introduce at least some principle of discontinuity into the model, it is argued that mechanisms of scapegoating exist in a *latent* state in every society, but are triggered by particular sets of political and economic conditions – slavery, imperialism, mass unemployment, the rise of Fascism, Thatcherism or whatever *deus ex machina* is preferred. This latency theory grants racist ideology its own special effect, but only by throwing its discourses outside history, and making them the static object of a general critique of 'human nature'. In practice, racist structures of feeling and belief are made to wait in the wings, in a state of suspended animation, and are only brought into the argument when it becomes clear that material conditions are not in themselves adequate to explain a particular outbreak of racism. Psychologism and economism here work hand in glove, not least in promoting the notion of racism as a 'necessary false consciousness', part of a 'natural' psychopathology of everyday life under capitalism.[54]

From a roots-radical position, the difficulty remains of how to recognise racism as a historical variable yet make it an entirely dependent, and dependable one, anchored to and coextensive with the history of specific populations of aggressors and/or victims. One solution has been to adopt an archaeological approach, peeling off layer after layer of historical evidence, digging back ever further and deeper, to get to the roots of racist discourse. This produces a version of historicism which reduces the meaning or effect of any conjunctual form to its conditions of origin and forms of development.[55] This, in turn, tends to make racist ideology something of a self-fulfilling prophecy, where nothing succeeds like historical success. It is to assume precisely what has to be explained – how a particular modality comes to be promoted within a specific strategy of class and ethnic hegemony. Moreover, how this operation is conducted, and where it looks, comes to depend on *which* type of racist ideology – and usually that means which ethnic referent – is privileged as paradigmatic. If it is primarily a matter of theoretical doctrine we are instructed to look no further than nineteenth-century scientific racism.[56] If, in contrast, it is seen as a wider cultural phenomenon, then we are directed to medieval pogroms, or the rise of the 'Enlightenment', and even to the roots of 'civilisation' in Ancient Greece or Rome. This is a major tendency amongst Jewish historians, who often operate with definitions which conflate the religious and scientific idioms of antisemitism.[57] Students of Black history, in contrast, have tended to emphasise the economic rationale of racism, limiting its origins to the institution of plantation slavery under capitalism, and its development to colonialism and unequal exchange.[58] Finally, if the accent is placed on political ideology, the key historical moments will be the rise of nationalism and the nation state, the phase of imperialism and the emergence of a modern apparatus of race relations.[59]

Where the history of racist ideology is made to start, the principles of periodisation and explanation which are applied to it thus indicates, and depends on a fundamental choice of premises about its definition and scope. Of course, at a purely descriptive level there is plenty of room for different kinds of historiography, some focussing on the economic, others on the political or cultural strands. The problems only arise when it comes to integrating these accounts into some kind of general theory. Here, as always, battle is joined between the idealists, for whom race is an idea which makes history (in the sense of animating racialist movements or policies), and materialists, for whom particular historical conjunctures (such as the colonisation of Africa or India), are reflected in particular mental structures which then become embedded in the whole social fabric.[60] Today the debate is complicated by the fact that idealism has developed a materialist edge, while materialism has produced a theory in which history is abolished in favour of structures which operate according to their own internal laws.

In the first case we have a theory of racist discourses, as 'technologies of power' operating through various institutional relays – the family, the education system, the mass media, and so on. Here, racist ideology is never the same old story; each of its codes has a distinctive history, its own repertoire of meaning. The distribution of these codes, and their modes of articulation is held to be the outcome of certain strategies, centred on what Michel

Foucault has called 'bio-politics' – the science of policing populations and their reproduction.[61]

This perspective has the advantage of bringing to light some of the more hidden and unconscious processes of racism, and also privileges the more subliminal forms of resistance to it. But it is not without its circularities; to define ideology as a discourse of power tends to reduce power to discourse; discourse in turn floats free of any external determinations and becomes a cause of itself as an effect.[62]

In the second case we have structural/functional models focusing on the processes through which racism is variously reproduced politically, economically and culturally.[63] Here, though, differences in the form, location and register of racist practices tend to be effaced before the uniformity of their function, in institutionalising patterns of discrimination and prejudice. Racism thereby becomes a cause of itself, as well as the sum of its effects, operating through a more or less seamless web of determinations. Such circular reasoning has one ideological payoff – it defines anything (or anyone) which does not actively interrupt the 'reproduction process' as racist. What a shame that it does not, and cannot, explain the real movement of history, and has to remain indifferent to the specific meaning of events.[64]

It is perhaps possible to envisage a division of intellectual labour in which functionalist models explained the persistence of racist ideology, and discourse analysis concentrated on its more innovative moments. But the problem remains of how to explain the relations between these structural and ruptural instances. How to explain why the racist imagination should be at its most inventive at times when its relay systems, far from undergoing any 'legitimation crisis', are functioning in a highly normative way?[65] One of the great virtues of roots radicalism is that it forces us to keep asking these kinds of question, even if, in doing so, it highlights the theoretical difficulties involved in answering them. Indeed, it could be argued that it is only in the attempt to go beyond this framework, *from within it*, that new paradigms of historical understanding are likely to emerge. So, from this starting point, let us try to take a further line of thought for a walk to try and grasp the roots of racism in a rather more radical way.

The strange case of Mr Savage and the Greek gorilla

Some first principles: ideologies have a material history as practices of representation inscribed in social relations of power. But this history is not of ideology's own making, it is governed by a wider set of political and economic forces, which establish the limits and conditions within which signifying practices have to work. However, the deep structure of ideology, its generative grammar, is in no way dependent on these factors: it belongs to the language of the Unconscious, the discourse of the Other, embodied in myths, rituals and fantasy. This language enters history only through the medium of its misrecognition, as a principle, not of change, but of compulsive repetition. Ideologies make history as specific strategies for disavowing history. That is their peculiar function and effect.[66]

What, then, is the relation between racist ideology as a structure of power and as a discourse of the Other? Let us illustrate it with a little case study of one of its key instances. Everyone knows the key role played by apes in the evolution of race thinking. Or do they? If you look up the entry for 'gorilla' in the standard Oxford English Dictionary, you come across the following:

An alleged African name for a wild or hairy man (strictly for female only). First used in Greek account of the voyage by the Carthaginian Hanno in 5th or 6th century BC.
'Another island full of savage people, the greater part of whom were women, and whose bodies were hairy, and whom our interpreters called Gorillae' (trans 1799).
Hence adopted and used by T. S. Savage to refer to apes (*Gorillae Troglodytes*, 1847) hence applied to black people.
'Others of the Haitian Negroes are the meanest looking Gorillas imaginable' Sir St John 1874.

Behind the insistent and apparently innocent little word 'hence', there lies the far from innocent suggestion, made with all the weight of historical philology, that the origin of a key word in nineteenth-century racist discourse can be traced to a Semitic text of the fifth century BC. How does such a respectable pedigree come to be manufactured?

Hanno's account of his voyage along the coast of West Africa was the subject of intense debate amongst nineteenth-century classical scholars.[67] What sites were colonised and how far did the expedition get? Was it Cape Verde or Cape Jube, the coast of Gabon, or only South Morocco? There are earnest discussions about trade winds, local weather conditions, navigation routes and the type of vessel used. But why should these scholars suddenly abandon their philological concerns to engage in speculative geography?

The answer is that they were anxious to establish historical credentials for the European conquest of Africa by tracing its antecedents to the 'civilising missions' of Ancient Greece and Rome. As Lord Lugard later put it 'As Roman Imperialism led the wild barbarians of these islands along the path of progress, so in Africa today, we are repaying the debt and bringing to the dark places of the earth, the torch of culture and progress'. In fact, it was even more important to demonstrate that the 'torch of culture and progress' had first been lit on Mount Olympus, and that Classical Greece was the birthplace of a new, superior and specifically European civilisation. But in order to do that it was necessary to deny systematically the Semitic and African roots of Hellenic culture. Under these circumstances the fact that Hanno's origins and that of his text were Punic, and thus were located at the intersection of Jewish and African influences, is conveniently ignored. Instead, he is turned into a kind of honorary Greek. The problems of translation, the fact that gorilla is a third-hand rendition into Greek of a Punic term, which was itself derived from a word which just may have been used by some unknown African tribe to denote a species of ape, all this is glossed over in favour of an obsessive preoccupation with comparing possible physical similarities in the terrain described by Hanno, and by European colonialists over two thousand years later.

Behind the shift in focus lies a whole network of assumptions – to the effect that Africa has no history, and its geography belongs to nature rather than culture.[68] Only on these terms can the colonial territories of the British Empire be compared with the kind of trading colonies set up by Hanno! Ironically, it was a Greek historian, Heroditus, who provided a real basis of comparison. The Phoenicians, he tells us, adopted a system of silent barter with the Africans. They would land and set out their goods, then retire to their ships. The Africans would then emerge from the forest, lay down the gold they thought represented a fair price, and in turn retire. The sailors would again approach and add or subtract their goods, and so on until both sides were satisfied, and the bargain struck. The difference between this process of visible and equal exchange, in which each partner respects the others terrain, and the trading practices of the early European colonists need hardly be stressed! It was just *this* comparison, which classicists could have made, in principle, which was foreclosed by their actual procedures of textual exegesis.[69]

There is, however, another dimension of misrecognition at work. How does it come about that a term allegedly first applied by Africans to apes should be so easily appropriated by Europeans and used to define them out of the ranks of humanity?

T. S. Savage (1847), in his treatise on the habits and customs of the gorilla, endorses its association with Black people but does so in quite a novel way. He writes:

> The orangs are believed by the natives to be human beings, members of their own race degenerated. Some few who have put on a degree of civilisation above the mass, will not acknowledge their belief in this affinity. The majority however fully believe orangs to be wild men of the woods, especially those tribes who live in their vicinity. They seem to be quite unaffected by our arguments in proof of the contrary.

African beliefs in certain correspondences between human and animal behaviour are here seen as symptomatic of their primitive culture or mentality: their 'indifference' to the arguments of scientific reason only confirms this view. The significance of their anthropomorphism is totally misread, because it represents an attitude to nature, and to animals, which is based on coexistence, not domination, and as such is profoundly subversive of Western beliefs.[70] The refusal of the 'natives' to entertain such ideas is used as yet further proof that their sense of kinship with animals must be understood in terms of proximity on an evolutionary scale.

Savage starts by citing the authority of Hanno to coin the term 'gorilla' for the African ape, even though the word itself can hardly be regarded as authentic, then he goes on to associate this creature with local superstitions, apparently unchanged since the fifth century BC, concerning 'wild men of the woods'. However the significant fact is that the Wild Man, in the form in which he appears here, is a specifically *European* invention. It was the Englishman, Lord Monboddo, writing in the 1770s who insisted that orang-utans were not animals but 'a race of men, left behind in the course of civilisation' and who even claimed to have seen troops of wild men living in the woods of Angola! But he was merely reiterating a traditional view.

The figure of the Wild Man and Woman had played a central role in the popular culture of Europe since the early Middle Ages.[71] In England 'wodewose', covered in hair and leaves and carrying clubs, were popularly supposed to haunt forests and other wild places and to kidnap or seduce passers by. This profane and highly sexed character was the antithesis of the moral order represented by the Catholic Church: it expressed everything which was repressed by the chivalric code of the nobility and which could not be brought under seigneurial cultivation and control. Not surprisingly, perhaps, this symbolism of wildness came to be associated with villeins, churls and other bondsmen, who were regarded as being of ignoble breeding and inferior race. It is easy to see then how the wodewose became a prototype for later perceptions of the African 'savage'. Shakespeare's Caliban, the Wild Man who name is an anagram of Cannibal, marked precisely the transition point.

It is the pre-history of Anglo-Saxon race thinking which is disavowed in the very instant that the ideology breaks new ground. T. S. Savage's, (1847) argument shifts the terms of racist misrecognition whilst conserving its underlying structure. Black people are no longer 'confused' with Wild Men. Instead, the confusion itself is attributed to them as a means of 'proving' that they are unable to recognise the true ontological status of the ape, and hence lack the full human faculties of reason. We have here the beginnings of a new theory of the innate inferiority of Black people, one which is founded not in nature, but in *culture*. But how does it come about that an anatomical study of the ape published in the 1840s should have pointed the way to this cultural racism?

To answer this we have to understand how a text always bears a double imprimatur – that of its author's unconscious relation to the subject matter, and of the way this is historically mediated by the wider conjuncture in which both author and text are produced. We have already suggested that T. S. Savage was writing at a time when Classical Studies were beginning to play a leading role in asserting the superior heritage of European culture. The importance of a classical education as a training for colonial administrators also increased dramatically in the Victorian period. Certainly it was important to the author to establish a classical pedigree for the object of his research, but his treatise is a work of physical anthropology, written in the language of an 'exact' natural science. What is striking in this respect is the indecision of his conclusions; it is here, I think, that the second dimension of the text, the author's own personal relationship to his subject matter, comes into play. In the final section of the monograph he writes:

> Any anatomist who will take the trouble to compare the skeleton of the Negro and the Gorilla cannot fail to be struck *at first sight* [my italics] by the wide gap which separates them. The difference between Negro and the Caucasian sinks into comparative insignificance. . . .

but then in the next paragraph he does a complete about turn and says:

> Yet it cannot be denied, however wide the separation, that the Negro and the Orang do afford the point where Man and Brute, *when the totality of their organisation is considered* [my italics] most nearly approach each other.

The immediate evidences thus unite White and Black, in essential human kinship, over and against the ape, but instead of following through on this, Savage turns away – to a consideration of habits and customs and the 'totality of organisation', to reinstate a great evolutionary divide. Is this simply a case of wanting to have it both ways and in the end the scientist capitulating to the racist? Isn't this the very formula of 'scientific racism'? Certainly the confident assertive tones of the first sentence sound like a man putting his intellectual adversaries to flight. Edward Long, who held that there were physical similarities between Africans and apes proving their common origin, is indeed someone who did *not* take the trouble to compare their skeletons. However, the somewhat tortuous construction of the sentence which follows, in marked contrast to Savage's normal, straightforward style, points perhaps to a more complex element. Is this a case of the man of science struggling to come to terms with the racist, and dimly aware of the contradiction? Or is the missionary here searching for a way to save the African from the civilising process? It may clearly be both, but linking them, and I think subsuming them, is a certain structure of ambivalence towards the whole subject matter, a structure which is at once historical and unconscious.

In the carnivals of the Middle Ages it was possible for young nobles to dress up as savages, and parade around as wodewose, in celebration of nature's freedom from culture's constraint. No such moments of ritualised role reversal were, however, available to the eminent Victorians who chose to carry the White Man's Burden in Africa. Their licensed excesses took quite different, military and economic, forms. But what of the 'wild man' within the straitjacket of these moral codes? There is plenty of evidence to suggest a certain return of the repressed – not least in the obsessive investigations of the Victorian sexologists and their 'anthropological' interest in 'exotic' pleasures of the body afforded by non-European cultures.[72] There is no sign of this, however, in the measured tones of this particular treatise! What we have instead is an intense and acknowledged concern to de-mythologise the ape accompanied by an equally involved but disavowed attempt to re-mythologise the African. These two operations are coupled together at several points in the text. The underlying ambivalence comes to the surface only at the very end – when the author first recognises his kinship with his 'namesake', and in the next moment dissociates himself from it.

We have no means of knowing why Mr Savage decided to take up the civilising mission in Africa. There is no recorded account of his life. It is dangerous, in any case, to infer motives, especially unconscious ones, from autobiographies; the pitfalls in placing a historical figure on the psychoanalytic couch are notorious.[73] It may be worth noting, however, that the Savages were an influential Bostonian family, with an obsession, shared by many 'New Englanders' then and now, about their antecedents. James Savage, a contemporary of T. S. Savage, published in 1867 a three-volume genealogy of New England settlers, tracing their ancestry back three generations. He established, for example, that his own family probably originated from Taunton in Somerset, where half the population were Savages in the reign of Queen Elizabeth I. If he had pursued his research a little bit further he might have discovered that 'Savage' was a popular epithet applied to those who lived in or near woods and other desolate places, and sometimes the name stuck. There is an Edricus Silvatus recorded as early as 1067 and Robert Le Sauvage was a Norman notable of the twelfth century. James Savage, was, however more than satisfied with a genealogical project which enabled him to conclude that 'in the century and a half from its colonisation by civilised people, a purer Anglo-Saxon race can be seen on this side of the Atlantic than on the other'.

Yet it was T. S. Savage who made the greater contribution to the foundations of Anglo-Saxon racism, and, paradoxically, by refusing to recognise any genealogical link between his patronym and his project of research. For instead of identifying the savage or wild man within his own cultural history, he uses the authority of Hanno and the Greeks to project it into the African. In this he is acting as a representative of both Western science and the civilising mission. The performative power of this text is thus directly bound up with its function as a discourse of the other. The result is a blindness which is all the more effective in being so selective, in the way it secretly organises the terrain of enquiry. How does this blindness manifest itself?

It is quite 'obvious' from Hanno's description of their behaviour that his 'gorillas' were, in fact, female dog-faced baboons.[74] Now it just so happens that this particular species of ape has a long history as a 'monstrous race', in the shape of 'cenocephali' (i.e. dog-faced 'men'). This figure is to be found in ancient Asian, Chinese and Egyptian iconography prior to its incorporation within classical teratology; it is, however, in its Hellenised form, and via Byzantium, that it is transplanted onto medieval maps and placed alongside 'Ethiopians' around the coast of Africa or India. Savage, who prided himself on his classical scholarship as well as his scientific acumen, was in principle ideally placed to make the connection between the mythical 'dog faces' and the real baboon, and thus track down the source of Hanno's confusion. But of course if he had embarked on this course he would have destroyed the classical pedigree of his object of study; he would have been forced to admit the non-European roots of Greek culture, and the development of 'primitive superstition' at the core of European thought. Anyway the whole fragile edifice, built on the superiority of Western culture, would have come crashing down around his ears and his own relation to the 'savage within' would have stood exposed.

What this example does at least show is that the hypothesis of a naïve racism born of ignorance or mere greed cannot be upheld. The principle of misrecognition is not empirical at all. The evidence of 'at first sight' is cancelled by a priori 'second thoughts'. The result is an imaginary animal, a Greek gorilla who is equipped with an impressive pedigree in order to give birth to a no less imaginary human – a savage without a history or a name.

Racist discourses necessarily supress their own historicity as a condition of denying that of other cultures. We learn nothing about the real relations or attitudes of Black people to their habitats from Savage or anyone of his ilk. A clue is hidden, however, in one of the terms he uses. 'Orang utan' means 'reasonable being who lives in the woods' in Malaysian, in other words the *antithesis* of the European wild man, who is by definition a dangerous and irrational force. Such reversals of meaning are only likely to come to light when a space has been created for them. It is, moreover, only at such points that elements of black culture which have been *deliberately* hidden from European history in order to protect a precolonial heritage from racist discovery and distortion, emerge in their own right, as a part of a dialectical process of re-evaluating the past in the light of the present. The paradigm for this moment of cultural liberation is given to us by a story invented by African slaves in the Caribbean at the end of the seventeenth century.

Apes, they suggested, were Black people who had decided to hide in the forest and who refused to learn to speak in order to avoid being captured and exploited by White people. Once the slave traders had gone they would re-emerge from their hiding places and resume their rightful human form. The myth thus turns the usual theory upside down by making use of an imaginary relation of Black people to apes, in order to signify their real relationship to Whites. Such constructs are the opposite of those to be found in roots radical texts. For rather than reinventing history to construct a retrospective myth of origins, a new myth of origins is here produced in order to encode a proper reading of history. This is a hidden history, not just because it has been suppressed or overlooked, but because it has chosen to both conceal and to communicate its message through the medium of a language which is structured like the unconscious – the language of myth.

As a general rule, subordinated cultures have tended to develop highly sophisticated narrative forms in which the terms of historical predicament are embedded in a special grammar of story-telling. This grammar requires protagonists to start from a position of weakness or lack, to overcome a series of obstacles by means of various ruses or magical instruments, and finally to accomplish their task by reversing the initial situation and/or restoring a state of power and plenty. Yet it would be wrong to reduce such stories to any formal 'skeleton' of meaning: the social context in which they are told, the material history of their transmission, plays just as important a part in determining their ideological effect. To read them properly at both these levels we need a more subtle and open framework of interpretation than that provided by either structuralism or Marxism alone and it is to this problem we must now turn.

Mapping the terrain – towards a multi-dimensional model

The question of ideology continues to bedevil contemporary theories of racism and much hangs on the outcome of this debate.[75] If ideology is held to consist of beliefs which merely reflect, justify or mystify social reality, then racial prejudice is treated as a secondary phenomenon and institutional racism is the main enemy. If, in contrast, ideology is granted an absolute autonomy from politics and economics, then educational interventions against racism assume higher priority but run the risk of substituting changes in personal attitude or societal values for structural reforms. Equally, reflection theories tend to assume a principle of correspondence between race, ethnicity and class; for example, anti-Semitism is held to have a real basis in the ethnic or class composition of the Jews, as well as to reinforce it politically. Against this, absolute autonomy models posit a radical discontinuity between these instances, arguing that their mode of articulation is arbitrary and has to be established concretely in each case. But pushed to an extreme this position would have to argue that there is absolutely *no* connection between the commercial occupations into which many Jews were forced and the image of them as 'exploiters' to be found in popular anti-Semitism.

One difficulty in arriving at a more satisfactory formulation is the strength of feeling and political self-interest invested in the question (itself an interesting ideological phenomenon); unfortunately, the attempt to take the hot air out of the debate by confining it to the more abstract realms of epistemology has not proved to be of much help either. To try and anchor a theory of ideology in a set of axiomatic or a priori principles which will hold good for all societies at all times, is not a very plausible project. Instead, we need to look towards the kind of model which allows for a *changing* relationship between ideology and other levels of the social structure, and can explain the specialisation of its forms and functions in terms of such variations.[76] What sort of intellectual resources can be committed to the task of building a more differentiated and multi-dimensional model of racist ideology?

One of the key maxims of modern thought is that the map is not the territory and the territory is both more and less than the map. Alfred Korzybski, who first enunciated the principle, was a logician and he meant that linguistic signs, in articulating our mental maps of the world, enjoyed a different logical status from the domains of material experience which they represented, in the same way that the word 'sugar' is not in itself sweet. To this, the structuralists later added the proposition that the meaning of 'sweet' depended on its opposition to 'sour', or some other 'value' as defined within a particular code of taste. The relation of signs to their material referents was therefore arbitrary or culturally constructed and could be changed.[77]

This apparently innocent rider, however productive its initial phase, quickly degenerated into an idealist position, whereby map was severed from territory and floated free to enclose language and ideology in each other's embrace. This in turn gave Marxists a chance to reassert an equally one-sided materialism which dissolved territory into base and map into superstructure, and made the latter reflect the former. From this vantage point, the meaning of sugar is far from sweet; it is bound up with its material history as a commodity, first as a bitter fruit of slave labour on Caribbean sugar plantations, and latterly as part of the unequal exchange between metropolitan capitalism and the Third World.[78]

Clearly, each side has got hold of part of the story – the two accounts complement and correct rather than cancel one another. For example, the profitability of slave plantations depended partly on the manufacture of European demand, and this in turn required the 'refinement' of brown sugar into white to 'suit the Anglo-Saxon taste'. Even then, the pattern of consumption was split along material lines, the rich eating the more expensive white sugar, and the poor brown. Only recently has the class and colour code switched its values of taste, with unrefined demerara becoming fashionably ethnic amongst the educated middle class, whilst white sugar, now recognised as a threat to health, becomes an ever more staple ingredient of the working-class diet.[79]

Map and territory are thus clear interdependent, but their relation is not fixed and does not belong to some a priori principle of correspondence. Territory is not a *tabula rasa* of sense impressions awaiting the imprint of false consciousness; map does not model or reflect 'external reality'. Indeed, there are many ideological phenomena which cannot be located at either level, but are produced solely through particular forms of interaction between them. Their paradigm, perhaps appropriately, is the mirage. Neither a pure hallucination, nor a pure environmental effect, the mirage is produced at the intersection between certain climatic conditions in the desert and a certain movement of desire on the part of thirsty travellers! Consequently, neither a degree in human psychology nor in the earth sciences, nor an intimate knowledge of the region, will protect you from believing the 'fake' evidence of your own eyes and setting out on a fruitless quest for a non-existent oasis. This might be a useful metaphor for the way ideology in general works but what does it tell us about the process of 'double inscription' of territory and map in concrete practices of representation?

Let us take the map to be a device for naming and fixing the unknown in such a way as to render it more accessible to various techniques of conscious control (social, physical or mental) which operate at the level of territory. What the map *unconsciously* represents is the drive for mastery which produced it, a desire to render the world as real and rational, by denying the existence of the Other as a locus of the unknown. From this omnipotent or Archimedean reference point the map constitutes a network of discrete meanings which are articulated to specific terrains of experience. These territories are always and already delimited by specific contexts and conjunctures; they are staked out by relations of power which are themselves traversed by human intentionality. If 'map' projects a space of desire in which power is disavowed in order to be exercised in Freuds 'other scene', then 'territory' anchors that dissociation to particular historical configurations of common sense. There is always a tension between the two. The movement of history always escapes the geography of the Unconscious.[80]

How does this map/territory model apply to the field of racist representations? At the level of map, a certain image of the body politic is constructed in terms of a set of constant topological relations (enclosure, separation, connectedness) which structurally exclude *and* define the Other. In doing this, the racist imagination, as we have seen, is highly mobile, operating across a whole range sites and sources, selecting and combining 'bits and pieces', and organising them into certain fixed chains of association (codes). In this way, each map draws a specific picture of the terrain on which racism describes its material effects. At this second level, a set of discourses and institutions fix designated subjects (races) to specific positions within a topography of power. It is here that the political geographies of class and ethnicity are formed and transformed. In moving from territory to map, we thus move from the patterns of prejudice to the designs of racist desire, from the dialectics of exploitation to those of envy.[81]

As an example of how this works in practice consider the system of apartheid in South Africa. At the level of territory it constitutes two separate domains of White and Black experience; the topography of discrimination which is here imposed by every means at the state's command confines the Black population to structural places ('homelands' or shanty towns, the secondary labour market, hidden economy, second class citizenship, for example) which 'spontaneously' confirms the material position assigned to them in and by racist ideology – 'the Blacks are fit for nothing better'; but it also constitutes the terrain of Black resistance and struggle which is changing the political geography of the country and with it the consciousness of a section of the White minority. However, the extent and direction of the shift in White racism is not simply a response to the pressures of Black militancy or external economic sanctions, it takes place not just at the level of territory but also of map.

Here we have to look at the conspiracy theories produced by the ideologists of apartheid. The Black movement is popularly supposed to be secretly guided and controlled by the 'hidden hand' of world Communism. In reality, of course, this hidden hand belongs entirely to the racist imagination. The splitting of Black and White in a 'law of separate development' produces a return of the repressed in unconscious as well as political terms. The more brutally the Black population is attacked in the desperate attempt to search and destroy this 'hidden hand', the greater the power which is attributed to it. Yet no matter how 'radical' the amputation, the hidden hand magically survives, as a kind of phantom limb of the body politic, to haunt apartheid with its presumed omnipotence, as well as to incite, and justify further, all too material, acts of butchery. At the same time, the actual Black 'hands' who service the domestic and industrial economy of White South Africa remain an obsessive focus of popular fantasies, on the part of the 'lager' society, an object of unconscious and disavowed racial envy, as well as a source of cheap labour.[82]

Apartheid is an example of strong correspondence betwen map and territory. Its symbolic topology and political geography all too faithfully reflect one other, for here the power of the racist imagination and the state are as one. Such strong forms of racism tend to be privileged by many Marxists. Unfortunately, this is not just because they are the site of major political struggles, but also because they support reductive theoretical explanations.

If we think of map and territory as two circles then in some cases they may be concentric – as in the case of apartheid – but in others they may only partially overlap, or even function quite eccentrically, reinforcing each other at a distance without any direct link – as we saw in our discussion of dominant and subordinate class racisms.

As an example of these possibilities, consider the different uses to which colonial maps have been put. Initially they were direct instruments of exploitation and conquest; to chart the 'unknown' continents of India and Africa was an all too material step towards their subjugation. But that in turn produced a new political geography of European settlement, and it is this topography of power, which, in a second moment, had to be mapped. In the process the history of African or Indian civilisation is effaced, not only at a material, but also at a symbolic level. As an example of the latter consider the role which these maps played in the classrooms of the Victorian board school. Their purpose, and that of the geography lessons organised around them, was to stretch the horizons of the working-class child beyond the confines of the slum neighbourhood, to embrace the globe with a proper, or rather a proprietorial, sense of Imperial pride. But if these maps sparked off the racist imagination of these children, it led them in a quite different direction, back to the very neighbourhoods from which it was hoped to liberate them and where, as we have seen, their constructs of territoriality both co-ordinated and staked their claim to local mastery. Imperial maps have, of course, long been expelled from the classroom, but it has not proved so easy to consign them to the dustbins of history. For no sooner placed there, than they become nostalgic symbols of the end of Empire, material signs of a 'world we have lost', even tourist souvenirs of an 'old country' and their market value increases accordingly. In this way they find a new role in a post-Imperial era.[83]

The relations between map and territory thus continually change over time, and in this way we can trace some of the more subtle shifts in the history of ideology. The tempo at which each level changes may also vary. Sometimes map and territory will be synchronised, in other cases they will be out of step. But there is no law of uneven and combined development to stipulate that one always and necessarily lags behind the other. Synchronisation is, in fact, often achieved only after a considerable period of disjuncture. For example, in the mid-Victorian period between the abolition of slavery and the heyday of imperialism, Anglo-Saxon race thinking went through a profound upheaval. As we have seen, the traditional genealogical models were displaced by a whole series of new theories. Yet the shift from religious to scientific racism involved a shift in codes, a redrawing of the ideological map, to which nothing immediately corresponded on the political terrain of 'race relations'. It was only with the subsequent introduction of new measures of surveillance and control – for example, the use of fingerprinting and other typologies to segregate dangerous populations both at home and in the colonies – that these wilder flights of the racist imagination could be said to have been conformed to a political *raison d'être*. What made the mid-Victorian efflorescence possible was precisely the conjunctural autonomy of race thinking, its localised freedom from the functional constraints of 'legitimation'; just as what impelled the institutional innovations of the later phase was a specific shift in the pattern of power within both industry and Empire.[84]

Racist assumptions become common sense only when and where map and territory effectively coincide, where the domains of conscious experience are organised in such a way as to always and already confirm the unconscious premises of myth, ritual and fantasy. The self-evidential character of common-sense racism is thus both transparent and impervious to countervailing forms of reason or experience as long as the map/territory relation remains intact. However, the realism of racist narratives does not have to depend on always telling the same old story; it is conveyed by the momentum generated by its own plots. If a 'master race' is to go on climbing to the top, to occupy positions where it can look down on everyone else and keep them in their place, it has to continually make new mountains out of old molehills. Even when it appears to be gripped by a profound stasis, the map/territory relation is never other than dynamic. The question of adequation, of how far racist representations provide an effective handle on the real world, arises only when their legitimating function is marginalised and/or has to be subordinated to a more imaginative role. How to conjure up a mountain when there are no longer any molehills in sight? It is here, as we have seen, that racist ideology is at its most inventive.

For when 'map' no longer corresponds to 'territory', the sky is the limit as far as representation is concerned. At this point we find ourselves impelled into a quite different universe of discourse, one ruled by international Jewish–Masonic conspiracies and 'racist' neutron bombs. However phantasmagoric these images, let us remember that under certain circumstances racist dreams can turn other people's lives into waking nightmares. Genocide, the ultimate racialist Utopia, may be a mirage in the sense that it represents a goal which can never be reached, since there are always survivors. But the compelling power of the mirage lies in the fact that it satisfies an existential imperative; it is precisely when its special effects of meaning are *not* locatable on any existing map, do not form part of any recognisable terrain, that the racist imagination can take its desires for reality. And the simplest way to make a mountain out of a molehill in an ideological landscape otherwise devoid of such features is to invent some moles who are invisibly undermining its foundations! The purpose of conspiracy theories is precisely to construct such a rationale; yet to make its plots seem like common sense may also entail shifting the grounds of material experience, by the use of *agents provocateurs*, or strategies of disinformation. Such theories are never 'just' fantasies. They often function as self-fulfilling prophecies. To call them mirages should not be to dismiss them, but to refer to their special conditions of existence in (a) a radical instability of meanings to be found in certain kinds of political climate; and (b) the role of conspiracies in giving these meanings a certain coherence and anchorage.[85]

Racialist conspiracy theories are not, however, the only kind of 'special effect'. We have already noted the delusion of authenticity generated by White people 'blacking up'. But such ritual trans-vestism is comparatively innocuous compared with the devices which have been developed in the name of human science. Colonial anthropologists, for example, fondly imagined that their ethnographic methods would enable them to 'penetrate' and 'capture' (*sic*) the essential contours of tribal society. But their charts of kinship systems, far from getting inside the Black experience of colonialism, only demonstrated the workings of a particular kind of rationality which, especially in its more abstract and universalising tendency, remains intrinsic to the imperialism of European thought. There are two different political lessons to be drawn from this. First, the terrain of oppression constructs experience in a way which is necessarily impenetrable from the vantage point of the oppressor even though its effects cannot be entirely effaced from their maps. On the other hand, it does not follow that the maps of racism spontaneously drawn by those subjected to it are necessarily 'correct'. For once again the territory is not the map. The attempt to collapse these two levels only points up the fact of their irreducible difference.

This model has certain implications for anti-racist strategies. For example, it may be argued that Black children do not need a map to find their way around multiracist Britain. Street and state racism constitute the terrain on which their everyday lives are lived; they know it 'like the backs of their hands'. This may well be true. But what is a strength at one level may be a weakness at another. It may be left to others to take on the roles of official interpreters and guides, and it is in this context that the emergence of an organic Black intelligentsia takes on its full historical significance, even if it produces a roots radicalism which on other grounds is problematic.

The issue is even more crucial when we consider how – and if – White children are to be introduced into the domains of Black experience. In many cases they are cast in the role of tourists, hunting 'multi-cultural' souvenirs. If this gives them material access to aspects of Black community and culture, they inevitably tend to select those bits which conform to their existing maps of 'proletarian ethnicity'. This provides them with certain street credentials! The critics of this approach, who point out, correctly, that it does not tackle the roots of popular racism, promptly go to the opposite extreme and produce the mirror argument to the effect that material factors are drawing White and Black youth on to shared terrains of experience, and that this will produce a common culture of resistance, even a new and revolutionary map of society. Unfortunately, all the evidence shows that responses to unemployment, on the part of young people, both Black and White, vary widely, according to a whole range of situational factors, and cannot be 'read off' in this way.[86]

The problem, then, is that most anti-racist interventions work along one dimension only – *either* map *or* territory. But to de-institutionalise racism will not in itself abolish the power of the racist imagination; this will continue to flourish through the media of popular culture long after its state forms have withered away; indeed, it may begin to stake out fresh territories in the vacuum thus created. Equally, driving the National Front off the streets may have a highly desirable effect on the political geography of 'race relations'; but it does not impinge on the racist image of the body politic daily reproduced through rumour, gossip and ritual insult, not to mention the gutter press. Finally, to demonstrate that racist arguments are nonsense in the classroom does not necessarily lessen the appeal of conspiracy theories as a source of myth and fantasy acted out physically as well as verbally in the playground.

One-dimensional approaches do not grasp the principles of articulation which make racism common sense, and consequently cannot shift the grounds on which the ideology reproduces itself. Racism Awareness Training (RAT) does set out to work at both levels, to make White people conscious of their personal implication in racist policies and practices. But it only makes the connection between strategies of domination and disavowal at the level of their surface representation in individual psychology or group dynamics. The material terrains of ideological struggle, and the deeper, more unconscious mappings of the racist imagination are both left untouched. As a result, RAT leaves White people feeling helpless and hopeless in the face of their collective historical responsibility for the oppression of Blacks; the only possible defence against this overwhelming sense of 'innate guilt' is to seek one's own personal redemption through that of the world; the result, all too predictably, is a political Messianism which mirrors in all its essential procedures the forms of prejudice which are supposedly being attacked.[87]

An alternative approach to anti-racist education must start out from a theoretical position which makes it possible to bring the hidden curriculum of racist ideology to the surface. But where is this curriculum to be found hiding if not in the history of education itself? A brief cartography of the codes which have informed its 'civilising mission' may, therefore, serve as a useful guide before we enter the minefield of current educational debates.

The codes of breeding

In many ways, the map we are going to draw turns the conventional projection inside out, or rather outside in. Anglo-Saxon racism is no longer seen as something first invented by slave traders or plantation owners to justify their exploitation of Black people in the colonies, and only subsequently brought home and applied to ethnic minorities in Britain. Rather, its essential idioms are generated from within certain strategic discourses in British class society, and from the very outset are applied across a range of sites of domination, both to the indigenous lower orders and ethnic minority settlers as well as to colonial populations overseas. In other words, racism is not something 'tacked on' to English history, by virtue of its imperialist phase, one of its aberrant moments; it is *constitutive* of what has come to be known as the 'British Way of Life'.[88]

Central to the development of this 'internal' racism was the construction of a code of breeding. Or rather, several variants of this. There is the aristocratic code, which first emerged in the late seventeenth century, linking notions of social pedigree and ancestral blood to a hierarchy of human sensibilities; and there is a bourgeois version which linked the practice of refinement to that of reason in a new way, by emphasising hierarchies of individual achievement based on inherited differences of 'intelligence' or 'natural aptitude'. The latter has an important variant – a model of racial degeneration focused on certain peoples and places as 'breeding grounds' of vice and disease. Finally, there is the reworking of these problematics in and through a distinctive proletarian code. We will look briefly at each in turn, trying to locate its distinctive features within the English social structure; I shall try to show how the complex negotiations between these codes served to connect certain strategic images of class and race to normative images of sexuality and reproduction and how in the process the civilising mission not only produced a new politics of the body, but its own body politic.[89]

But first things first: why and how did selective breeding cease to be simply a practice of animal husbandry and begin to function as the basis of a hegemonic racist code?[90] It is significant that this occurs at the point where material practices of aristocratic and peasant inheritance begin to lose ground to more dynamic forms of capital accumulation as a means of ensuring the reproduction of class positions from generation to generation. It is at this point that the original restricted meaning of race, as denoting a particular line of dynastic descent (a *metonym* for generation) gives way to a wider set of connotations and becomes a *metaphor* for the body politic as a whole. Race becomes part of an *ideology* of inheritance through which the aristocracy asserts its hereditary entitlement to govern, either against the claims of a rising bourgeoisie (as in most European countries) or as a means of transforming itself from a feudal *rentier* class into 'gentleman capitalists' as occurred, uniquely, in Britain.[91]

What made this country such a special case was the *hybrid* character of the governing élite which presided over the Long Transition: an aristocracy which had become thoroughly bourgeois in its economic outlook, and had reason to play down any Norman ancestry, allied itself to members of the new manufacturing classes who aspired to the lifestyle of the gentry. Each partner used the other as a means of denying its own origins (whether high or low born) while legitimising its own special destiny to rule. What cemented this alliance, and gave it such ideological solidity, was a myth of class *monogenesis*, linked, as we've seen, to an image of the 'free-born Englishman'. That myth was the central construct of the code of breeding.

In and through this code, natural and cultural breeding, pedigree and good taste came to be linked in quite a new way; not only could inner mental and moral qualities be derived from outward physical characteristics, but the ambiguity of the term 'breeding' – its double connotation – meant that 'superior sensibility' could be represented both as something innate *and* as something which could be acquired by those who had a special 'calling' for it. This enabled the aristocracy to go on believing that they were the exclusive possessors of a special patrimony – breeding, after all, was in the blood – and their privileged position had nothing to do with their capital investments in plantation slavery or the enclosure movement. 'Young bloods' – younger sons whose inheritance was rendered problematic by the law of primogeniture and who consequently sought to make their fortunes in the colonies – had an especially strong, if disavowed motive for adopting this view and for seeing themselves as a class, and race, apart. At the same time the bourgeois could turn gentleman, by mastering the arts and crafts of refinement, or having his children instructed in such etiquettes before marrying them into the ranks of the lesser nobility, whilst still holding to the motto, emblazoned on so many newly-acquired escutcheons, that 'class tells' and 'breeding will out'.[92]

The code furnished a new generic principle for classifying and hierarchising human beings, yet one which was also closely modelled on feudalism's three estates. At the top were the English ruling class 'the naturally cultured', who bore the indelible marks of superior breeding in both senses of the word; below them were a class of uncultivated humans, who shared the status of domesticated pets or well-bred farm animals, occupying a space midway between the salon and the jungle; this was the group who might be civilised. And at the bottom were those subhumans of entirely savage disposition, wild beyond any possible redemption. This schema produced a number of special effects. First, it drew a line between those with breeding who might be allowed, even encouraged, to intermarry, and those who merely bred – whose 'promiscuity' must be kept in check. In this way it enabled the governing élite to practice what might be called a double standard of miscegenation, to absorb 'new blood' without diluting its patrimony, whilst condemning such practices amongst the lesser breeds. Moreover, it could pursue its fascination with the hybrid and with monstrous births, without for a moment suspecting that its obsession had anything to do with its own mixed origins. It was not, of course, possible for the aristocracy to compose a class racism centred on the idea of 'pure and noble blood' – there is no equivalent of Count Gobineau in early British race thinking – but it could now identify with the Noble Savage as one of Nature's Gentlemen, whose breeding, unlike its own, was untainted by the corrupting influence of bourgeois 'materialism'. At the same time the civilising mission became an *inherited vocation*; the White Man's Burden could be carried only as a special calling on the part of those few chosen by superior rank and birth – it was a duty and a sacrifice imposed upon them 'as officers and gentlemen'; others were not fit to be standard-bearers of the 'master' race.

Nevertheless, the terms of the historical compromise meant that bourgeois ideals had to be incorporated within the aristocratic code. Possessive individualism had to find a home within its logic of race and class ascription. As a result, breeding had to be associated with certain *private* properties of personality which in turn resumed the public bourgeois virtues of industriousness and thrift. *Reason*, or at least a certain calculating rationality, was thus promoted as the distinguishing feature of human individuality, a condition of full admittance to civil, and hence civilised, society. In the process, its meaning underwent a subtle transformation; it took on an expressive, even an aesthetic, dimension. Reason became the *practice of refined sensibility*, the mark of superior intellect. In this way the code of breeding helped to give birth to an aristocracy of learning, which would supervise much of its later development.[93]

Was Reason an innate faculty or could it be acquired? Was it an impartible or partible inheritance? Was it a universal characteristic of human beings, or the prerogative of the chosen few? These debates were not only about deciding who was placed where in the Great Chain of Breeding; they defined the limits and conditions of the civilising mission itself, the role which this nascent intelligentsia would play within it. There is no better sign of the internal dynamics of British race thinking than the fact that its initial focus was on a 'home-grown' savage; eighteenth-century Society was fascinated by 'wild children' – no longer mythical creatures but real children of 'common origin' who had been abandoned by their parents in remote areas of the countryside and who had grown up without apparent contact with human beings. Here was a real, live test case, both for the code and the civilising mission. Were these children reasonable beings, even if they lacked articulated speech, or were they stuck in their wild state? For the first time a specific pedagogy and curriculum was developed and applied. Its aims were succinctly spelt out:

> Receive them and with tender care
> for reasons use their minds prepare
> shew them in words their thoughts to dress
> to think, and what they think express
> their manners form their conduct plan
> and civilise them into Man.'[94]

In one way or another this set of instructions continued to motivate movements of educational reform, at home and in the colonies, throughout the nineteenth and early twentieth centuries. The regimes of reason might vary in location and organisational form; they might be punitive, rehabilitative or purely pedagogic in design; they might be sited in African mission schools, or British public schools, juvenile reformatories or adult asylums; but underlying them was the same equation: to be civilised was to exercise a system of rational control over bodily impulses; to be primitive was to fail to defer these gratifications; to educate was to discipline the body and improve the mind. Ever since the Puritan revolution the educated classes held to the view that the body was the heart of unreason, the site of 'base pleasures' and vulgar instincts as against the higher and more refined faculties. But it took the code of breeding to turn this view into common sense, and to use it to draw a web of correspondences between the relations of parent and child, man and woman, teacher and pupil, bourgeois and proletarian, sane and lunatic, master and subject race.[95]

As the code spread its net ever wider, the crucial issue was whether its positions were fixed once and for all or whether they could be accounted for in terms of some more dynamic model of inheritance. In negotiating this problem, the code split into two variants, each offering its own solution. The first started by fixing reason as a specialised property belonging to certain superior types of brain, but then gave it a more dynamic reading as 'purposeful behaviour' indexed to particular kinds of criteria of competence. Reason gradually lost its link with refinement and was given a new and purely instrumental definition modelled on the economic or bureaucratic rationality of a modern society. Reason, in other words, became operationalised as intelligence, a 'mental trait' which was supposed to measure a set of dynamic and adaptive functions, yet could still be fixed in terms of its statistical distributions amongst different populations. Intelligence quotient (IQ) ratings produced through increasingly sophisticated psychometric tests not only gave a pseudo-scientific basis to evaluation of performance, but also took on an increasingly important symbolic function. Each 'degree' of intelligence carried its own set of entitlements; IQ itself became a kind of patrimony passed on from generation to generation, something which 'proved' that some people were congenital idiots and others born with brains.[96]

The issue of whether reason was innate or acquired thus shifted on to new terrain; intelligence might either be a measurement of natural aptitude and as such 'a God-given gift', or it might be used as an incremental index of achievement and personal drive. It might be transmitted under the sign of vocation or career. *Both* constructions were grist to the mill of competitive individualism, and served equally well to rationalise inequalities based on class or 'race'. Under the auspices of the code intelligence became a euphemism for the inheritance of cultural capital, making success or failure, especially within the education system, seem to be a product of personal disposition rather than structural inequality in society. The largest study to forge the link between heredity and intelligence was carried out in Britain in the interwar period and proved to its own satisfaction at least that the success of aristocratic families in business politics or the professions had nothing to do with their networks of patronage and preferment, but was governed solely by their intellectual abilities. Seen in historical perspective, the significance of Burt's study is that it fused (and abused) the findings of modern biology and sociology to confirm the message of an all-too-traditional class racism – that breeding was in the blood.

The influence of social Darwinism on the code was profound. Here was a model which enabled each 'race' or class to be ranked at a specific place on the evolutionary ladder according to certain fixed traits which signified its degree and mode of individual adaptation to a common competitive environment. The theory succeeded in integrating the aristocratic ideology of inheritance with bourgeois paradigms of career in a way which gave the civilising mission a renewed vocation – to bequeath the legacies of culture to those less fortunately endowed.[97]

The potential kinship between the civilised and savage estates could now be explicitly signalled in developmental terms. For as one early evolutionist put it, 'man in the course of life progresses from the mere animal to the intellectual creature, just as the most civilised nations had been in their infancy, no less uncultivated'. It was suggested that every individual in the process of socialisation recapitulated the stages of societal development, moving from Stone Age baby to rational 'modern man'.[98] Certain individuals and societies had simply got stuck at an infantile stage: the task was to help them grow up! This theme was given an even more bizarre twist by juvenile reformers who argued that the problem with modern society was that, unlike 'primitive culture', it provided no rite of passage from childhood into adulthood. The result was a lot of adolescent 'storm and stress'. The answer was to design new kinds of youth organisation which would embody these missing ritual links. So just as the more privileged strata in colonial societies were initiated into the profane mysteries of the British public school system, the more delinquent and deprived children of the working class were encouraged to explore the 'sacred secrets' of tribal initiation rites. In the various woodcraft movements which sprang up in the 1890s, as in the later character-building industry which sought to span all classes, adolescents were sent off to hunt and gather good deeds in the Great Outdoors, in the belief that by learning to survive in these 'primitive' environments, they would also learn to control the wild man or woman within; having safely regressed to the state of the (hopefully) noble savage, they would progress to some approximation of the Christian gentleman.[99]

Much has been made of the role of the late-Victorian public

schools and youth movements in popularising the values of imperialism and even proto-Fascism. Certainly in the arcane rituals of the Kibbo Kith Kindred, which drew equally on Blatchford's *Merrie England* and Rider Haggard's *She*, one can discern the seeds of an incipient 'National Socialist' *jugends ideologie*. But its influence was minimal; the larger woodcraft organisations deliberately eschewed such 'mumbo jumbo' and stressed their function in providing safe and rational forms of recreation. The National/Popular, I have suggested, found its way into working-class culture by other routes than these. The real significance of these movements lay elsewhere in giving an institutional form and legitimacy to a developmental psychology, built on a class racism which in one form or another continues to shape much contemporary policy and practice, in both education and the youth service. What we are dealing with here is the *hidden* curriculum of racist ideology.

There was always a risk inherent in encouraging a strategy of self-improvement amongst the 'lesser breeds', that they might yet grow up to assume their independence in quite other ways. Civilising racism was always race thinking against time. This sense of foreboding which darkened the skies of Empire long before its actual sun began to set, found expression in another, explicitly eugenic version of the code. From the 1860s onward official concern about the 'quality of British stock' became increasingly focused on the resistance offered by the working classes to the civilising mission itself. One early reformer complained:

> They live precisely like brutes, to gratify the appetites of their uncultivated bodies, and then die, to go whither they have never thought, cared or wondered . . . Brought up in the darkness of barbarism, they have no idea that it is possible for them to attain any higher condition; they are not even sentient enough to desire to change their situation . . . they have unclear, indefinite, and indefinable ideas of all around them; they eat, drink, breed, work and die; and the richer and more intelligent classes are obliged to guard them with police.[100]

For the Social Darwinists, this was clear evidence of a failure to adapt to the new conditions of urban and industrial life. But others pointed the finger at those very environments as being responsible for a degeneration in manners and morals. The poverty and squalor of the slums and the degrading conditions of factory labour were all factors in undermining the 'natural bonds' of family life and they paved the way for every kind of vice. In the Great Debate which ensued, opinion was about equally divided as to whether the working classes had brought misfortune on themselves, or whether they were the hapless victims of circumstances beyond their control. Both positions were, in a sense, reconciled in a compromise formula which divided the working class into 'respectables' who were capable of self-improvement and self-help, and the 'rough' who were not – the good natives and the bad.

In the former role, as we have seen, the working class could be assimilated into the 'life of the nation'; in the, latter they remained a 'race apart'. The code helped to make that demarcation possible by establishing a firm 'hereditary' relation between habits and habitat. As a result, the threat posed to those with Breeding, by those 'who merely bred' was made to take on a more definite and sinister shape.

The great fear of the Victorian bourgeoisie was that the concentration of the dangerous classes (the labouring and immigrant poor) in dangerous places (the street and other resorts of popular pleasure) at a dangerous time (adolescence) would lead to rampant promiscuity as well as mob rule. The population would explode in a double sense. This feeling of alarm is signalled in a new set of images which mapped the 'lower depths' of the city and the psyche on to each other. A new topography of urban derogation emerges featuring sewers and cesspits, swamps and jungles, rookeries, and so on, all of them 'fertile' breeding grounds of crime and vice of every kind. These are not just 'mental' maps; they stake out a new terrain of sanitary intervention by the state.[101]

The civilising mission took on specific tasks of population control – to police the working class through the family, to privatise its practices of sexuality and confine them within the legal framework of marriage, and in general to submit all forms of popular pleasure to the regime of reason, if not refinement. Through a whole network of social welfare agencies, those who merely bred were to be trained to reproduce in a way which diminished rather than enlarged their powers of social combination.[102] But what if this strategy failed? There was a second line of defence.

One effect of the 'breeding ground' thesis with its attendant moral panics was to focus concern about the condition of the people away from 'the State of the Nation', and towards 'the Alien Threat'. Investigation into the real relations between poverty, overcrowding, ill-health and crime became implicated in quite another discourse centred on purely imaginary relations between dirt, disease and the immigrant presence. There is no better example of this interleaving than F. Engels' account of the Irish quarter in Manchester:

> Whenever a district is distinguished for special filth the explorer may safely count on meeting chiefly those Celtic faces, which one recognises at the first glance as different from the Saxon physiognomy of the native. The Milesian deposits all his garbage before his house door, as he was accustomed to do at home, and so accumulates the pools and dirt heaps which disfigure the working people's quarters . . . The Irishman loves his pig as the Arab his horse, eats and sleeps with it, his children play with it, roll in the dirt with it . . . filth and comfortlessness prevail . . . the southern facile character of the Irishman, his crudity which places him little above the savage, his filth and poverty, with such a competitor the English working man has to compete, and even if the Irishman should force his way into other occupations enough of their old habits would cling to them to have a strong degrading effect on their companions in toil.

Engels shows us here just how materialist the racist imagination can be. Dirt is both an obsessive refrain and a mirage; it dissolves into myriad forms as soon as the 'explorer' tries to grasp its substance, and in this way leads him ever deeper into the racist mire. This momentum is maintained through a perpetual oscillation between territory and map. At the first level the structural processes which confined these Irish workers to the worst slums, and the most menial and manual of jobs, 'spontaneously' confirm their association with dirt, and this in turn produces the evidence of their 'disgusting habits'. But if Engels can treat the

Irish like dirt, it is because of what dirt symbolises at another level – namely *human matter out of place*.[103] The Irish are here explicitly portrayed as a backward peasantry who do not fit in to the more advanced English working class, and who are not fitted 'by nature' to do so.

For other commentators, the Irish simply represent the unacceptable face of Celtic nationalism. To associate them with dirt here takes on a specific political (as well as moral) connotation in the context of demands for Home Rule. For within this scheme of things only the 'English born and bred' are allowed to enjoy a positive, *organic* relation to their native soil; Fenians, in contrast, having been relegated to the inorganic properties of dirt, are turned into a kind of 'bacteria' of the body politic.

This immediately mobilises another function of dirt, as a material and symbolic carrier of disease. Within the code of breeding, disease becomes an explicitly racist metaphor, signifying a lethal process of degeneration attacking the health and well-being of society. At the limit, ethnic minorities with political demands come to be identified with an invasive and highly contagious virus, which must be isolated if the body politic is to survive. Certainly the strategies of segregation and screening to which these populations have been intermittently subjected owe as much to procedures for dealing with epidemics such as cholera as they do to routine immigration controls.[104]

Breeding in its negative connotation associated unrestrained libido with the hidden hand of disease, and served to concentrate programmes of moral hygiene against both on the immigrant presence. It was in this context that the religious and scientific registers of racism most easily converged. The imagery of pollution and taboo constantly fed off and amplified the idioms of epidemiology and other medical discourses to construct the immigrant as a parasitic 'host'. It is perhaps significant that it was the Irish in Britain who were the first and foremost 'beneficiaries' of this joint enterprise.

In most internal histories of Anglo-Saxon racism it is the Black and Jewish presence which is given most weight. The Irish are ignored, pushed into the 'Celtic fringe'.[105] This partly reflects the fact that at the level of political geography, or 'race relations' the Irish in Britain have been effectively rendered invisible. But this in itself points to the pivotal role which the Irish question has played in constructing the more hidden agendas of English race thinking. This role is *not* a matter of historical pattern and priority – it is not to do with the fact that the colonisation of Ireland provides a model for that of the West Indies, or that Little Ireland in Manchester sets the scene for the Whitechapel Shtetl. The Irish diaspora in any case has its own unique logic and meaning.[106] What concerns us as cartographers is rather what the Irish are made to *unconsciously* represent in and by the code of breeding:

(a) in its scientific register *a missing evolutionary link* between the 'bestiality' of Black slaves and that of the English worker

(b) in its politico-moral register, a principle of *ideological contagion* between heretical currents of European 'free' thinking (anarchism, republicanism, socialism) associated with the Wandering Jew, and a domestic tradition of radical dissent.

In other words, the Irish question did not just mean 'Home Rule' and the loss of British territory; it signified a threat to the body politic, at quite another and more symbolic level. It mapped out a potential space of alliance between *all* the alien populations and ideas which the British ruling class most feared. That is why in popular caricature the Irish have been made to take on so many borrowed negative traits; the ape-like features of the 'African savage', combined with the cut-throat gestures of a 'Jewish vampire'; a proletarian in rags wearing the hat of anarchy.[107]

The overdetermination of the stereotype is actually encoded in the special name given to the Irish – Milesians, descendants of the legendary Spanish King Milesus. This 'race' was supposedly the product of interbreeding between Moors and Marrains, that is, between Africans who had Hispanic roots and Spanish Jews who were forcibly converted to Christianity. This hybrid status did more than confirm the Irish as a 'monstrous race'. It set them apart, made them a special case. Once isolated within this magic circle, all sorts of conjuring tricks could be performed to make the Irish in Britain disappear; they could be assimilated through the civilising mission of their own Catholic Church, or converted to the British way of life via trade unionism. Most of all the image of their political threat could be dissolved into its parody.

The paddy joke is one place where the different elements of the code meet up;[108] paddy's lack of refinement and reason, 'his congenital stupidity', is here symbolised by his proverbial absence of family planning. His catholic tastes (in food and drink) are another sign that he does not fit in. But this dangerousness is de-fused by turning it into mere social incompetence; it is precisely at this point that ethnicist humour turns into a sick racist joke. For it is in and through the figure of 'Paddy' that racist theories of intelligence and moral degeneration were linked and relayed through popular culture to become common sense.

What, though, of the *internal* connection between immigration control and the civilising mission? What chain of associations does the code embed and fix within the hidden agendas of these two apparently conflicting areas of policy? The answer lies buried in the deep structure of the code, in the generative grammar of its misrecognitions. So let us look for it with the aid of the map we have devised.[109]

The racist problematics of breeding involve a specific *perversion* of inheritance. In the normal process of generational transmission the child grows up to inherit the place or functions of the parent; there is a transfer of power entailed in the succession of positions. But under the developmental laws of racism no such transfer occurs. The only condition under which a subject race is allowed to 'grow up' and become 'civilised' is if it first surrenders its birthright (that is, its own cultural legacy) and receives instead an intransitive patrimony of origins and destinies. This process of unequal exchange is at the heart of the whole civilising enterprise, and is today pretty well demystified. What is less remarked is the direct bearing it has on the moral anatomies mapped out by the racist imagination.

When race replaces generation as a signifier of patrimony, images of reproduction are split in a peculiarly perverse way. At one pole there is the body ideal of the master race; this is an ancestral body, immaculately conceived, desirable precisely because it leaves nothing to be desired. In the British case, as we have seen, it is a body of reason and refinement rather than pure blood. What is 'ideal' about it, is that within these imaginary relations of inheritance the body ceaselessly *regenerates* itself by repressing both its sexuality and its history. These, however, return 'by the back door' in the body image constructed for the subject race. This is a body in which everything desirable has been made lacking, a body made up of denigrated bits, unified only in the image of its monstrosity. This monster, through its polymorphous perversity represents a purely *degenerative* power of reproduction; its sexuality makes history, 'by the bad side', as a hidden hand, a secret principle of catastrophe. Thus sexuality and history which threaten the closed reproduction of the master race and are expelled from its body ideal, reappear under a negative sign in the sphere of circulation, where they are associated with the anarchic presence of the subject race. This mapping in turn opens up a space for the positioning of immigrant labour within the field of racial myths and fantasies.

However, if immigrant labour is constituted as a special object of this 'anti body' politic this is not just down to the workings of the racist imagination! It corresponds to its material positioning as a site of exploitation under capitalism. Capital requires reserve armies of labour to be free to circulate according to the anarchic demands of the market. This labour must be reproduced from day to day, but *not* from generation to generation, since the latter involves the state in considerable additional expense. Migrant labour appears to 'fit the bill', but only on condition that immigrants do not become settlers, or press their claims for social justice. For at that point the contradiction between the circulation and reproduction of their labour power comes to a head. Under these conditions their very mobility makes them an amorphous political threat, while if they put down roots they are seen as an intolerable economic burden. It is the terms of this contradiction which are articulated in a displaced and condensed form, in the ideological constructions of the code of breeding.

This operation which I have tried to describe in its successive forms, is represented diagrammatically in Figure 1.1. The code thus establishes a chain of correspondences, both real and imaginary, between the positions of master/subject race (map) and the properties of capital/labour (territory); in the process a structural contradiction (reproduction/circulation) is both misrecognised and magically resolved – through a *double* set of relations to the body politic.[110] This double inscription occurs whenever the code is effectively totalised, and all its registers (theoretical, moral, behavioural) are integrated into a single, comprehensive set of ideological practices. The code may then operate silently, or in a verbally elaborated form, may be enunciated as a political programme or moral norm, or simply be acted out, without changing its hegemonic role: to ensure that there is *no* context in which Jews, Blacks,

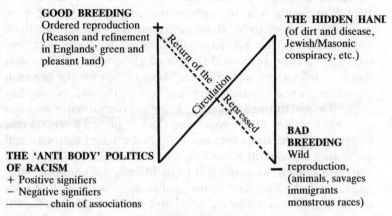

Figure 1.1

Irish, and so on are not treated as inferior beings as a matter of course and common sense.

Normally this requires that the code be institutionalised, either through the state apparatus, or through the everyday rituals of 'legal' subjectivity which constitute civil society, or both. However, the tensions which exist between state and civil society ensure that hegemony is never total, and it does not have to be in order that 'double inscription' takes place. For example, in the case of the Black community in post-war Britain, strategies of state racism and working-class prejudice have combined their effects at the level of territory whilst operating quite independently of one another to map the 'British way of life'. In other cases ethnic minorities may find themselves trapped on specific terrains of discrimination, yet do not spark off the racist imagination; the situation of the Turkish or Greek Cypriot communities may be an example of this; alternatively, a group may focus popular myths and fantasies precisely because of its success in breaking out of the positions assigned to it in the topography of power; the second-generation Jewish community is an obvious case in point. In the course of its history the same community may thus change position, just as different strata within it may be subjected to more or less totalised forms of racism.

Using this kind of model, it may, therefore, be possible to establish the principles of covariation between the trajectories of particular ethnic groups and of the specific types of racism to which they have been subjected, without reducing one to the other. A good deal more concrete comparative research would have to be undertaken before such an analysis could be made with any confidence. However, on the basis of the foregoing discussion there are one or two tentative conclusions which may be reached, regarding the peculiarities of the British case. The code of breeding evolved in and through successive historical compromises between different fractions of the governing class; it played a central role in cementing the links between class and ethnic hegemony and organising the civilising mission; from the outset biological and cultural signifiers were integral to its idioms, not so much alternatives as complementary terms used to construct a myth of class origin based on a racialised ethnicity; finally a perverse (split) representation of generation and sexuality was essential to its operation and served to inscribe patrimonies of reason and refinement within a problematics of inheritence where 'breeding was in the blood'.

Two rather more general points perhaps need to be made: first, racist ideology, however totalising in scope is not necessarily totalitarian. It becomes so only when hegemony breaks down and racist norms are directly enforced throughout society by the coercive power of the state. The development of a specialised apparatus of race relations has successfully pre-empted such a situation occurring in post-war Britain. The function of race relations management is to *de*totalise the code of breeding, to absorb ethnic minorities as separate and subordinate fractions of the working or professional classes, whilst holding popular racism in check. It is through this set of interventions that the civilising mission has finally succeeded in producing a specialised body politic of its own.[111] Second, the more totalising the code, the more fragmentary and context-bound other subordinate instances of racism become. For example, the more working-class racism has been 'outlawed' by the state education system, the more selective and intensive its operations have become in the community; but if we want to understand why this happens, and also just how the racism of the dominant class succeeds in becoming the dominant ideology of racism in society, we would be well advised to pay attention to the sources and sites of common-sense prejudice as these emerge 'from below' and it is to these we must now turn.

Tarzan and the jungle bunnies – class, race and sex in popular culture

Implicit in much of the argument so far has been the view that innovations in the idioms of popular racism during the post-war period have not arisen from the need to update the imperial legacy, or to blame immigration for Britain's terminal economic decline, but are the result of a sharpening contradiction between map and territory within the field of existing ideological practices. The White working class is being motivated to assume imaginary positions of mastery at a time, and in places, where its real forms of subjection are being forced ever closer to the material domains of Black experience in terms of unemployment, the hidden economy, and police harassment. It is in the attempt to dissolve or resolve this contradiction, by displacing or condensing its terms, that new themes, new chains of association have been produced. And it is in the realm of popular culture, in particular in its representation of sexuality, that we can find this process at work; both remaking racism as common sense, and opening up new possibilities of cultural negotiation between Black and White youth.

Popular culture is often written about as if it were the mere effect of a collision between dominant and subordinate ideologies, or some kind of open space where discourses circulate, and are distributed to various social determinations, in order that hegemony may go on being reproduced. Against this I want to argue that if the racist imagination is here at its most productive *and* most vulnerable, it is because popular cultures are always changing their own terms of reference; making history by actively constituting and anchoring new constellations of meaning.[112]

How then, does racism work through popular culture? First, via narrative themes, embedded in rumour, gossip, and jokes, which relay myths of racial origin and function as condensed statements of racist belief. Second, these 'mythemes' encode certain unconscious patterns of relation between Self and Other centred on idealised fantasy images of the body, and its 'monstrous' negation. Finally, myth and fantasy continually reverse into one another through rituals of misrecognition. It is at this intermediate level that racist stereotypes are constructed and enacted through specific modes of address, most especially in the form of ritual insults. Repertoires of verbal abuse are the cutting edge of popular racist discourse, not only because they offer an open invitation to physical injury in the context of the social encounters which they regulate, but also because it is here that the racist imagination is at its most dynamic in mapping out new territories of prejudice.[113]

Consider for a moment the derogatory epithets which have been applied to Black people. Into the already overcrowded bestiary of racist insult (sambo, coon, wog, nignog, spade, and so on) there entered a new creature around 1960: the jungle bunny. In countless streets and playgrounds this 'monster' sprang to linguistic life, and spread (or bred) until it became the most popular term of abuse directed by White working class youth against Black people. But where did it come from? Rabbits are not, after all, to be found in African rain forests! At first sight the jungle bunny's credentials seem straightforward enough. It links a popular racist myth (Blacks come from the jungle) to popular sexual fantasies (Blacks breed like rabbits) to reinforce a racist misrecognition (Blacks are animals). The insult also contains an embedded injunction (Blacks should go back to the jungle where they belong). In this way destinies are fixed to origins, prescriptively as well as ascriptively; the insult could be regarded as a condensed statement of support for enforced repatriation and/or tighter immigration controls, couched in the language of popular culture.

So do we have here a simple transcription of the dominant code of breeding, a symptom of its hegemonic penetration into working-class culture? Or is its provenance somewhat more complex? The term 'jungle', for example, is nothing if not a keyword in the history of racism, especially in the hidden curriculum of its civilising mission. Originally a Sanskrit word meaning a wild, uncultivated place inhabited by dangerous animals and spirits, it was appropriated by nineteenth-century colonial administrators and applied abusively to characterise 'native' habits and habitats throughout the Empire. Subsequently it was brought home and applied to the 'dark continents' of the working-class city. Urban jungles, concrete jungles, even blackboard jungles, where mobs of youth rampaged, and decent citizens feared to tread, were headline features of the popular Press throughout the 1960s. But it was not only spectacular youth cultures (mods, rockers, skinheads and so on) who were targeted in this way: the ghetto areas, the large housing estates (such as London's Broadwater Farm Estate) where, by courtesy of racialist housing policies, large numbers of Black people were forced to settle, were vilified in similar terms. The media message was that 'these people' had brought their 'primitive cultures' with them and turned these 'civilised amenities' into jungles of crime and vice.[114]

The jungle addressed in the insult is, therefore, not just an imaginary place of Black origins associated with the colonial past – it is the contemporary inner city as constructed in moral panics where White youth find themselves positioned alongside their Black peers as 'animals and savages'. But if the insult points to a potential recognition of shared predicament along one of its dimensions, along another it works to foreclose just that possibility: the entry of 'bunny' into the jungle story sees to that. I asked a group of White working class boys, with pronounced racist views, to give me their associations to the word. 'Bunny' for them, first of all, meant 'slag' or 'whore' after the eponymous heroines of *Playboy* magazine. It also signified someone who was 'all mouth' and rabbits on (rhyming slang: rabbits paw = jaw): shades of the cockney singing duo, Chas and Dave. It was also a synonym for a 'div', someone who doesn't have their wits about them and is easily conned (Teddy Boy slang); and finally, of course, it meant someone who was timid, or fearful and scared of authority (as in the popular song 'Run, rabbit, run'). The term thus encompasses *all* the attributes which are most despised in these lads' culture.[115]

What happens, then, when the two terms are put together? If a Black boy is called a jungle bunny by one of these young racists, he may choose to ignore the insult and walk away. But that 'only proves' to these lads' satisfaction that Blacks are 'running scared'; if, however, he loses his temper and threatens to hit them, then that only goes to show that 'Blacks can't take a joke, and are no better than savages'. If he 'bad names' them back, and *then* walks off, 'Blacks are all mouth'. No matter which way he responds, he confirms that he *is* a 'jungle bunny' in their eyes. All insults have this self-fulfilling, performative function. Moreover, it is a basic rule of racist discourse that its objects cannot become subjects without confirming its predicates. Racist insults 'stick' in so far as they succeed in trapping their victims in this double bind. In this case the Black boy is offered a choice between being termed 'running scared' – and hence 'out of order', in terms of the masculine code of territoriality, or 'running wild', and thereby constituting an 'outrage' to public propriety.

If this bunny has been transformed from the friendly little playmate of toddlers' first storybooks into an adolescent monster, it is because it plays a further role in the racist jungle story. In so far as it is gendered feminine its mixture of social timidity and rampant fertility is a simple rendition of the sexual double standard (virgin/whore). But its location in the urban jungle gives it a masculine connotation as well. The jungle bunny is a *potent* figure forging the link between sexuality and social combination in a way which epitomised for these lads, the very threat of black power. This was a physical prowess they secretly envied, even idealised, though in the jokes and stories they told it was derided and treated with contempt. As myth reverses into fantasy, denigrated features are transformed into secret sources of identification, while fear and fascination continue to oscillate unacknowledged beneath the surface bravado.[116]

Embedded in this structure of racist disavowal there lies a more hidden set of class and gender relations. First, on the lived terrain of exploitation, capital and patriarchy combine to 'unite' immigrant and youth labour in the same generic categories of ancillary, servicing and 'skivvy' jobs, closely associated with women's work in the home. Moreover, the youth wage, like the 'immigrant' wage, has this in common with the female wage – that it is *not* a family wage, and does not meet the full intergenerational costs of reproducing labour power within the domestic sphere. In the case of girls this results in the multiple oppressions of gender, race and class becoming articulated into a single domain of material experience. A spontaneous sense of shared predicament is thus relatively easy to sustain. But for boys the situation is much more fraught with contradiction, and involves a very different kind of map. They live their class subjection through the proto-domestic features of their labour, but in such a way as to dissociate themselves from both by assuming imaginary positions of mastery linked to masculine 'prides of place'. As we have seen, under certain conditions, these prides may get expressed through racist practices; moreover, the counter-assertion of 'hardness' is not just in relation to male elders; the apprenticeship to working-class inheritances also involves mastering techniques for 'feminising' and belittling other lads, and ritual insults are a favoured medium for this.[117]

For a White lad to call a Black boy a jungle bunny, is thus a means of shifting from a one-down position (feminine/youth) to a one-up one (male/elder) which is thereby claimed as exclusive prerogative. But there is a 'Catch 22' to this; for Black working-class boys operate the *same* strategy to assert their own 'hardness'. Their repertoires of ritual insult are no less developed. 'Jungle bunny', for example, may be capped by 'powder puff'. Now it is the White boys' turn to be 'shown up' as 'soft like a girl', hence 'queer' or 'bent'. The exchange of jeers and taunts in the context of a street or playground encounter may well escalate into physical violence, to prove 'who rules round here'. But this is not the only possible scenario. The very fact that they are conducted through the mechanisms of male rivalry implies some recognition that Black and White are peers of the same proletarian public realm. Whereas insults by definition articulate unequal positions, banter is more symmetrical. It may support multi-ethnic friendships between boys by reinforcing a common macho stance. As a medium of social exchange it may even serve to neutralise the racist component of the message. If one Black boy calls another a 'jungle bunny' it will be read as a term of friendship not abuse, a mark that they are 'best mates', by very virtue of the fact that they can share its use against its racist connotation. What in one context is a term of racial hatred communicating a violent intent, may, in another, signal the message 'this is play' promoting a brand of inter-ethnic humour which can serve as a powerful diffuser of tensions. Ritual, in symbolising conflictual positions can pre-empt the passage to the act.[118]

However, because all these negotiations rest on a hidden structure of disavowal, patterns of identification remain highly unstable. Some ethnic attributes may be idealised because of their positive class and gender associations, whilst others are denigrated. Most typically, of course, many White working-class boys discriminate positively in favour of Afro-Caribbean subcultures as exhibiting a macho, proletarian style, and against Asian cultures as being 'effeminate' and 'middle-class'. Such boys experience no sense of contradiction in wearing dreadlocks, smoking ganja and going to reggae concerts whilst continuing to assert that 'Pakis stink'. Split perceptions, linking double standards of gender, ethnicity and class are increasingly the rule.[119]

One reason why these context-bound forms of prejudice are so hard to get to grips with, is that they rest on a set of unspoken positions which are deeply entrenched within popular culture and which are voiced through many of its heroes. I asked my group of thirteen-year-olds whom they would most like to be like and a variety of stars from the world of sport and popular music were mentioned without any consensus being reached. Then one boy, somewhat shamefacedly, admitted to Tarzan being his 'childhood' hero and all the group instantly agreed: Tarzan still ruled OK, as far as they were concerned!

At first sight, there is nothing particularly mysterious about the continuing popularity of the Tarzan myth. He represents a masculine body ideal in which the whole code of breeding is enshrined. He is quite literally a noble savage. Born of aristocratic parents, but abandoned, he grew up as a 'wild child' in the African jungle, uncorrupted by bourgeois ways and wiles (unlike the real English aristocracy) and possessing a body which 'leaves nothing to be desired'. Tarzan's body is *not* defined by sexual difference – Jane is merely there to support its narcissistic properties – but it does express an absolute identity with its class and racial ancestry. For 'breeding will out' and Tarzan is soon Lord of the Jungle, master of all he surveys. And, like all clever civilisers, he learns the natives' (that is, the animals') languages in order to get them to do his bidding. Even when he is at his wildest, uttering savage whoops and cries, he remains a born aristocrat, one of Nature's gentlemen.[120]

The way in which these boys 'read' the story did not, however, conform to its plot line in the dominant version of the code. For them, Tarzan was above all a *White ape*, someone who possessed all the physical qualities they secretly admired in both apes and Black people. To identify with Tarzan was to assume these qualities, without associating themselves with either. Moreover, as a 'wild child' who makes good, who comes out on top without having to conform to the dominant conventions of educated society, he represents a position with which working-class children in particular can identify. Playing at Tarzan on the streets of their inner-city neighbourhoods licensed them to 'behave like savages' whilst maintaining their supremacy as 'Lords of the Urban Jungle' over and against both the Black presence *and* the civilising mission. In this way they succeed in 'squaring the circle', turning a code which puts them down into a device for affirming the superior patrimony of being not only white and male but also working-class 'born and bred'.

It is the figure of Tarzan who in a sense makes it possible to snare the bunny within the jungle of racist ideas; as a hidden operator between myth and fantasy, he constitutes the unspoken position of power from which the insult is issued and the stereotype is made to stick. For if the White ape and the Black rabbit are made to magically cohabit the same universe of discourse, it is only to reinstate, in these boys' own language the great divide between those with breeding and those who merely breed. By this circuitous route, and without for a moment knowing it, these 'Jack the lads' managed to join the 'young bucks' of another period and class as erstwhile playboys of the Western world.

Feminists and anti-racists have laboured mightily to put Tarzan and the jungle bunnies out of business, to replace them with positive images and alternative heroes and heroines. The enterprise has not had much success; partly because of the authoritarian and insensitive way in which it has often been conducted, and partly because it has not understood the dynamics of popular racism. Moreover, behind many recent initiatives aimed at achieving greater equality of educational opportunity there has been an undialectical view of gender, race and class. It is assumed that these are homologous structures, that to undermine one is to weaken the others, and that methods which are effective in one sphere can be transplanted elsewhere.[121] I have tried to show why these assumptions are false. There is no fixed or direct principle of correspondence. Sexist imagery may at one moment add injury to racist insult, and in the next, unite White and Black boys in displays of male chauvinism; the shared experience of sexism may in one setting bring girls together, and in another polarise them through the operation of a racial double standard.

The reception of the anti-racist message is similarly over-determined in its contexts of transmission within the school. For example, if a Black teacher disciplines a White pupil for a racist remark, that action implicitly relays a message from outside the classroom itself – to the effect that the Black community, which the teacher here represents, will not passively stand by and tolerate racial abuse, but will use whatever power its members can command to defend themselves and prevent further attacks. But if the teacher happens to be a woman, and the pupil is male, here disciplinary intervention is likely to be read in quite a different way – as that of a mother telling off a naughty child – and it will be resisted from a sexist as well as (or rather than) a racist standpoint. If, however, the anti-racist teacher is also White, the intervention is much more likely to be decoded by the pupil in class terms, as the expression of an arbitrary state authority, which is 'siding with the Blacks against us'.

The existence of such variables points to the need for an overall policy. But the difficulty here is that the cultural negotiations amongst young people which both reproduce *and* interrupt the links between racism and sexism often take place as part of a wider process of *class* resistance to the civilising mission of the school. In so far as educational interventions are made into these arenas they may well provoke a reaction which reinforces all the negative aspects of the school counter-culture; the idioms of popular racism which are already in circulation within the White working class community may then connect up with and legitimise other kinds of popular resentment against schooling. And this is clearly a situation which racialist youth organisations can and do exploit. If we are to be in a stronger position to pre-empt such moves we need to look more closely at the underlying premises of our own anti-racist policies and practices.

Reasons (not) to be racist

There is a famous etching by Goya entitled 'The Sleep of Reason Produces Monsters', which shows the artist slumped over his desk and surrounded by a crowd of eerie, bat-like creatures, representing phantoms of the imagination which have escaped the grasp of the conscious mind. This picture has come to symbolise the project of the Enlightenment – to make the more recalcitrant and hidden aspects of the human personality yield up their secrets so that they can be better understood and controlled, and society can be organised along more orderly and rational lines. Today, that project survives nowhere more strongly than in the role assigned to education and social science in the struggle to overcome the monstrous images of popular prejudice. If Goya's etching were to be redone today it would show reason and racism locked in mortal combat to win the hearts and minds of the young.

I have argued that this is a false picture. The practice of reason is deeply implicated in the history of Anglo-Saxon race thinking. In fact, if the creatures of the racist imagination have aroused the intelligentsia from its slumbers it has either been to rationalise and operationalise them as the basis of new technologies of surveillance and control, or to use them as yet further evidence of the 'primitive superstitions' which hold sway amongst the masses.[122]

Teachers, who are after all supposed to be the guardians and inculcators of reasonable behaviour in the young, are especially prone to hold this latter view. The most widely-held theory about the causes of popular racism is still that it is the product of ignorance and/or irrational fear. This is often linked to a deficit model of working-class culture. The common sense of the staffroom is that 'those kids' don't know any better than to be racist because their parents or peers have not equipped them with the intellectual or experiential resources to think any differently about difference. Middle-class culture, in contrast, is usually seen as a haven of tolerance, understanding, appreciation of diversity and other liberal values. Teaching against racism is thus all too easily incorporated within the traditional remit of the civilising mission to the working class. Reason and tolerance is made the prerogative of the 'educated classes' while 'unreason' and racism becomes inherent traits of the rest. It is in and through this very construction that a specifically middle-class form of racism is being mobilised – that is, a racism centred on an ideology of innate intelligence and natural aptitude, and the congenital lack of these qualities on the part of those 'less fortunately' endowed. In adopting what they take to be an anti-racist position, these teachers are, in fact, simply redirecting their middle-class prejudice, from Black to White working-class students. This, in turn, tends to produce a curious double standard in teachers' perceptions of racism in the classroom. They are highly sensitised to the possibility of racist innuendo in the behaviour of those working-class pupils, especially boys, whom they regarded as 'trouble' in other contexts, whilst they are far more permissive of – or blind to – the more subtly racist attitudes of middle-class pupils and girls, whom they view in any case as 'sensible'.

If racism is seen as an illogical belief system, and working-class culture as dominated by irrational forces, then it is clearly not too difficult to conceive of some elective affinity between the two. So the argument goes, if Black immigrants are made the scapegoat for material and social problems suffered by the more deprived sections of the White community, it is because the latter do not understand the real reasons for them. The answer must, then, lie in the application of reasoned argument to analyse the true causes of unemployment; teaching materials which give the true historical facts about Empire, or the reasons for immigration, will enable working-class students to realise that Black and White share common problems and that their real enemies are the state and capital. The problem with this kind of rationalist pedagogy is not just that it rests on an inadequate theory of racism; it fails to grasp the fact that popular racism does not rely on 'theories' in the sense of worked-out beliefs about society; as we have seen, it is primarily a behavioural ideology, one which works through everyday cultural practices to shape basic bodily images of Self and Other. The racist imagination constructs its own objects of perception and its own internal procedures of consensual validation in a way which is quite impervious to theoretic logic. Lessons in 'race relations' are, therefore, so much grist to its mill. Moreover, this approach implies academic methods of instruction, which spell instant boredom to many pupils, especially those who are already alienated from school. Thus resistances to the pedagogic medium *and* to its anti-racist message become intertwined to ensure that these pupils live up to their teachers' expectations of them as apprentice racists.[123]

It is certainly the case that there have been plenty of racist ideologues who have drawn on the language and philosophy of irrationalism, albeit in a highly calculating way; but it would clearly be absurd to conclude from this that all racists are suffering from a special kind of thought disorder, or emotional disturbance! The project of constructing some kind of mass psychology of racism has always foundered on the fact that whatever instance of psychopathology is identified with extreme racist beliefs, it can also be found distributed just as widely amongst other populations. There are plenty of 'rigid authoritarian personality types' to be found in the anti-racist movement, for example, and it may well be that some of them are splitting off or repressing the 'bad' parts of the Self associated with excretory functions, and projecting it onto the Other in the form of White racists! However, to regard racist or anti-racist attitudes as simply a rationalisation of conflicts located elsewhere in the psyche rather than in society is in itself a rather interesting example of displacement. Therapeutic models of intervention based on such ideas are either impracticable – you cannot lay a whole society out on the couch – or else treat the problem as having to do with a deviant minority, rather than being the social norm that it is.[124]

If neither pedagogic nor psychiatric regimes of reason have had much success with popular racism, is a good dose of 'experience' a better remedy? Experiential learning is currently much in vogue for use with 'non-academic' pupils and who wouldn't rather go on a trip to Barbados, or the local Gurdwara, than sit in the classroom listening to Sir? But experience has shown that these impressions, memorable and rewarding though they may be, do not in themselves shift the grounds of common sense. For those who have a strong ontological stake in racism – who cannot stand the touch, sight, sound or smell of Black people – familiarity only 'breeds' more contempt; for the majority, material experiences of other cultures, however positive, do not seem to deconstruct negative stereotypes; each operates at a different level of ideology; map and territory remain insulated from one another; what *is* learnt is how to manage and reduce cognitive dissonance, how to say 'some of my best friends are Black', with greater credibility than before. The system of split perceptions and double standards remains intact and indeed may well be reinforced.[125]

The enlightenment model of anti-racist work, whether its epistemology is rationalist or empiricist, fails to break with the deficit view of working-class culture, and treats racism as a form of false consciousness which is intrinsic to it. Whatever the strategy of demystification proposed, the reasons which young people themselves give for holding racist views are regarded as rationalisations, mere 'epiphenomena', and are largely ignored. This does not put the teacher or youth worker in a strong position to enter into the 'extra-curricular debates' in which such issues are largely decided. Consider the following piece of common sense, from a popular peer group spokesman with active racialist sympathies:

Everyone's a racist in one way or another, whether they admit to it or not. Everyone prefers their own kind. I was brought up to live in a white society; it runs through me, like a stick of rock. Can you imagine Britain with a black queen? People all over the world used to look up to the British way. That's why they all wanted to come over here, even the blacks. That's when the problems started. Black and white just don't mix. It's no good just blaming Thatcher. She's just sticking up for white people's rights because no-one else will. We're supposed to be living in a democracy – that means the rule of the majority – and the majority is white.

Such arguments are entirely logical within the framework of class and ethnic hegemony, and indeed reproduce its effects to the letter. They clearly have to be engaged with, rather than dismissed. But on what terms?

There is a school of thought which argues that working-class racism, far from being a product of 'unreason', is an entirely rational and realistic response to competition with immigrants for scarce resources in the housing and labour market. The solution is, therefore, simple – more jobs and houses equals less racism. The equation is attractive, not least because it gives the economistic demands of the labour movement the status of a moral crusade against racism without having to do anything to put its own house in order; but it does not add up. There is no simple correlation between market conditions and ideological relations. Moreover, to make racist positions a rational choice is tantamount to giving these arguments the status of a realist account, without in any way problematising their construction.[126]

Instead, it should be possible to grant that racist discourses produce forms of rationality which are specific and adequate to their purpose, whilst representing the real in an entirely imaginary and perverse way. Racist arguments are specious not because they are formally illogical (although they may be), but because their rhetorical object – race – is a construct to which nothing real corresponds in the subject to which it is addressed. Furthermore, the construction of this object exerts a special effect on the reasoning which is employed on its behalf.[127] For example, the peculiar notion of historical causality which is built into racist conspiracy theories bears the indelible imprint of what I have called the perversions of inheritance. This is an operation in two stages: to begin with the movement of history is reduced to a law of generations – that is, to genealogy. Just as one generation begets or causes its successor, so one historical event is supposed to cause or beget another. Then this *post hoc propter hoc* logic is made to function as the hidden hand of 'race' in history: first the Blacks arrive in Britain, then unemployment rises, therefore the Blacks are taking our jobs. The line of argument thus plots a network of invisible genealogical links between what are structurally discontinuous (though spatially or temporally contiguous) realities to produce, in this case, a catastrophe theory of immigration.

A further example is the *sui generis* character of racist ascriptions. The abusive generalisations which recognise subjects only as generic representatives of their 'race' is based on a special paralogical form which removes 'some' as a category between all or none. Thus:

> (Some) young Blacks are criminals.
> Errol is a young Black.
> Therefore Errol is a thief.

Equally, it may work through the identification of subjects by predicates; thus:

> Criminals are people who fail to conform to society.
> Rastas are people who fail to conform to society.
> Therefore Rastas are criminals.

Now, rightly, it has often been pointed out that such reasoning is characteristic of all kinds of unconscious or primary process thinking, and is not unique to racism. My argument, is that the generative grammar of racist discourses is not only dependent on such processes, but also organises and articulates them in a special way.[128]

Of course, no philosopher is going to persuade the police that the statements given above are either false or racist, for they constitute the operational logic of the daily routines through which the law criminalises large numbers of Black youth.[129] Map and territory here coincide to reinforce each other's 'rationality'. In this situation it is understandable why sections of the anti-racist movement are now concentrating their efforts on dissuading people from racist practices, not by appeals to reason, but by taking direct action. Here there are two main approaches: first there is what might be called the physical force tendency where the aim is to police the physical behaviour of the ethnic majority and to use 'remedial violence' against anyone who makes physical attacks against the minority community. The logic of reprisal is meant to act as a deterrent, and to signal clearly to apprentice racists what is in store for them if they put their beliefs into practice. The justification for this method is that violence is the only language that this kind of racist understands, and that it is better to teach them a lesson they won't forget sooner rather than later. The second line of attack might be called the moral force tendency and has been adopted by some councils and local education authorities. Here the aim is to police language and social behaviour, to outlaw negative stereotypes, and make positive images as defined by ethnic minorities themselves a normative practice of representation. Although disciplinary action is taken against anyone found guilty of committing any public statement of racial prejudice, the main thrust is to use the threat of moral denunciation as a means to impose a form of self-censorship, which interrupts or inhibits the production of racist utterances.

These are strong-arm tactics, and they have an unpleasant ring in liberal ears. But perhaps it is worth remembering that they are dealing with an unpleasant reality – the escalation of physical and verbal attacks on the Black community, which more liberal methods have proved powerless to check. There is some evidence that such sanctions are proving effective in making racism a 'no-go area' for White working-class youth, and are in one way or another shutting racists up. However, the question remains whether methods which may be appropriate for dealing with hard-core racists are also suitable for working with the majority of rather more silent or passive followers of ideological fashion. Recent experience in schools suggests that the answer is a decisive 'no'.

For a school to adopt an anti-racist policy is to explicitly signal to ethnic minority communities its commitment to fight racism in all its forms.[130] That must obviously include a policy of identifying and punishing any display of racist sentiment on the part of pupils, as well as staff. But this means that dealing with popular racism becomes essentially a matter of classroom discipline, albeit one which now takes on a higher political saliency. In so far as it does, it is likely to reinforce strategies of resistance which working-class pupils are already deploying against other aspects of school discipline. In its most benign form the teacher may be subject to racist 'wind-ups' with pupils deliberately exaggerating their own feelings and beliefs in order to provoke a response. If the teacher treats it seriously, as a disciplinary matter, then he or she is shown up as someone who can't take a joke; if he or she ignores it, then the pupil has 'got away with it'. The more usual response, however, is for pupils to simply play it cool, giving an outward display of conformity whilst inwardly maintaining the same racist position, which may then be all the more vehemently acted out as soon as the teacher's back is turned. This kind of Jekyll and Hyde racism, which is a function of teacher/pupil interaction may then connect up with wider patterns of split perception. The attempt to censor the popular culture of racism through disciplinary means thus encounters a whole series of resistances which may produce a number of unintended counter-effects. Racism may be silenced in the classroom only to appear in an even more virulent form in the playground. Various strategies of disavowal may be mobilised, and silent racism may continue to rule. If, out of desperation, the school resorts to asking pupils to report incidents of racial harassment to the staff, then the association between 'anti-racist' and 'school sneak' or 'teacher's pet' is made complete, and even those who are not involved in the school counter-culture are likely to close ranks.

There are a number of reasons why such attempts to legislate against ideology fail. In the first place they are forced to adopt technologies of surveillance and control which are identical to those already exercised by the state and sometime to deploy them in an even more extreme form. Interestingly enough, the propaganda produced by both physical and moral forcers often explicitly mimics the discursive strategies of totalitarian power.[131] 'Racist Beware – Elwar is watching You' says one well-known campaign flyer issued by East London Workers Against Racism. Haringey Council issues an invitation for a conference on housing and ethnic minorities, entitled 'Stamping Out Racism', which positions the reader as having his or her face stamped on, in sad fulfilment of George Orwell's prophecy for the world after 1984.

The battle for young hearts and minds will clearly not be won by such means. When it is no longer possible to 'call a spade a spade', because the level of connotations, which is always open to multiple associations, including racist ones, has been shut down 'By Order', then denotation itself becomes a mere exercise in the language game of Power. But when meanings can no longer be subject to negotiation, it becomes impossible to question or contest their ideological construction. The chronic repetition of 'correct thought' is probably the quickest way to kill the development of any critical awareness; when the anti-racist message is only the same old slogan we can be sure that young people will not listen to it!

No one seriously engaged in anti-racist education would entertain such a purely repressive strategy. This is not unfortunately, true of some political activists, of an authoritarian persuasion. Yet they are their own worst enemies, for in their failure to understand and engage with the unconscious reasoning of racism, they run the risk of reproducing it within their own practices of representation. The examples just given illustrate this all too well. But perhaps more worrying in the long term is the continued prevalence of conspiracy theories within sections of the anti-racist movement. Here we find the same paralogics as with racist discourse, only applied to different referents, of course:

(Some) Whites are racialist.
John is White.
Therefore John is a racialist.

or

Racialism divides and rules the masses.
Capitalism divides and rules the masses.
Therefore racialism is a capitalist plot
to undermine the working-class movement.

The 'hidden hand' belongs to a different agent, but the principle, or rather *petitio principii*, is the same. Moreover, the strategic imagery is drawn from the same source. Racism is held to 'breed' in certain environmental conditions (inner city decay, mass unemployment, for example) and is treated as a highly contagious 'ideological disease', something people catch from each other through personal contact, and which, if left unchecked, will infect the the whole body politic. The 'answer' is, therefore, to institute various 'screening procedures' to isolate the 'carriers' and prevent them spreading the virus further, and/or eradicate its 'breeding grounds'. We can perhaps see here just how hegemonic the code of breeding has become, how far it has succeeded in pre-empting alternative modes of thinking, so that even, and especially those movements which set out to oppose it, end up using its terms. The result is that racist and anti-racist movements mimic each other's discourse, shadow each other's every move, like Harpo and Groucho Marx in *Duck Soup*.

Why, in practice, has it proved so difficult to move beyond this mirror phase? One reason, I think, is that political polarisation around the issue of 'race' and ethnicity so often occurs in societies like that of Britain, where the class structure has proved capable of absorbing these tensions without fundamental change. Asymmetrical relations of power are routinely represented through symmetrical ideologies of the Other in a way which leaves the basis of hegemony intact. This can generate some very vicious circles. For example, because of the discrimination they face, members of ethnic minorities have to continually assert their rights; yet, in a racist society, even the smallest gesture of self assertion runs the risk of being interpreted as a sign of 'unreasonableness' or 'trying to take over'. This reaction in turn encourages Black/Irish/Jewish people to regard all members of the ethnic majority, whatever their actual class position or social behaviour, as belonging to the same, globally oppressive power structure. Under these circumstances, any individual statement of less than total support for any action taken by any Black/Irish/Jewish organisation is likely to be read as a full blown racist attack against the whole community. And this in turn provides further ammunition for those who wish to portray the legitimate demands of these communities for social justice as being the ravings of fanatics.

Perhaps the major task facing educationalists at the present time is to help find a way out of such vicious circles, and one minimum condition for that is to ensure that educational policies and practices do not themselves contribute a further twist. The history of recent initiatives is not entirely encouraging in this respect. Despite some notable advances in reforming the curriculum so that it is more responsive to the cultural and linguistic diversity of pupils, and in the professional advancement of ethnic minority teachers, little progress has been made in tackling the subroutines of racism to be found in staff room and pupil cultures.[132] Neither appeals to reason or experience, nor moral or physical force have shifted this mule. One major obstacle here is the question of persuasion. Charges of political brainwashing, indoctrination or worse frequently fly around whenever the taken-for-granted assumptions of racist common sense are confronted.[133] The liberal or multi-cultural position rightly resists the compulsory morality of 'positive images' but fails to recognise the forms of hidden persuasion which exist in the educational system and the wider society. Anti-racists are much better at highlighting these dimensions of hegemony, but if they use the most sophisticated theoretical work to expose the hidden ideological manoeuvres of racism, they no less strenuously exempt their own practices of propaganda from similar critical scrutiny. This double standard seriously undermines any heuristic claims that might be made for the educational value of introducing anti-racist materials in the classroom.

There is a growing recognition that neither approach in itself is up to the task of making racism genuinely unpopular. Clearly there are elements in both which need to be defended and extended, but unfortunately no simple or easy synthesis is likely to emerge. The problem is indeed one of method, or rather the lack of it. For it is at the level of pedagogy that the failure of commitment and imagination has been greatest. In one sense this is surprising, since there does exist a set of teaching methods which expressly sets out to challenge the élitist educational norms embodied in the civilising mission and to explore popular culture as an alternative source of really useful knowledge. Yet in another sense Cultural Studies, as it has been developed in schools only has itself to blame for its lack of impact. Its ethnocentric origins in the Eng. Lit. tradition initially limited its application to creating a space within which the racist (and sexist) elements of White working-class youth culture could have free play; more recently, under the impact of emergent cultural politics in the Black community, it has become the vehicle for a roots-radicalism which tends to be highly ethnocentric in its concerns. Nevertheless, this is an active pedagogy in which students are encouraged to read between the lines, not only in various mass media, but also in their own everyday cultural practices.[134] For example, students might examine the ideology of teenage romance by taking apart photostories from popular magazines and putting together alternative versions of their own; this in turn might open up discussion about real, as opposed to idealised relations between boys and girls. Such methods do not rely on the logistics of 'experience' or the formal logic of 'structuralist analysis'; they have been specifically designed for 'non-academic' students and they can be used to elicit and give expression to cultural materials which resist or are repressed by racist discourses, as well as to expose racist representations to critical scrutiny. This approach may help White working-class youth to recognise what is suppressed in their own culture by its racist articulations as well as sensitising Black students to the points where racist images have succeeded in penetrating and distorting their own frames of self-reference.[135]

As an example of what is particular to this method, and how it differs from other approaches, consider for a moment the possible uses of the Anansi stories in the multi-ethnic classroom.[136] From an anti-racist perspective, Anansi is a political hero, a symbol of popular resistence to colonialism, a Black 'Spiderman' who will just not be kept down. Such a reading, whilst quite valid, does involve some 'recontextualising' of the stories, even in some cases a rewriting. Moreover, White children are not likely to identify with this revised version as readily as Black. In multi-cultural readings, Anansi tends to be presented as a figure in Afro-Caribbean folklore, occupying a similar role to that of the Yoruba or Winnebago Trickster: he even has a European parallel in the shape of the Good Soldier Schweik. This approach *de*contextualises the stories, turning Anansi into an historical figure, an anthropological curiosity, in a way that robs the texts of much of their contemporary relevance for children.

For the Cultural Studies teacher, in contrast, the main interest lies in exploring the possible relations between Anansi and his White opposite number, the Spiderman who stalks the streets, and pages of American comics. Both sets of stories might be read to the class, and the children asked to note similarities and differences between the Black and White 'Spidermen'. They would then be asked to make up their own comic story in which the two characters meet. This in turn would serve to open up a discussion about popular heroes produced by dominant and oppressed cultures. In this way, Black and White children would be invited to negotiate about meanings on an equal footing, to explore the grounds of their own and each other's readings of this material as well as the cultural politics of the texts themselves. And if, finally, it is the Anansi stories which prove the more genuinely persuasive, it will be because they contain more of the complexities and ironies of life, because Anansi in both his vulnerability and his cunning is more human than the magical omnipotence and mechanical plots offered by the Spidermen comics. For what the children should be learning through this and similar exercises is to become more sensitive – we might even say allergic – to slogans, stereotypes and one-dimensional imagery of every kind.

The kind of approach I am arguing for, thus tries to connect with what is most progressive in both multi-cultural and anti-racist teaching, whilst adding a dimension of its own which overcomes some of the more negative features of both. But I am certainly not offering a panacea. It is intended merely to indicate one possible direction for a renewal of educational initiatives at a time when these are thin on the ground and face increasing difficulties on all sides. Many of these difficulties stem from structural resistances to change in both the education system and the wider society. These have been amplified by the Thatcherite administration, but they will not disappear with Thatcherism. Their form and function is analysed elsewhere in this book (see Chapters 2 and 3).

To focus on the ideological dimensions of racism as I have done in this chapter is not to argue that changing hearts and minds is the only, or even the most important way to produce a less racist society. Unless the political conditions and economic foundations of hegemony are shifted, then such changes will be superficial and all too easily reversed. But, equally, anti-racist or multi-cultural policies will not translate into a lasting and effective reform of practice as long as the majority of the population continue actively or passively to resist them. Under these conditions, all that ideological analysis can do is pinpoint some of the stumbling blocks which have been built in to particular social formations. It may not be possible to bulldoze them out of the way; indeed that would be counterproductive; but it may be possible to find ways round them. It is one of the essential tasks of education as a genuinely civilising process to open up these alternative routes to young people not as part of a long forced march towards 'Truth', but as a means of exploring for themselves the discrepancies between map and territory, where other kinds of meanings wait to be brought to creative life.[137]

I have tried to demonstrate a method of analysis which answers to these terms of reference. In doing so I have argued for a model which not only allows racist discourses to 'speak' at a number of different levels, but helps pinpoint their changing principles of articulation, as these are governed by particular contexts and conjunctures. I have outlined a number of substantive theses regarding the differences and similarities between anti-Semitism and colour prejudice, the contradictory features of working-class racism *vis-à-vis* 'national/popular' discourse and the central role of the code of breeding in linking class and ethnic hegemony. At the same time I have tried not to lose sight of the inner workings of the racist imagination, relating its characteristic practices of reason, to a deep structure of myth, ritual and fantasy in which images of the body are organised according to a split representation of sexuality and generation. In this way I have tried to draw together some of the threads of recent research in psychoanalysis, cultural studies and social history. Above all by locating the peculiarities of Anglo-Saxon racism in the internal history and contradictions of British society, I have tried to indicate how to build a framework within which it is more possible to cross-reference between the Jewish, Irish and Black experiences in this country without either reifying them or reducing them to some lowest common denominator. This seems to me to be a precondition for moving beyond the mirror phase of ideological struggle towards a radicalism which is less rooted in ethnocentric concerns. Finally, by looking at popular culture as a complex site of negotiation between gender, ethnicity and class, I have suggested one possible focus for work with young people which may help make racism less popular and education more so. In these long years of Britain's decline, when the rancorous clash of contested wills and legacies completes and complicates the perversions of inheritance, it still seems important to hold on to a more generous vision of human possibilities, even if it becomes ever more imperative to ground them in realistic principles of hope.

Notes and references

1. The research on which this chapter is based was carried out as part of a wider study of changing patterns of political socialisation in Britain funded by the Leverhulme Trust. The writing up of this material was completed under the auspices of the PSEC/CME Cultural Studies Project, at the Institute of Education, London, and was funded by the Gulbenkian, Baring, Hilden and Sir John Cass Foundations. I would like to thank the many colleagues who have read and commented on earlier drafts, especially Jagdish Gundara, Billy Nowathe, Bob Ferguson and Bob Catterall. Professor Basil Bernstein continued to provide much needed stimulus and support.
2. See Hilberg (1973) Davidowicz (1979) and Mosse (1978). Also Arendt (1951).
3. See Sartre (1948).
4. For a psychoanalytic reading of the Unconscious and its relation to racist ideologies and institutions, see Sibony (1976) and (1983). Sibony has located the 'mirror phase' not just in a general formula of ideology and subjectivity but in precise mechanisms of power and perversion in which racist positions and practices are structurally reproduced.
5. See Mullard (1980) for a critique of multi-culturalism.
6. For a critique of anti-racist ideology, its limits and conditions, see Sibony (1986).
7. On splitting and the 'coconut' phenomenon, see Fanon (1970).
8. On animal categories as terms of derogation, see Leach (1964), Poliakov (ed.) (1975) and Thomas (1983). On the comparison between Black and Irish in Britain, see Lebow (1976).
9. For a recent restatement of the 'physicalist' position, see Smith in Rex and Mason (eds) (1986).
10. See for example Griffin (1986) and the recent film *Soul Man*. For a general overview of liberal strategies of conscientisation, see Rich (1984).
11. The best account of anti-Semitism and its relation to the Jewish question is to be found in Rodinson (1983). Rodinson's resolute stance against ethnocentrism, whether Jewish, Arab, or whatever kind, has inspired much of what follows.
12. On the strategic role of merchant capital, see Fox and Genovese (1983) and also Rey (1973); on the symbolism of the wandering Jew, see Dundes *et al.* (1986); on the vampire as an economic metaphor, see Moretti (1983); and on the thematics of the 'hidden hand', see Poliakov (1980).
13. See Holmes (1979) and Poliakov (1974).

14. On the medieval iconography of 'monstrous races', see Friedman (1966), Wittkower (1977), Lascaux (1983). For a general overview of racism in feudal societies, see Delacampagne (1983).

15. On the changing status of labour in the transition from feudalism to capitalism, see Hilton (1970 and 1976) and Corrigan (1977); on the relation to slavery, see Williams (1963), Verlinden (1970) and Patterson (1980); and on changing modes of representation, see Duby (1980).

16. See Bolt (1971) and Lorimer (1978).

17. On the rise of scientific racism, see Rose (1976) and Lewonton *et al.* (1982). On the forms of Western rationality, see Foucault (1970). On the strategic role of the monster in articulating reason and racism, see Tort (1979).

18. See Poliakov (1975).

19. See Lorimer (1978).

20. On the white slave trade, see Bristow (1983); on popular anti-Semitism, see Robb (1954), Freedman (1978) and A. Lee in Lunn (ed.) (1980). The latter book contains some useful material on images of a range of immigrant groups. On the link forged between Blacks and Jews in the Middle Ages, see Cutler and Cutler (1986).

21. See, for example, G. Langmuir's 'explanation' of medieval anti-Semitism in Langmuir, *et al.* (1978); and for a contemporary rationale on the same lines, Ray (1985).

22. This definition derives from Sibony (1981) and refers to the historical and discursive foundations of the ideology in a problematic of *generation*, as well as to its perverse logic of *generalisation*. This formulation has the advantage over the textbook definition (i.e. moral or mental qualities of inferiority/superiority inferred from physical characteristics) in that it does not conflate racism with sexism or ageism, whilst pointing to possible principles of articulation between them.

23. The various positions taken up on the relative status of race and ethnicity are well rehearsed in Rex and Mason (eds) (1986). The ethnicist tendency is best represented in the work of Epstein (1978) Van den Berghe (1981) and Wallman (1978). For a critique, see Kahn (1981).

24. Class analytic models are currently polarised between Weberian and Marxist perspectives. See the contributions of J. Rex and H. Wolpe in Rex and Mason (1986); also the overview by Solomos (1986). For a discussion of the role which sexual divisions play in reproducing ethnicity, see Yuval Davis (1980).

25. See Rodinson (1983).

26. Recent attempts to develop a Gramscian perspective on race, class and ethnicity include Hall (1980a), Sarup (1986) and the work of Genovese (1971). For the original formulation of hegemony, see Gramsci (1971). For current attempts to ground this problematic within a revised reading of national/popular ideology, see the discussion in the next section. See also Mouffe (1979).

27. See CCCS (1982a) and Hall *et al.* (1978) for a discussion of the construction of race as site of political intervention and debate in the post-war period.

28. See Simmel (1971) and Ellis Thomas (1982).

29. The most persuasive advocacy of an English tradition of national/popular

radicalism is to be found in the work of E. P. Thompson (Thompson, 1963 and 1978a). For a consideration of the national popular as a central motif in post-war Marxist historiography in Britain see Schwartz in CCCS (1982b). The linkage of this motif to ethnicity is discussed in Shanin (1986) and to racism by Miles (1982). A structural model within which such multiple articulations could be explained is developed by Laclau (1977). The basis of a Gramscian reading in the context of English history is provided by Nairn (1970 and 1977). In what follows I have drawn on the work of both these authors, in the belief that it is necessary to try to achieve a synthesis between structural and cultural interpretations.

30. The prevalence of racist practices, both personal and institutional, within the English socialist movement is now well documented, for both historical and contemporary periods. On anti-Semitism in the British Left, see Billig (1984) and S. Cohen (1984). On anti-Irish prejudice, Curtis (1968); and on colour prejudice, Winter (1973). See Miles and Phizaclea (1980) for an overview; also Reinders (1968).

31. The original pioneering essay by Hill (1958) continues to set the agenda for research; unfortunately he does not consider the strategic role of the Jewish Question. This deficit is remedied by Poliakov (1974) who, however, ignores the class problematics of the Norman yoke. The most detailed account of the Readmittance Debate is by Katz (1982).

32. On plebeian culture see Thompson (1974). On the post-Chartist settlement and its role in cementing links between people, nation and race, see Lorimer (1978) and Nairn (1970). The Victorian reconstruction of pre-Norman history as an Anglo-Saxon idyll is considered by Girouard (1981) and its effect on images of labour by Wiener (1981).

33. On the 'Great Debate' see Semmel (1960); on the re-formation of working-class culture in the late Victorian period see Stedman Jones (1983); also Lorimer (1978).

34. See P. Cohen (1979) on territoriality in relation to class, and Suttles (1968) on its ethnic dimension. See Humphries (1981) for evidence of its racialisation in the Edwardian period.

35. See P. Cohen (1981) on the crystallisation of public propriety in the 1890s, and Storch (1977) on its emergence in the mid-Victorian period.

36. On the 'corporatism' of British working-class culture, see Nairn (1964b) and the study by Meacham (1977); see also Roberts (1971). Recent theoretical debate on this issue can be found in Critcher and Clarke (eds) (1979). On the structure of the proletarian public realm, see Negt and Kluge (1975).

37. On the 'social imaginary' see Castoriadis (1975); for the application of this concept to the study of nationalism see Anderson (1983).

38. The 'divide and rule' thesis is still popular on the Left. See, for example, Edgar (1977).

39. There is a dearth of local historical studies which have a comparative basis, but see Humphries (1981). For the recent past, see Miles and Phizaclea (eds) (1979) and Cashmore (1986). The outstanding comparative study of contemporary patterns is Hewitt (1986). For an attempt to link historical and contemporary material in a local case study see Mungan and Pearson (1976).

40. On the links between discourses of patriarchy and Empire in Victorian Britain

see Davin (1978) and Cunningham (1972); On imperialism as an adventure story for boys, see Green (1980) and Mackenzie (1987); on the ideologies of kith and kin, see Bratton (1986). See also Mangan and Walvin (1987).

41. There has been considerable debate on the relation between imperialism and working-class culture. Price (1972) in his study of popular attitudes to the Boer War argues that its implantation was never very deep. In contrast, Mackenzie (1984) seeks to demonstrate that popular culture was a major vehicle for diffusing racist and imperialist images. The present line of argument seeks to go beyond these either/or positions. See also Williams (1985). On the role of political organisations during this period, see the contributions to Kennedy and Nicholls (eds) (1981). On the links to emergent Fascist movements, see Rees (1979). Again, comparative local research on the bases of support for these movements is badly needed in Britain.

42. It is sometimes argued that the East End is a special case on account of the deep and long-standing implantation of extra-parliamentary movements of both Right and Left. Their precise strength during the inter-war period is open to doubt, see Lunn and Thurlow (1980). It is clear, however, that Communist and anarchist ideas were a major element in the local culture of the Jewish working class. See Fishman (1975) and White (1981). This may have helped to push other sections of the East End community towards Fascist politics. The contradictory features of local anti-Semitism are well documented in Samuel (1981). White (1986) in his study of Campbell Bunk in Islington, argues that it was the chauvinism of such communities which armoured them against Fascist ideology. The East End is thus not so much an exception as a particular instance of a general rule that there is a tension between the everyday practices of popular racism and their political articulation. See Dandeker (1985) for an overview of current debates on Fascist ideology and its social bases.

43. On the pattern and level of support for the National Front see Marsh (1976), Weir (1978) and the research summarised by Billig and Cochrane (1983); on its rationale, see Miles and Phizaclea (1979); for a local case study of its social phenomenology see Cohen (1988).

44. On the phenomenon of Powellism see Nairn (1970b and 1977). For the dockers response Lindop (1987).

45. This is well documented in Walker (1977). See also Rees (1979).

46. The term is originally Freud's (1930), referring to ethnic rivalries. For an analysis of these transformations in post-war capitalist society see Lasch (1980) and Berman (1982), also Martin (1981); on youth culture, see Cohen (1980); on subculture, ethnicity and style, see Hebdige (1979); for a local case study of the impact of these changes, see Robins and Cohen (1978).

47. On the rise of Thatcherism and its role in reconstructing the 'national-popular' see Hall and Jacques (1983). For a different interpretation, which stresses the independent politicisation of race, see *Race and Class* (1983) and Gilroy (1987).

48. See Barnett (1982) for a general conjunctural analysis. See Harvey (1983) on the media coverage.

49. The main argument for a 'new' racism is either based on innovations in theoretical ideology (namely the appeal to socio-biology or cultural pathology)

or a shift in behavioural ettiquettes-racism as 'silent discourse'. See Barker (1981) and Reeves (1983). However, in so far as socio-biology proposes to apply the findings of animal ethology to human society, it is located firmly within the problematics of Social Darwinism, even if some of Charles Darwin's propositions are questioned. Moreover arguments about 'cultural pathology' are scarcely new; they were being applied to the Irish in the 1860s (see Curtis (1971)). Similarly, racist discourse has often operated in an unvoiced register, especially in 'polite society', in the presence of its subjects, or in the face of resistance. To silence racism under these conditions only implies a change in *mode*, not *code*. What is important is not that these contemporary forms of race thinking or talking are new – they are not – but the role which they play in the current conjuncture. But that can only be specified in terms of a wider historico-structural analysis of the ideological and social framework, in which they are operating. See later sections of this chapter for further discussion of this point.

50. Perhaps the most elegant exposition of the Whig interpretation is Mason (1962). For a critique of ethnocentrism in history text books, see Chancellor (1970) and Preiswend and Perrot (1975). For a detailed case study of the perversions of historical interpretation in the heyday of Empire, see Said (1980) and Bernal (1987).

51. See Owusi (1986) on the development of the ethnic arts movement, and Gilroy (1987) on its cultural politics.

52. Roots radical historiography has been largely based around oral history projects and the promotion of ethnic studies. See, for example, the important work carried out by such organisations as the Irish in Britain History Centre, the Museum of the Jewish East End, various Caribbean Studies Centres and the Tara Arts Centre. The best examples of roots-radical history are Fryer (1984) and Visram (1986). The intellectual foundations of roots-radicalism are developed by Robinson (1983). Despite the title of his book (*Black Marxism*) the author rejects Marxist class/race analysis in favour of a national/popular perspective on Black struggles.

53. See the interesting attempt to ground roots-radicalism within a new problematics of class rather than ethnicity by Ramdin (1987) and Gilroy (1987). On the general problems of using history as a vehicle for ideological axe-grinding see Ferro (1984).

54. The work of Poliakov (1974) has been criticised by Rodinson (1983) for its tendency to reduce the history of anti-Semitism to the reiteration of an 'eternal hatred' for the Jew. A similar reading of the Irish question can be found in Curtis (1984), and is also to be found in 'race bound' theories of colour prejudice. What I have called the latency theory is especially prevalent in attempts to construct historical psychologies, or 'psycho-histories', of racism. See the classic study by Adorno (1950) and the work of Kovel (1970). For an account of racism as a mode of false consciousness, see Gabel (1975).

55. For a critique of this kind of historicism, see Hobsbawm and Ranger (eds) (1983).

56. On racism as theoretical ideology, see Banton (1977) and Rose (1976).

57. See, for example Gager (1978) and Abel (1981). Rodinson (1983) has developed an effective critique of these traditional readings of the Jewish question.
58. See, for example, Williams (1963), Rodney (1974) and Emmanuel (1984). The traditional Marxist or political economy approach to racism is conveniently summarised in two books produced by the Institute of Race Relations (IRR, 1982).
59. For an example of this type of analysis, see the classic study by Arendt (1951) and the work of Rich (1984 and 1986).
60. For a good contrast between the materialist and idealist readings of ethnic history, compare Leon (1970) and Poliakov (1974) on the Jewish question, or Cox (1948) and Minz (1966) on Black struggles and slavery.
61. On 'bio-politics', see Foucault (1977 and 1979); on discourse and the microphysics of power see Foucault (1980). In this chapter I have preferred to use the term 'body politic' in view of the links which it connotes between medieval and modern discourses (Elias, 1978) and also because it refers to the way the body is used as a natural symbol of power relations (Douglas, 1970b).
62. Foucault's position has been criticised for its lack of purchase on the material history of power by both Vilar (1973), and from a rather different but still Marxist point of view, by Timpanaro (1976).
63. The revival of structural/functional models of explanation is due largely to the influence of Louis Althusser who insisted on the reproductive dynamics of ideological practices within both state and civil society. See Althusser (1971). This model proved especially attractive for theories of immigrant labour under capitalism. See Miles (1982b).
64. For a trenchant critique of Althusserian structural/functionalism see Ben-Tovim and Gabriel (1978).
65. In the work of the Frankfurt School it is always assumed that the primary function of any ideology is to legitimate existing patterns of authority and power in society. See Habermas (1976). Hence only if this function is 'in crisis' can a new ideology emerge into prominence. Undoubtedly this analysis is heavily influenced by the experience of the rise of Fascism in Germany.
66. This, more dialectical, view of the relationship between History and the Unconscious in shaping and 'overdetermining' cultural practices has developed in areas where semiology and psychoanalysis have entered into the closest engagement with social history. See, for example, the work of Moretti (1983). On the methodological implications of this convergence see Ginzberg (1980). Both these works have influenced what follows.
67. The earliest and apparently most influential translation and commentary of Hanno's text was Falconer (1797). There were twenty further 'readings' of Hanno produced in the nineteenth century. For an overview, which also locates Hanno within an African problematic see Marcy (1947).
68. On Victorian images of Africa, see Curtin (1965); also Bolt (1971).
69. For a general discussion of the role of classical studies in constructing a Eurocentric vision of history, see the important analysis by Bernal (1987). On the role of Ancient Greece in the development of African political thought, see Mazrui (1965).

70. For the history of Anglo-Saxon ideas about nature, animals and 'inferior species', see Thomas (1983), for African attitudes, see Turnbull (1975); on the general history of Africa see Davidson (1977) and Rodney (1974).

71. The 'Wodewose' may in fact be a transformation of *benign* tree spirits to be found in popular, pre-Christian cultures, which in turn derive from classical Indian mythology. See Wittkower (1977). Their malevolent functions increase the more they are made to mark the domination of nature by culture. See Bernheimer (1956) for the Middle Ages and the contributions to Dudley and Novak (1972) for the subsequent history of this figure. The relationship between the return of the repressed in European culture and elements of African or Asian civilisation is discussed in a somewhat speculative fashion by Duerre (1984). See also the somewhat more sober reflections by Hirst and Wooley (1982).

72. On the role of carnivals, see Bakhtin (1968); on ritual reversal, see Turner (1969): on the civilising process, see Elias (1978); on the licensed excesses of Victorian imperialism see Cairns (1965); and for the 'sexological' fascination with exotic cultures, see Said (1980).

73. See Savage (1864). On the relation of autobiography to history, and the dangers of reading one into the other, see Lejeune (1975). On the paternal metaphor as a source of body imagery and site of disavowal, see Sibony (1974).

74. See Zuckerman (1932) and Sahlins (1959) on the social life of monkeys and apes. For their changing image in history, see Thomas (1983).

75. The best overview of the debate is by Solomos (1986).

76. This model retains the notion of the relative autonomy of (racist) ideology but rejects the Athusserian clause concerning 'determination in the last instance' by the economy. There is no a priori assumption about the role which political and economic structures play in either producing, undermining or relaying ideological forms; but, equally, the meaning of these forms is not read off from either their immediate function or their historical conditions of existence, that is, both functionalist and historicist explanations are rejected.

77. On Korzybski's original formulation, see Bateson (1973) and Baudrillard (1986). For the structuralist analysis of myth, see Levi-Strauss (1968 and 1977); and for the methods of social semiology, see Barthes (1984).

78. As an example of the language/ideology closure, see Cowards and Ellis (1977) and for a restatement of the traditional base/superstructure model see Sivanandan (1973 and 1976).

79. See Mintz (1985) on the history of sugar, and Hebdige (1986) for an essay in the cartography of popular taste.

80. Serres (1977) has produced the most sophisticated model of how spaces of representation are transformed in the transition to capitalism. In particular he is concerned to relate the mappings of myth to specific topographies of power. For a psychoanalytic reading of the map/territory relation, see Rosolato (1978); for a literary evocation, see Calvino (1974).

81. In this model the principle of relative autonomy is founded on the *double inscription* of ideological practices in what I have called map and territory. It is not the case that the map/territory distinction as it is used here corresponds to the traditional opposition between deep and surface structure, or latent

and manifest function. The difference between map and territory is a difference in their respective patterns of overdetermination by Unconscious and Historical processes. This theoretical perspective does have some similarities with that of Carter (1987). His study of the construction of Australia in the journals and journeys of the first settlers explores some of the key tensions in map/territory relations at the heart of the colonial enterprise. But the notion of inscription deployed in his essay in spatial history owes more to phenomenology and post structuralism, than it does to psychoanalysis or cultural materialism, and in that sense differs from approach advocated here.

82. On the history and structure of apartheid, see Woods and Bostock (1986). It should perhaps be stressed that in South Africa we are not dealing with a situation of class and ethnic hegemony, but with a totalitarian regime in which an ethnic minority has coercively imposed its rule on an ethnic majority and is using every means in its power to exclude this majority from the body politic. In this case there is little attempt to win the consent of Black people to their subjugation; the battle for hearts and minds is waged elsewhere, in the foreign and diplomatic spheres.

83. On the mapping of Empire, see Carter (1987); on Imperialism as a geography lesson in the elementary school, see Roberts (1971) and Mackenzie (1984); on the ethnocentric construction of mental maps see Gould and White (1986); on history as a commodity form, see Wright (1985) and Hewison (1987). For the history of cartography, see South (1980).

84. See Cairns (1965) and Eldridge (1973). Also for a general overview of the period Hobsbawm (1968) and Lorimer (1978).

85. On the logic of racist conspiracy theory, see Poliakov (1980) and Sibony (1981).

86. See Cashmore (1986) and Hewitt (1986).

87. For an exposition of RAT methodology, see Katz (1978); and for a critique of RAT, see Sivanandan (1985). On the psychopathology of political Messianism, see Cohn (1957).

88. The immanent critique of Anglo-Saxon racism was first developed by Lorimer (1978) and Hechter (1975).

89. The pioneering study by Elias (1978) has set the agenda for research on the code of breeding. The work of Johnson (1970, 1976 and 1977) provides a Gramscian reading of the development of the educational ideologies in Britain, within which this code was inserted.

90. For popular or lay theories of selective breeding, see Thomas (1983) Blackman (1977) and Jacob (1974).

91. The pivotal role of ideologies of inheritance is suggestively indicated by Thompson (1978b). See also the contributions to Ross (ed.) (1979). However, the reading of the 'peculiarities of the English' adopted here is much closer to the historico-structural analysis proposed by Anderson (1964 and 1986) and Nairn (1964 and 1970).

92. On the 'pure' form of aristocratic racism, see Drevyer (1979). On its genesis as a bourgeois ideology, see Lewonton *et al.* It is unfortunate that there has been little or no attempt to examine the negotiation between the two, but see Lorimer (1978). There is, however, an extensive literature on the cultural relations between the two classes. See in particular Scott (1982) and the study

by Gray (1979), the former stressing the continued dominance of aristocratic power, the latter the emergent forms of bourgeois hegemony.

93. The development of an aristocracy of learning, the tensions between its role as a traditional intelligentsia (in Gramsci's terms) and as a *corps d'élite* of public administrators or 'evangelical bureaucrats' is traced in Anderson (1968), Johnson (1977) and Wiener (1981).

94. Quoted in Dudley and Novak (eds) (1972). On the role of the Wild Child in the Enlightenment see Tinland (1982) and Malson (1969) and especially the commentary by Mannoni (1972). See also Hirst and Wooley (1982).

95. A good deal of research remains to be done to unpack this network of correspondences and identify their relay systems in the British context. The work of Foucault (1977) has inspired studies by Jones and Williamson (1979), which, though suggestive, fails to anchor the analysis within a historico-structural framework of class negotiation. A recent paper by Bauman (1984) not only provides a critique of Foucauldian extrapolation, but locates this set of oppositions within the class problematics of the Enlightenment, especially the privileged role which the European intelligentsia gave itself in and by its theories of society.

96. On the ideology of intelligence and natural aptitude, see Rose (1976), Bisseret (1979) and Bourdieu (1984).

97. On the codes of inheritance, apprenticeship, vocation and career, see P. Cohen (1986).

98. The theory of recapitulation was elaborated by Stanley Hall in his influential study on the psychology of adolescence (Hall, 1908). For a commentary on Hall's theories, see Hendrick (1986).

99. See Springhall (1977), Blanch (1979) and Mangan (1986a, b).

100. Quoted in Storch (1977).

101. A whole literary genre grew around this problematic, with titles such as *Town Swamps and Social Bridges*, *The Seven Curses of London*, *Low Life Deeps* and *London Shadows*. On the theme of urban degeneration, see Stedman Jones (1976).

102. See Donzelot (1978) on the relation between social welfare and population control.

103. On the symbolism of dirt, see Douglas (1970a). For its history as a site of unconscious fantasy, see Laporte (1982), and as an expression of class relations, see Corbin (1987). See also the study by Kern (1975).

104. The relation between epidemiology, policing and moral panics about the 'dangerous classes' crystallised in the late nineteenth century around the Contagious Diseases Acts. See the study by Walkovitz and Walkovitz (1973). Loewenstein (1954), in his psychoanalytic study of anti-Semitism, emphasises the role of syphilis. The issue has gained topical importance, of course, in the context of Acquired Immune Deficiency Syndrome (AIDS).

105. See Hechter (1975) and Jones (1971); on the history of the Irish question in Britain, see Dangerfield (1976); on the cultural invisibility of the Irish in Britain, see Hickman (1984) and O'Brennian (1985).

106. On nineteenth-century Irish migration and settlement in Britain, see Lees (1979) and Gilley and Swift (1985); also Miles (1982b).

107. On racist stereotypes of the Irish in Victorian Britain, see Curtis (1968 and 1971).
108. On the history of paddy jokes see Parsons (1983) and Kerrigan (1981). For an analysis of ethnic humour, see Leach (1979) and on its symbolic function, see Douglas (1968).
109. The model presented here builds on the analysis of Sibony (1986).
110. On the body as a 'natural symbol' of real power relations, see Douglas (1970b); on its social function as a bearer of imaginary relations of power see Dolto (1982). The term 'body politic' as it is used here recovers the dual function of the body, at the level of both territory and map. On its cultural history see Kern (1975).
111. For a concrete analysis of the articulation between racist codes and Fascist ideology, see the pioneering study by Faye (1980); on the 'detotalising' function of the race relations apparatus see Sarup (1986).
112. This more dynamic view of popular culture has usually been stressed by historians rather than sociologists. See, for example, Ginzberg (1980a) and the contributions to Yeo and Yeo (eds) (1981).
113. The law of 'reversal' between myth, ritual and fantasy was first stated in the seminal study of Valabrega (1967), and has been elaborated in the context of kinship and Oedipal relations by Green (1977). This tripartite structure is here considered to be integral to the productivity of the racist imagination.
114. See, for example, the study by Troyna (1981).
115. On the culture of the 'lads', see Willis (1977) on its school context and Robins and Cohen (1978) for its community setting.
116. The structure of racist disavowal is theorised by Sibony (1976 and 1986).
117. For a discussion of these dynamics in the traditional code of working-class masculinity, see Cohen (1986). On the wider context see Thewelert (1987).
118. On symmetrical and complementary rules, see Bateson (1973); on ritual insult, see Labov (1971) and Robins and Cohen (1978); on racist banter, see Hewitt (1986).
119. On the double 'double standard', see Hewitt (1986).
120. On Tarzan and the noble savage as themes in popular culture, see Street (1975), and Newsinger (1986).
121. The conflation of race, sex and class is characteristic of certain recent initiatives by the ILEA. See, for example, ILEA (1983); also Brittan and Maynard (1984).
122. See Bauman (1984).
123. A rationalist pedagogy anchored to a traditional Marxist reading of racism has been developed by the Institute of Race Relations and the Association for Curriculum Development. See IRR (1982).
124. For the association of racist beliefs with various instances of 'latent psycho-pathology' see Adorno, *et al.* (1950), Reich (1975) and Loewenstein (1954). For a therapeutic model of anti-racist work, which draws on some of these ideas as well as more recent feminist psychologies of oppression, see Green (1987).
125. The experiential approach to multi-cultural learning is well illustrated in the

recent teaching pack produced by the Community Education Trust (1986). For a critique of this approach, see Hall (1980b).

126. Miles (1982b) advances a 'functionalist' explanation of working-class racism which, while it is careful to distance itself from such crude extrapolations, does nevertheless underwrite the view that it would diminish under improved economic conditions. Weberian models of status competition also have their champions – see Banton (1983) – and have been strengthened recently by the introduction of rational choice models of ethnic segregation (Hechter, 1986).

127. For much of what follows, see Sibony (1976).

128. On the para-logical structures of racist thought, see Gabel (1975) and Sibony (1976).

129. See, for example, Gilroy (1982).

130. On the logistics of anti-racist teaching, see Brandt (1987).

131. On the discursive strategies of totalitarian ideologies, see Faye (1980).

132. See Troyna and Williams (1986).

133. On the moral panic about anti-racist education, see Murray (1986).

134. See Ferguson (1981).

135. This methodology is developed in Cohen (1987).

136. For the original stories see Sherlock (1979); and for an imaginative 're-creation' giving the stories an overtly political slant as well as a more authentic creole, see Salkey (1973). For a general discussion of their significance see Kemoli (1981). For an analysis of American comics as a form of cultural imperialism see Dorfman and Mattelart (1975).

137. On the methods of critical pedagogy, and how they differ from the normative/prescriptive models associated with political propaganda/recruitment, see Shor (1980).

Bibliography

Abel, E. (1975) *The Roots of Antisemitism* (London).

Adorno, T. W. *et al.* (1950) *The Authoritarian Personality* (New Haven).

Althusser, L. (1971) *Lenin and Philosophy* (London).

ALTARF (1984) *Challenging Racism* (London).

Anderson, B. (1983) *Imagined Communities* (London).

Anderson, P. (1964) 'Origins of the Present Crisis', *New Left Review*, 23.

Anderson, P. (1968) 'On the components of national culture', *New Left Review*, 59.

Anderson, P. (1986) 'The Figures of Descent', *New Left Review*, 161.

Arendt, H. (1951) *The Origins of Totalitarianism* (New York).

Bakhtin, M. (1968) *Rabelais and His World* (Cambridge, Mass.).

Banton, M. (1977) *The Idea of Race*, (London).

Banton, M. (1983) *Race and Ethnic Competition* (Cambridge).

Barker, M. (1981) *The New Racism* (London).

Barnett, A. (1982) 'Iron Brittania' *New Left Review*, 134.

Barthes, R. (1984) *Writing Degree Zero* (London).

Bateson, G. (1973) *Steps towards an Ecology of Mind* (London).

Baudrillard, J. (1986) *Simulacre et Simulation* (Paris).

Bauman, Z. (1984) 'Ideology and the World View of Intellectuals', paper given to the Conference on Ideology, Polytechnic of Central London.

Berman, M. (1982) *All That is Solid Melts into Air* (New York).

Ben-Tovim, G. and Gabriel, J. (1978) 'Marxism and the Concept of Racism', *Economy and Society*, 7/2.

Bernal, M. (1987) *Black Athena* (London).

Bernheimer, C. (1956) *The Wild Man in the Middle Ages* (Chicago).

Billig, M. (1984) 'Anti-Jewish Themes and the British Far Left', *Patterns of Prejudice* 181 and 182.

Billig, M. (1979) *Psychology, Racism and Fascism* (Birmingham).

Billig, M. and Cochrane, M. (1983) 'Youth and Politics', *Youth and Policy*, 8.

Bisseret, N. (1979) *Education, Class Language and Ideology* (London).

Blanch, M. (1979) 'Imperialism, Nationalism, and Organised Youth' in Clarke and Critcher (eds) (1979).

Blackman, J. (1977) 'Popular Theories of Generation' in Woodward and Richards.

Bloomfield, J. B. (ed.) (1979) *Class, Party, Hegemony* (London).

Bolt, C. (1971) *Victorian Attitudes to Race* (London).

Bourdieu, P. (1984) *'Entretien sur Racisme'*, *Constellations*, 5 (Paris).

Brandt, G. (1987) *The Realisation of Anti-Racist Teaching* (Brighton).

Bratton, J. S. (1986) 'Of England, home and duty' in MacKenzie and Duane (1986).

Bristow, E. (1983) British Jewry and the Fight Against the White Slave Trade, *Immigrants and Minorities*, 2/2.

Brittan, A. and Maynard, M. (1984) *Sexism, Racism and Oppression* (Oxford).

Cairns, H. A. C. (1965) *Prelude to Imperialism 1840–1890* (London).

Calvino, I. (1984) *Invisible Cities* (London).

Carter, P. (1987) *The Road to Botany Bay* (London and Boston).

Cashmore, E. (1986) *The Logic of Racism* (London.)

Castoriadis, C. (1975) *L'Institution Imaginaire de la Société* (Paris).

Chancellor, C. V. (1970) *History for the Masters* (Bath).

Centre for Contemporary Cultural Studies (CCCS) (1982a) *The Empire Strikes Back* (London).

CCCS (1982b) *Making Histories* (London).

Clarke, J. and Critcher, C. (eds) (1979) *Working Class Culture* (London).

Cohen, P. (1979) 'Some Notes of Researching Territoriality' *Schooling and Culture*, 4.

Cohen, P. (1980) 'Subcultural Conflict and Working Class Community' in S. Hall (ed.).

Cohen, P. (1981) 'Policing the Working Class City' in J. Young (ed.) (1981).

Cohen, P. (1986) *Rethinking the Youth Question* (London).

Cohen, P. (1987) *Racism and Popular Culture* Working Paper 9 Centre for MultiCultural Education (London).

Cohen, P. (1988) 'On the other side of the tracks' in *Contemporary Issues in Geography Education*, vol. 4, no. 1.

Cohen, S. (1984) *That's Funny You Don't Look Antisemitic* (Leeds).

Cohn, N. (1957) *The Pursuit of the Millenium* (Oxford).

Community Education Trust (1986) *Let's Grow Together* (London).

Connerton, P. (ed.) (1976) *Critical Sociology* (Harmondsworth).

Corbin, A. (1987) *The Foul and the Fragrant* (Leamington Spa).

Corrigan, P. (1977) 'Feudal Relics or Capitalist Monuments – Notes on the Sociology of Unfree Labour', *Sociology*, 2/5.

Coward, R. and Ellis, J. (1977) *Language and Materialism* (London).

Cox, O. C. (1948) *Class, Caste, and Race* (New York).

Cunningham, H. (1972) 'The Language of Patriotism', *History Workshop*, 12.

Curtin, P. D. (1965) *The Image of Africa 1780–1850* (London).

Curtis, L. (1984) *Nothing But the Same Old Story* (London).

Curtis, L. P. (1968) *Anglo-Saxons and Celts* (Connecticut).

Curtis, L. P. (1971) *Apes and Angels – The Irishman in Victorian Caricature* (Washington, DC).

Cutler, H. and Cutler, H. (1986) *The Jew as Ally of the Muslim – The Mediaeval Roots of Anti-Semitism* (Notre Dame).

Dale, R. *et al.* (1976) *Schooling and Capitalism* (London).

Dandeker, C. (1985) 'Fascism and Ideology', *Ethnic and Racial Studies*, 8/3.

Dangerfield, G. (1976) *The Damnable Question – A Study of Anglo-Irish Relations* (London).

Davidson, B. (1977) *A History of West Africa* (London).

Davin, A. (1978) 'Imperialism and Motherhood', *History Workshop*, 5.

Davidowicz, L. (1979) *The War Against the Jews* (Harmondsworth).

Delacampagne, C. (1983) *L'Invention du Racisme–Antiquité et Moyen Age* (Paris).

Dolto, F. (1982) *Image Inconscient de la Corps* (Paris).

Donaïgrodski, H. P. (1977) *Social Control in 19th-Century Britain* (London).

Donzelot, J. (1980) *Policing the Family* (London).

Dorfman, A. and Mattelart, A. (1975) *How to Read Donald Duck* (New York).

Douglas, M. (1968) 'The Social Control of Cognition – some factors in joke Perception', *Man* (NS) vol. 3.

Douglas, M. (1970a) *Purity and Danger* (Harmondsworth).

Douglas, M. (1970b) *Natural Symbols* (Harmondsworth).

Drevyer, A. (1979) *Le Sang Epuré* (Brussels).

Duby, G. (1977) *The Chivalric Society* (London).

Duby, G. (1980) *The Three Orders – The Imaginary in Feudal Society* (London and Chicago).

Dudley, E. and Novak, M. (eds) (1972) *The Wild Man Within* (Pittsburgh, Penn.).

Duerre, H. P. (1984) *Dream Time* (London).

Dundes, A. *et al.* (1986) *The Wandering Jew* (Toronto).

Edgar, D. (1977) Racism, Fascism and the Politics of the National Front, *Race and Class*, 19/2.

Eldridge, C. C. (1973) *England's Mission 1868–1880* (London).

Elias, N. (1978) *The Civilising Process: Vol. I The History of Manners* (Oxford).

Ellis Thomas, D. (1975) 'The Making of Minorities' in *Multi-Cultural Teacher*, 5.

Emmanuel, A. (1984) *Unequal Exchange* (London).

Engels, F. (1969) *The Condition of the Working Class in England* (London).

Epstein, M. (1978) *Ethos and Identity* (London).

Ernst, S. and Maguire, M. (eds) (1987) *Living with the Sphinx* (London).

Falconer, T. (trans.) (1797) *The Voyage of Hanno* (London).

Fanon, F. (1970) *Black Skins, White Masks* (London).

Faye, J.-P. (1980) *Languages Totalitaires* (Paris).

Ferguson, R. (1981) 'Race and the Media' in *Multi-Racial Education*, vol. 9, no. 2.

Ferro, M. (1984) *The Uses and Abuses of History* (London and New York).

Fishman, W. (1975) *East End Jewish Radicals* (London).

Foucault, M. (1965) *Madness and Civilisation* (London).

Foucault, M. (1970) *The Order of Things* (London).

Foucault, M. (1977) *Discipline and Punish* (London).

Foucault, M. (1979) *The History of Sexuality 1: The Will to Truth* (New York).

Foucault, M. (1980) *Power/Knowledge* (London).

Fox, E. and Genovese, E. (1983) *The Fruits of Merchant Capital* (Oxford).

Freedman, M. (ed.) (1978) *A Minority in Britain* (London).

Freud, S. (1930) *Civilisation and its Discontents* (London).

Friedman, J. (1966) *The Monstrous Races in Medieval Art and Thought* (Toronto).

Fryer, P. (1984) *Staying Power – The History of Black People in Britain* (London).

Gabel, J. (1975) *False Consciousness* (Oxford).

Gager, J. (1983) *The Origins of Antisemitism* (Oxford).

Genovese, E. (1971) *In Red and Black* (New York).

Gilley, S. (1978) 'English Attitudes to the Irish 1789–1900' in L. C. Holmes (ed.) (1978).

Gilley, S. and Swift, R. F. (eds) (1985) *The Irish in the Victorian City* (London).

Gilroy, P. (1982) 'Police and Thieves' in CCCS (1982a).

Gilroy, P. (1987) *There Ain't no Black in the Union Jack* (London).

Ginzberg, C. (1980a) *The Cheese and the Worms* (London: Intro.).

Ginzberg, C (1980b) 'Freud, Morelli and Sherlock Holmes' *History Workshop*, 9.

Girouard, M. (1981) *The Return to Camelot* (New Haven, Conn.).

Goody, J. (ed.) (1978) *Family and Inheritance* (Cambridge).

Gould, P. and White, R. (1986) *Mental Maps* (Boston, Mass.).

Gramsci, A. (1971) *Prison Notebooks* (London).

Gray, R. (1979) 'Bourgeois Hegemony in Victorian Britain' in J. B. Bloomfield (ed.).

Green, A. (1977) 'Atomes de parente et relations oedipiennes' in Levi-Strauss (ed.) (1977).

Green M. (1987) 'Women in the Oppressor's Role – White Racism' in Ernst and Maguire (1987).

Green, M. (1980) *Dreams of Adventure, Deeds of Empire* (London).

Griffin, J. H. (1986) *Black Like Me* (London).

Habermas, J. (1976) 'Problems of legitimation in late capitalism' in Connerton (1976).

Hall, Stanley (1908) *The Psychology of Adolescence*, 3 vols (New York).

Hall, Stuart, *et al.* (1978) *Policing the Crisis* (London).

Hall, S. (1980a) 'Race, Articulation and Society' in UNESCO, *Socoiological Theories of Race and Colonialism* (Paris).

Hall, S. (1980b) 'Teaching Race' *Multi Racial Education*, 9/9.

Hall, S. (ed.) (1980c) *Culture, Medica, Language* (London).

Hall, S. and Jacques, M. (eds) (1983) *The Politics of Thatcherism* (London).

Harvey, R. (1983) *Gotcha – Media Treatment of the Falklands* (London).

Hebdige, D. (1979) *Subculture – the meaning of style* (London).

Hebdige, D. (1986) *Hiding in the Light* (London).

Hechter, M. (1975) *Internal Colonialism in the British Isles* (Berkely, Cal.).

Hechter, M. (1986) 'Rational Choice Theory' in Rex and Mason (1986).

Hendrick, H. (1986) 'Personality and Psychology', *Youth and Policy*, 18.

Hewison, R. (1987) *The Heritage Industry* (London).

Hewitt, R. (1986) *White Talk, Black Talk* (Cambridge).

Hickman, M. J. (1984) 'The Irish in Britain' in Altarf (1984).

Hilberg, R. (1973) *The Destruction of the European Jews* (London).

Hill, C. (1958) 'The Norman Yoke' in *Puritanism and Revolution* (Oxford).

Hilton, R. H. (ed.) (1976) *The Transition from Feudalism to Capitalism* (London).

Hilton, R. H. (1970) *The Decline of Serfdom in Mediaeval England* (London).

Hirst, P. and Wooley, P. (1982) *Social Relations and Human Attributes* (London and New York).

Hobsbawm, E. J. (1968) *Industry and Empire* (Harmondsworth).

Hobsbawm, E. J. and Ranger, T. (1983) *The Invention of Tradition* (Cambridge).

Holmes, C. (ed.) (1979) *Antisemitism in British Society 1876–1939* (London).

Holmes, C. (ed.) (1978) *Immigrants and Minorities in British Society* (London).

Holtsmark, E. B. (1964) *Tarzan and Tradition* (New York).

Humphries, S. (1981) *Hooligans or Rebels* (Oxford).

Husbands, C. (ed.) (1982) *Race in Britain – Continuity and Change* (London).

Inner London Education Authority (ILEA) (1981) *Race, Sex and Class Guidelines* (London: ILEA).

Institute for Race Relations (IRR) (1982) *Roots of Racism/Patterns of Racism* (London).

Jacob, F. (1974) *The Logic of Living Systems – the History of Heredity* (London).

Jackson, T. (1963) *The Irish in Britain* (London).

Johnson, R. (1970) 'Educational Policy and Social Control in Early Victorian England', *Past and Present*, 49.

Johnson, R. (1976) 'Notes on the schooling of the English working class' in R. Dale *et al.* (1976).

Johnson, R. (1977) 'Educating the Educators' in H. P. Donajgrodski (1977).

Jones, C. and Williamson, H. (1979) 'Birth of the Schoolroom', *Ideology and Consciousness*, 6.

Jones, S. (1986) 'White Youth and Jamaican Popular Culture', unpublished PhD, Birmingham University.

Jones, W. R. (1971) 'England Against the Celtic Fringe', *Journal of World History* 13/1.

Katz, D. (1982) *Philosemitism and the Admittance of the Jews into England 1603–1655* (California).

Katz, J. (1978) *White Awareness – A Handbook for Anti-Racist Teachers* (Oakland, Cal.).

Kahn, J. (1981) 'Explaining Ethnicity', *Critique of Anthropology*, 16/4.

Kemoli, A. (1981) *Caribbean Anansi Stories* (London).

Kennedy, P. and Nicholls, A (eds) (1981) *Nationalist and Racialist Movements in Britain and Germany before 1914* (London).

Kern, S. (1975) *Anatomy and Destiny* (London).

Kerrigan, C. (1981) 'The Same Old Joke', *Irish Studies in Britain*, 2/1.

Kovel, J. (1970) *White Racism – A PsychoHistory* (New York).

Labov, W. (1971) 'Rules for Ritual Insults' in D. Sudnow *et al.* (1971).

Laclau, E. (1977) *Politics and Ideology in Marxist Theory* (London).

Langmuir, G. *et al.* (1978) *Les Juifs dans l'histoire* (Leiden).

Laporte, D. (1982) *Histoire de la Merde* (Paris).

Lascaux, G. (1983) *Le Monstre dans l'art occidental* (Paris).

Lasch, C. (1980) *The Culture of Narcissism* (London).

Lebow, R. N. (1976) *White Britain and Black Ireland – the influence of stereotypes on colonial policy* (London).

Leach, E. (1979) 'The Official Irish Jokester', *New Society*, 20.

Leach, E. (1964) 'Animal Categories and Verbal Abuse' in E. Lenneberg (ed.) (1964).

Lee, A. (1980) 'Aspects of working class responses to the Jews in Britain' in K. Lunn (1980).

Lees, L. (1979) *Exiles of Erin* (Manchester).

Lejeune, P. (1975) *Le Pacte Autobiographique* (Paris).

Lenneberg, E. (ed.) (1964) *New Direction in the Study of Language* (MIT).

Leon, A. (1970) *The Jewish Question* (New York).

Lewonton, R. *et al.* (1982) 'Bourgeois ideology and the origins of biological determinism', *Race and Class*, 24.

Lindop, F. (1987) 'Responses to the speeches of Enoch Powell by the London Dockers', paper given to Labour History Conference, London.

Loewenstein, R. (1954) *Christians and Jews – A Psychoanalytic Study* (London).

Lorimer D. (1978) *Colour, Class and the Victorians* (Leicester).

Lunn, K. (ed.) (1980) *Hosts, Immigrants and Minorities* (Folkestone).

Lunn, K. and Thurlow, R. (eds) (1980) *British Fascism – Essays on the Radical Right in Inter-War Britain* (Oxford).

Mackenzie, J. (1984) *Propaganda and Empire* (Manchester).

Mackenzie, J. (1987) 'The Imperial Pioneer, Hunters and the British Masculine Stereotype' in Mangan and Walvin (eds).

Mackenzie, J. and Duane, P. (eds) (1986) *Imperialism and Popular Culture* (Manchester).

Macciocchi, M. (ed.) (1976) *Elements pour une analyse du Fascisme*, 2 vols (Paris).

Malson, L. (1969) *Wolf Child* (London).

Mangan, J. (1986) *The Games Ethic and Imperialism* (London).

Mangan, J. and Walvin, J. (eds) (1987) *Manliness and Morality* (Manchester).

Mannoni, O. (1972) 'Itard and His Savage', *New Left Review* 74.

Marcy, G. (1947) 'Le Periple d'Hanno dans le Maroc Antique de M. J. Carcopino', *Journal Asiatique*, vol. 234.

Marsh, A. (1976) 'Who Hates Blacks?', *New Society*, 28.

Martin, B. (1981) *The Sociology of Cultural Change* (Oxford).

Mason, P. (1962) *Prospero's Magic* (Oxford).

Mattelart, A. and Siegelaub, G. (eds) (1975) *Communication and Class Struggle* (New York).

Mazrui, A. (1965) *Greece in African Political Thought* (London).

Meacham, S. (1977) *A Life Apart – The English Working Class 1890–1914* (London).

Miles, R. (1982a) 'Racism and Nationalism' in C. Husbands (ed.) (1982).

Miles, R. (1982b) *Racism and Migrant Labour* (London).

Miles, R. and Phizaclea, A. (eds) (1979) *Racism and Political Action* (London).

Miles, R. and Phizaclea, A. (eds) (1980) *Labour and Racism* (London).

Mintz, S. (1966) 'The Caribbean as a socio-cultural area', *Journal of World History*, vol. 9, no. 4.

Mintz, S. (1985) *Sweetness and Power* (London).

Moretti, F. (1983) *Signs Taken as Wonders* (London).

Mosse, G. L. (1978) *Toward the Final Solution* (London).

Mouffe, C. (1979) *Gramsci and Marxist Theory* (London).

Mullard, C. (1980) *The Social Context and Meaning of Multi-cultural Education* (London).

Mungan, G. and Pearson, G. (1976) 'Paki Bashing in a North East Lancashire Cotton Town' in *Working Class Youth Culture* (London).

Murray, N. (1985) 'Anti-Racists and Other Demons', *Race and Class*, 27/3.

Nairn, T. (1964a) 'The British Political Elite', *New Left Review*, 23.

Nairn, T. (1964b) 'The English Working Class', *New Left Review*, 24.

Nairn, T. (1970a) 'The British Meridian', *New Left Review*, 60.

Nairn, T. (1970b) 'Portrait of Enoch Powell', *New Left Review*, 61.

Nairn, T. (1977) 'The Twilight of the British State', *New Left Review*, 101/2.

Negt, C. and Kluge, G. (1975) 'Structures of the Proletarian Public Realm' in A. Mattelart and S. Siegelaub (eds) (1975).

Newsinger, J. (1986) 'Lord Greystoke and Darkest Africa', *Race and Class* 28/1.

O'Brennian, S. (1985) 'The Invisible Irish', *Irish Studies in Britain*, no. 7.

Owusi, K. (1986) *The Struggle for Black Arts in Britain* (London).

Parsons, B. (1983) 'Mad Micks and Englishmen – A Historical look at Anti-Irish Racism', *Irish Studies in Britain*, 6.

Patterson, O. (1980) 'On Slavery', *New Left Review*, 117.

Phizaclea, A. and Miles, R. (1979) 'Working Class Racist Beliefs in the Inner City' in R. Miles and A. Phizaclea (1979).

Poliakov, L. (1974) *The Aryan Myth*, (London).

Poliakov, L. (ed.) (1975) *Hommes et Bêtes* (Paris).

Poliakov, L. (ed.) (1980) *Causalité Diabolique* (Paris).

Preiswend, E. and Perrot, F. (1975) *Ethnocentrisme et Histoire* (Paris).

Price, R. (1972) *Imperialism and the Working Class* (London).

Race and Class, (1983) *British Racism – The Road to 1984*.

Ramdin, R. (1987) *The Making of the Black Working Class in Britain* (London).

R. R. Ray, (1985) 'Racism and Rationality', *Ethnic and Racial Studies*, 8/3.

Reeves, F. (1983) *British Racial Discourse* (Cambridge).

Reinders, R. (1968) 'Racialism on the Left', *International Review of Social History*, vol. 1.

Rees, P. (1979) *Fascism in Britain* (Hassocks).

Reich, W. (1975) *The Mass Psychology of Fascism* (Harmondsworth).

Rex, J. (1986) 'The role of class analysis in race relations' in Rex and Mason (1986).

Rex, J. and Mason, D. (1986) *Theories of Race and Ethnic Relations* (Cambridge).

Rey, P.-P. (1974) *Les Alliances des Classes* (Paris).

Rich, P. (1984) *White Power and the Liberal Conscience* (Manchester).

Rich, P. (1986) *Race and Empire in British Politics* (Cambridge).

Robb, J. H. (1954) *Working Class Anti-Semite* (London).

Roberts, R. (1971) *The Classic Slum* (Manchester).

Robins, D. and Cohen, P. (1978) *Knuckle Sandwich* (Harmondsworth).

Robinson, C. J. (1983) *Black Marxism* (London).

Rodinson, M. (1983) *Cult, Ghetto, State – The Persistence of the Jewish Question* (London).

Rodney, W. (1974) *How Europe Underdeveloped Africa* (Washington DC).

Rose, S. (1976) 'Scientific Racism and Ideology' in H. and S. Rose (1976).

Rose, H. and Rose, S. (1976) *The Political Economy of Science* (London).

Rosolato, G. (1978) *La rélation d'Inconnu* (Paris).

Ross, C. (ed.) (1979) *Patronage, Pedigree and Power* (Gloucester).

Sahlins, M. (1959) 'The Social Life of Monkeys, Apes and Primitive Man', *Human Biology*.

Said, E. (1980) *Orientalism* (London).

Salkey, A. (1973) *Anancy Score* (London).

Samuel, R. (ed.) (1981) *East End Underworld* (London).

Sarte, J.-P. (1948) *The Jew and the Anti-Semite* (New York).

Sarup, M. (1986) *The Politics of Multi-Racial Education* (London).

Savage, J. (1864) *A Genealogy of Settlers to New England* (3 vols) (Boston, Mass.).

Savage, T. S. (1847) *A Description of the habits and customs of Gorilla troglodytes* (London).

Scott, J. (1982) *The Upper Classes* (London).

Schwartz, B. (1982) 'The People's History' in *Making Histories* (London: CCCS).

Semmel, B. (1960) *Imperialism and Social Reform* (London).

Serres, M. (1977) 'Discours et Parcours' in C. Levi-Strauss (ed.) (1977b).

Shanin, T. (1986) 'Soviet Theories of Ethnicity', *New Left Review*, 158.

Sherlock, P. (1979) *Anansi the Spiderman* (London).

Shor, I. (1980) *Critical Teaching and Everyday Life* (Montreal).

Sibony, D. (1974) *Le Nom et le Corps* (Paris).

Sibony, D. (1976) 'Quelques Remarques sur l'affet ratial' in Macclocchi (ed.) (1976).

Sibony, D. (1983) *La Juive – une transmission inconscient* (Paris).

Simmel, G. (1976) *On Individuality and Social Forms – Selected Writings* D. Levine (ed.) (Chicago).

Sivanandan, A. (1973) 'Race, Class and Power', *Race and Class*, 14/4.

Sivanandan, A. (1976) 'Race, Class and the State', *Race and Class*, 17/4.

Sivanandan, A. (1985) 'RAT and the degradation of Black struggles', *Race and Class*, 26/4.

Smith, M. G. (1986) 'Pluralism, race and ethnicity' Rex and Mason (1986).

Solomos, J. (1986) 'Varieties of Marxist Concepts of Race, Class and the State' in Rex and Mason (1986).

Springhall, J. (1977) *Youth, Empire and Society* (London).

South, S. (1980) *A History of Cartography* (London).

Stedman Jones, G. (1976) *Outcast London* (London).

Stedman Jones, G. (1983) *The Language of Class* (London).

Storch, R. D. (1977) 'Problems of Working Class Leisure' in Donajgrodski (ed.) (1977).

Levi-Strauss, C. (1968) *Structural Anthropology*, vol. 1 (London).

Levi-Strauss, C. (1977a) *Structural Anthropology*, vol. 2 (London).

Levi-Strauss, C. (ed.) (1977b) *L'Identité* (Paris).

Street, B. (1975) *The Savage in Literature* (London).

Sudnow, D. *et al.* (1971) *Studies in Social Interaction* (Chicago).

Suttles, G. (1968) *The Social Order of the Slum – Ethnicity and Territory in the Inner City* (London, Chicago).

Thewelert, K. (1987) *Male Phantasies* (London).

Timpanaro, S. (1976) *On Materialism* (London).

Tinland, F. (1982) *L'homme Sauvage* (Paris).

Thomas, K. (1983) *Man and the Natural World* (Cambridge).

Thompson, E. P. (1963) *The Making of the English Working Class* (London).

Thompson, E. P. (1974) 'Patrician Society, Plebeian Culture', *Journal of Social History* 24.

Thompson, E. P. (ed.) (1978a) 'The Peculiarities of the English' in *The Poverty of Theory* (London).

Thompson, E. P. (1978b) 'The Grid of Inheritence' in J. Goody (ed.) (1978).

Tort, P. (1979) *L'ordre et les Monstres* (Paris).

Troyna, B. (1981) 'Images of Race and Racist Images in the British Mass Media' in *Mass Media and Mass Communications* (Leicester).

Troyna, B. and Williams, J. (1986) *Racism, Education and the State* (London).

Turner, V. W. (1969) *The Ritual Process* (New York).

Turnbull, C. J. (1975) *The Forest People* (London).

Valabrega J.-P. (1967) Le Probleme Anthropologique du phantasme in *Désir et Perversion* (Paris).

Verlinden, C. (1970) *The Beginning of Modern Colonisation* (London).

Van den Berghe, P. L. (1981) *The Ethnic Phenomenon* (New York).

Vilar, P. (1973) 'Writing Marxist History', *New Left Review*, 80.

Visram, R. (1986) *Ayahs, Lascars and Princes* (London).

Walker, M. (1977) *The National Front* (Glasgow).

Wallman, S. (1976) 'Race Relations or Ethnic Relations', *New Community*, 6.

Walkovitz, D. and Walkovitz, J. (1973) 'We Are Not Beasts in the Field', *Feminist Studies*.

Weir, S. (1978) 'Youngsters in the Front Line', *New Society*, 2 April.

Wiener, M. (1981) *English Culture and the Decline of the Industrial Spirit* (Cambridge).

Williams, E. (1963) *Slavery and Capitalism* (London).

Williams, K. (1985) *Imperialism, Colonialism and the Culture of Empire* (London: BFI).

Willis, P. (1977) *Learning to Labour* (Hants).

Winter, J. M. (1973) 'The Webbs and the Non-White', *World Journal of Contemporary History*, 9/1.

Wittkower, R. (1977) *Allegory and the Migration of Symbols* (London).

White, J. (1981) *Rothschild Buildings* (London).

White, J. (1986) *The Worst Slum in North London* (London).

Wolpe, H. (1986) 'Class Concepts, Class Struggle and Racism' in Rex and Mason (1986).

Woods, D. and Bostock, M. (1986) *Apartheid* (London).

Woodward, J. and Richards, D. (eds) (1977) *Health Care and Popular Medicine in 19th Century Britain* (Brighton).

Wright P. (1985) *On Living in an Old Country* (London).

Yeo, S. and Yeo, F. (eds) (1981) *Popular Culture and Class Conflict* (Sussex).

Young, J. (ed.) (1981) *Capitalism and the Rule of Law* (London).

Yuval-Davis, N. (1980) 'Bearers of the Collective', *Feminist Review*, 4.

Zuckerman, S. (1932) *The Social Life of Monkeys and Apes* (Oxford).

Part II

Policies

2

Two-Tone Britain: White and Black Youth and the Politics of Anti-Racism

Paul Gilroy and Errol Lawrence

After the lid was finally blown off Brixton in April 1981, the late Sir Ronald Bell appeared on BBC's 'Nationwide' to explain that Afro-Caribbean youth's 'rootlessness' was the principal cause of the riots. The essence of his argument was that this 'rootlessness' was a consequence of attempting to transplant 'alien' people with 'alien' cultures on to English soil. Growing up in a country that was not theirs, Afro-Caribbean youth failed to develop a sense of belonging; their essential identity, their *roots*, lay elsewhere. A few days later, Gordon Brook-Shepherd, political editor of the *Sunday Telegraph*, made explicit some of the ideas which underpin this view. In an article entitled 'Where the blame for Brixton lies' (19 April 1981), he contrasted the Afro-Caribbean's failure to be 'digested' by 'Mother England' with the Asian's apparent success. The Asians had integrated better 'for the paradoxical reason that they (had) stayed different':

> Their religion and language have stayed different (whatever proficiency they require in English) and this, alongside their *whole* culture, has bound them tightly together both as communities and as families – this family bond being something, incidentally, which many white as well as black parents would envy. [Our emphasis.]

The 'cohesive family bond' generated by their staying different was of particular importance to Brook-Shepherd. It had apparently

121

produced Asian youth who were 'passive' yet hard-working; happy yet seriously studious. This imagery contrasted favourably with the unruly Afro-Caribbean youth of Brixton, who had been 'playing a new and gruesome variation of the game of cricket', using 'bricks for balls and plastic police shields for bats'.

Within this scheme, Afro-Caribbean family life does not provide the same cohesiveness as does that of Asian people; and this has something to do with the Afro-Caribbean's *lack* of a whole culture. According to Brook-Shepherd, the 'old plantation relationship' has produced a situation in which Afro-Caribbean people do not recognise themselves as essentially foreign:

> They came to us from the oldest part of the Empire with the *same* religion and a *colourful variant of the same language.* They expected to find a ready made niche in what *they thought* would be a familiar society. [Our emphasis.]

The superficial similarities between Afro-Caribbean culture and English culture become a part of the explanation about why it is *Afro-Caribbean* youth who riot. In Brook-Shepherd's view, Afro-Caribbeans are neither fish nor fowl. They are not English enough to be easily assimilated, but neither are they different enough or their culture 'whole' enough for there to be a basis upon which they can bind themselves 'tightly together' as communities or as families. Indeed, Afro-Caribbean youth, in Brixton at any rate, are said to have 'slipped completely from the control of their parents'. Brook-Shepherd's references to the confused and disorganised nature of Afro-Caribbean cultural practices are put more starkly by Richard West in a two-part article written for the *Daily Telegraph* on 10/11 August 1981. He makes the connections this way:

> Jamaica and Brixton have many problems in common, like dope, Rastafarianism and violent crime. But there are other social problems affecting *all* British West Indian countries . . . *single parent families, harsh corporal punishment at home* yet lack of discipline at the school and *at a deeper level, the psychological wounds going back to slavery.* [Our emphasis.]

These 'social problems' appear in Britain at this point in time, argues West, because Afro-Caribbean brought them here, and reproduced them in their 'disorganised' family structures.

These ideas about Afro-Caribbean youth and Afro-Caribbean family structures are not new; they have been formulated within the ideology about the 'nation' and 'race' which has been constructed since the mid-1960s. Within the Conservative Right, culturalist explanations have long since replaced environmentalist notions. Where environmentalism talks about 'alienation' as a product of disadvantage and discrimination, this brand of 'biological culturalism' sees 'rootlessness' as the inevitable consequence of people with different traditions and 'alien' cultural practices settling in Britain.

These sets of ideas are used to provide a framework for understanding why Afro-Caribbean youth riot. The riot in Bristol in 1980 came as a 'surprise' only because St Paul's had not, at that point, been recognised as an area with 'race relations problems'. After the April riot in Brixton, on the other hand, 'surprise' was expressed not so much at the fact of rioting as at its intensity. By then the common-sense wisdom was that riots were likely to occur wherever there was a large Black, and particularly Afro-Caribbean, presence. The sheer scale of the 'nationwide' riots in July 1981 disrupted this wisdom for a while. It was not only that the rioting spread so quickly from area to area but also the fact that rioting occurred in areas without an appreciable Black presence; indeed in areas without a Black presence at all. In our view, an adequate understanding of why Black and White youth rioted during those few weeks, must pay attention to shared experiences of being young, working-class and living under crisis conditions. This does not mean that we can afford to ignore the different histories of struggle that came together in that brief moment. On the contrary, we will argue that the struggles of black youth and the relationship between Black culture and the sub-cultures of White working-class youth are of crucial importance.

During the riots there was a concerted attempt to play down or erase altogether the role that racist practices had played in precipitating them. In part this took the form of stressing that Black *and* White youth were equally involved. If this was so then the riots couldn't have had anything to do with racism, could they? Thus, although the *Daily Mail* of 6 July headlined its news of the second night's rioting in Toxteth 'Black War on Police', and emphasised Chief Constable Kenneth Oxford's explanation that gangs of

> young, black hooligans . . . hell-bent on a confrontation with the police (had only subsequently) been joined by an element of whites who latched onto the pickings from the looted shops.

These arguments fed into more general attempts to explain the events in terms of youth hooliganism, permissiveness, lack of parental control, inner-city decay and unemployment. Either criminal elements were mounting a sustained and premeditated attack on the most obvious symbols of authority, or 'youth' were implementing the perception that there was 'no future' for them in Britain. The discovery of young children on the frontlines raised the question of discipline in the home and for a few days this topic dominated discussion of the riots. Most papers thoughtfully averaged out the ages of the youth as being between 'ten and fourteen'. The *Daily Mail* of 8 July asked 'Don't Their Parents Care?' and, dismissing unemployment and 'racial tension' as possible contributory factors, gave a negative reply to its own question by portraying the improbably scene of parents in the courtroom, seeming 'no more concerned than parents waiting to see the maths master on Speech Day'. This scenario was strengthened by the 'authentic' voices of working-class parents: 'Well, you've got to let them have their play, haven't you? There's only the streets'; 'We were out ourselves, having a jar, so how the hell could we know what he was up to?' and common sense made the connections between parental neglect and rioting. In her televised broadcast, Prime Minister Margaret Thatcher spelt out the consequences of 'falling standards' within the family. 'A free society will only survive if we, its citizens, obey the law and teach our children to do so.'

Despite the widespread denial of *racism* in the news coverage, feature articles and long-term appraisals clearly expressed the feeling that *race* was a key factor in the rioting. The *Sunday Mirror* of 12 July 1981, for example, carried a centre-page feature entitled 'The Lost Children', in which a report about the dissatisfaction of youth in general and society's culpability in allowing resentment to fester, was accompanied by a large photograph of a Brixton scene. *The Guardian* despatched a reporter to St Paul's – which was *not* an area of rioting at the time – to speak to a generation of Afro-Caribbean youth apparently 'lost in limbo'. This was translated in a cartoon in the same issue (11 July), into a picture of a Sambo-like figure doing 'the limbo' as part of a 'Civil Unrest Circus'. *The Financial Times* of 11 July 1981 spoke about the 'Outbreak of an alien disease . . . to which the body politic has no immunity', even as it tried to maintain the idea that the problem was one of 'youth' *per se*. It is worth noting that openly racist groups share this language of 'alien diseases', although they also claim to have the cure . . . repatriation. This theme too was urgently discussed throughout the summer months, particularly after Enoch Powell had intervened to warn the 'nation' that 'you've seen nothing yet' (*Daily Mail* and *The Sun* 10 July 1981). It was left to Powell's soul brothers on the Conservative right to spell out the significance of the racial theme. In the *Daily Express* of 6 July 1981, Eldon Griffiths (MP and Parliamentary Adviser to the Police Federation) placed 'racial violence' supreme amongst the upsurge 'of violence of all kinds – industrial and political, personal and international', that made it necessary to ask, 'Can We Really Afford NOT To Arm Our Police?' Prophecying future riots, he argued that:

Ten years ago such a prophecy would have been dismissed as irresponsible. But after Brixton and Bristol, Notting Hill and Lewisham, Southall and Toxteth, who can say that racial violence does not threaten the social fabric of Britain?

While the *Sun* of 10 July 1981 made the point graphically in the same week with a cartoon depicting a snake called 'Race Hate' strangling Britain, Ronald Butt in *The Times* of 9 July 1981 talked of the organisations who were peddling 'even in *the classroom*, black hatred for white society'. To suggest that 'racialism' was endemic in British society was, he said, to risk 'alienating the vast majority of ordinary decent (i.e. white) people . . . and everyone can think out the consequences of that for himself'.

The corollary of all this was that the young Blacks were indeed the 'problem'. Later in the year and in response to the Scarman Report, Peregrine Worsthorne 'blurted out the truth' that Lord Scarman had apparently not been able to bring himself to reveal:

Brixton is the iceberg tip of a crisis of *ethnic criminality* which is not Britain's fault . . . but the fault of the ethnic community itself, from whom the cure must come, as has the disease. (*Sunday Telegraph*, 29 November 1981) [Our emphasis.]

We will discuss later how criminality comes to acquire an 'ethnicity'. For the moment we want to draw attention to the fact that by this time the riots had been racialised. The earlier concern with a 'general problem' of bad parents and undisciplined children had retreated into the 'common-sense' scenario of 'race relations', leaving the 'problem' of Black youth and crime, once again, as the primary means of signalling Britain's 'moral' as well as economic decline. The country was 'going to the dogs' because the Blacks were here.

Some historical connections

The themes of race, youth, violence and crime have not always been knitted together in this way. Racist images of Black sexuality and idleness, which had sedimented into common sense during the colonial period (Lawrence, 1982), were certainly updated in the 1950s through the media's association of Blacks with prostitution and drug-dealing. These ideas were also picked up by sociologists and historians who were beginning to research in and around the field of 'race relations'; although always careful to draw a line between the 'disreputables' and the 'respectables', they nevertheless theorised the disreputables' involvement in crime in terms related to the whole group, in particular the nature of the 'sending society' and the customs and mores of the 'immigrants'. Apart from the activities of 'pimps and drug-dealers' – discussed collectively in the literature as 'café society' or 'ruffianboys' – concern was also expressed about West African students who, it was felt, might respond to Britain's 'colour bar' either by turning to communism or by spreading the bad word to the detriment of Britain's economic interests, once they returned home. This theme meshed into anxiety about the process of 'decolonisation', in which images of restless natives and violent savages had been revitalised in response to anti-colonial movements, particularly the Mau Mau movement in Kenya.

However, in an era in which Britain 'had never had it so good', worries about the Blacks were peripheral in comparison to the 'moral panics' about the activities of mainly White working-class male youth at home. Such anxiety was not in itself a new phenomenon. Working-class youth had been the object of concerned social commentary since the 1880s (Humphries, 1981; Blanch, 1979). Nevertheless, the form this concern took in the post-war period was qualitatively different. Although the anxiety about youth in this period expressed fears about the direction and pace of post-war change, it is no accident that the 'moral panics' about youth should have occurred at precisely the point where Black cultural forms became incorporated into the subcultures of White, working-class youth.

In America, where the music which was to become the Teddy Boys' anthem originated the connections between White youth subcultures and Black culture were keenly felt and clearly expressed. Although rock 'n' roll was a bleached and sanitised version of Afro-American rhythm 'n' blues, it produced a storm of protest both north and south of the Mason–Dixon line. The moral threat that this 'nigger music' posed to a generation of White American youth was concretised in the image of the 'asphalt jungle' and personified in the figure of 'Elvis the Pelvis', who unashamedly modelled his 'sexual' hip movements on Black acts as he tried to bring a Black feel to the way he sang his songs. These connections were noted in Britain as well. Jeremy Thorpe, for example, discussing the film 'Rock Around the Clock' on *Any Questions* and making no distinction between jazz and rock 'n' roll, prefaced his remarks about the film thus: 'I'm a lover of music . . . I don't like jazz, it's the music of the jungle'. Revealing that he was 'one of the few people' actually to have seen the film, he poured scorn on the 'fuss' that had accompanied its release. 'It's a fourth-rate film with fifth-rate music', he contended, 'It's musical *mau mau* that's what it is, *musical mau mau*.' At which point the audience enthusiastically applauded.

This snippet points to the way in which racial themes which now predominate in discussions about 'youth and the crisis' were already present in a submerged way in the discrete moral panics that were constructed around White youth in previous periods. The associations that were made between 'musical mau mau', drugs, teenage violence and sexual permissiveness were a product of years of racial conflict in the USA but they were, of course, also consonant with British ideas and theories about adolescence. The activities of White youth further cemented these associations. While the activities of the boys were reported largely in terms of their violence (wrecking cinemas, 'gang' fights, and so on) many of the other theories gravitated around the activities of the girls. They were the ones who followed 'the wild ones into battle', 'egging on' the boys to violence on Bank Holiday afternoons, or who were 'discovered' to 'have been sleeping around with youths carrying the recognised weekend kit, purple hearts and contraceptives' (*Daily Telegraph*, 31 August 1965 in S. Cohen, 1980). The imagery here derived its power from the double standards that operate for girls and boys. For boys, 'sowing a few wild oats' has always been considered a part of growing up to 'manhood'; 'good girls' on the other hand just 'don't do that sort of thing'. In a milder form, this kind of idea was also evident in the incredulous but patronising coverage of 'Beatlemania'. At one level the 'screaming' and 'swooning' at pop concerts was handled as an aspect of the 'hysteria' appropriate to young women going through the 'natural stage' of puberty, even if its public expression was regarded as not quite right for British girls. But there was also the hint that such public expression was itself prompted in some way by the 'jungle music'. Taken together, this bundle of ideas and imagery confirmed that there was something very 'wrong with young people today' and that whatever it was, was organically linked with the deterioration of standards in Britain. As *Tribune* of 10 April 1964 put it, 'there is something rotten in the state of Britain and the recent hooliganism at Clacton is only one manifestation of it'.

The proximity of White youth to Black culture in America, which had generated rock 'n' roll, was not at that time a prominent feature of urban life in Britain. In any case the Caribbean people who were here and whose culture closely resembled that of the Afro-Americans, brought with them musical traditions which although developing from the same roots as the Afro-American variety had branched off in a different direction. Even Blue Beat which was developed in close dialogue with rhythm 'n' blues was different enough for the Teds not to recognise the connections. In the American context, rock 'n' roll could express an ambiguous and vicarious identifcation with the oppressed Blacks, but these meanings were not available to the English Teddy Boys. Instead, the music was received as *White* American music – even Black acts marketed under the rock 'n' roll banner being thought of as 'White' until films featuring them reached these shores. In this situation, the reproduction of racist common sense within the Teddy Boy subculture went uncontested and in contrast to the racist skinheads, their attacks upon their Black neighbours were embarked upon without any sense of contradiction. Indeed, the ideas which sanctioned these attacks were reinforced by the media and it is evident that the government shared many of the same assumptions. In 1957, for example, the Home Office required the police to ascertain certain facts about the Black population. Of the six questions they were asked to answer, two related to criminal activity and a third to the rate of illegitimacy amongst 'West Indians'.

After the Notting Hill race riots of 1958 the then Home Secretary, R. A. Butler, argued that the 'difficulties arose partly through vice' but reassured the nation that:

> I think it very likely that the government in the new session will seek a power of deportation. I believe that would deal with undesirable residents and give me the same power as I have in dealing with aliens.

As the subcultural space opened up by the Teddy Boys was colonised by a new generation of youth, the influence of Black cultural forms became more explicit. The mods replaced rock 'n' roll with soul and constructed a style based partly on their perception of Black 'cool', members of the hard core signifying their closeness to Black culture by imitating Jamaican Creole. White musicians – not for the last time – turned to the whole range of Black American musical traditions (rhythm and blues, jazz, the blues, and so on) in order to revitalise rock music. A procession of dead and/or forgotten blues artists, in particular, were wheeled in to receive belated acknowledgement of their part in the 'rock explosion' and to play music which most Blacks had long considered out of date. White singers and musicians were looking to recreate an 'authentic' (that is, Black) sound which would nevertheless appeal to White audiences. Mick Jagger's stage act, for example, is reputed to have been based on that of James Brown. Undoubt-edly, by pouting his 'negro-like' lips he was able to emphasise the

Black connection, adding to his 'authenticity' and 'sex-appeal' at one and the same time. For lesser mortals it was a case of living out, through imagination and/or drugs, the 'negro condition'. However, although both mods and musicians, for their own different reasons, were seriously interested in Black music, few were actually aware of the day-to-day pressures under which Blacks lived on both sides of the Atlantic. Hebdige (1979) and Chambers (1976) have noted a tendency to romanticise the lives of Black people but this criticism has been set in the historical context of the overt racism of the Teddy Boys and skinheads. If the response of the teds to the presence of black people was openly hostile and that of the skinheads (mark I) ambivalent (beating up Asians at the same time as they attended dance halls with Afro-Caribbean youth), then the mods were sympathetic or at least neutral. Indeed, during the 1960s the sympathetic noises of the mods, and later the hippies, were enough to convince some people that racism would atrophy with the older generation. What the sociologists and subcultural theorists tended to miss was the extent to which this romantic imagery was underpinned by racist common sense. In part this is due to the fact that the mods' common sense had been partially *transformed*. Not only did some of them live in the same neighbourhoods as Black people, but their preference for Black music meant that they also shared some of the same dance halls. As well as sharing this leisure space, some Blacks were also one source of the drugs that the mods used. In order to preserve these connections, then, overt signs of racism needed to be suppressed. Thus the kinds of racist stereotypes held by the Teds were replaced in the case of the mods by less immediately offensive imagery. For example, ideas about Black people possessing natural rhythm (preoccupied with dressing-up and only out for a good time) were retained and reconstructed in soul and disco culture which defined Blacks as the smartest and the best dancers. Some Black youth would indeed have been better dancers but only because they were already familiar with the music and the dance styles that went with it, and would have been practising the steps and movements from a very early age. However, then, as now, the practice in schools of channelling black youth into physical activities and away from academic work had the effect of training black youth in these practices (sport, and so on) at the same time as their disproportionate success at school level reinforced, for White youth, the image of Blacks as naturally gifted in and equipped for such activities as running, dancing, and so on. Black people's ways of dancing, dressing and having fun were not viewed as aspects of a *different* culture which provided them with *different* sets of rule and *different* ways of being. Instead, White youth's racist common sense *naturalised* the cultural differences; Blacks were by nature happy-go-lucky, colourful, rhythmic and amoral.

In Afro-American and Afro-Caribbean cultures, music has been a powerful medium for communicating the community's political experience and for organising its consciousness. Black women have participated equally in this and they have also made use of music to express their distinctive struggles against racism and patriarchy. As Blacks have come to dominate pop culture, these messages have also become available to Whites. The Supremes, Donna Summer, Randy Crawford and Diana Ross defined sexuality, femininity and style for many young Whites. The liturgy of gender conflicts which female soul singers preach has meaning for White girls too, particularly if they are involved in relationships with the Black boys who are often seen as the sharpest dressers and best dancers in soul and disco culture. All this has been ignored by 'subculture theorists' who have only looked at masculine forms in addressing the issue of race.

The emergence of middle-class youth on to the scene in the mid-1960s added further complications to the already tricky relationship between White youth and Blacks. Precisely because they were of a different class, their identification with Blacks was purely on a cerebral level. Their disdain for the then contemporary black music (soul, rock steady and early reggae) actively prevented even the kind of relationship the mods had had. Their concern with individual enlightenment and 'inner peace' led them instead in the direction of the cultures of Britain's Black Asian population. Paradoxically, the interest in 'Eastern mysticism' did not signal an engagement with the Asian people living here. The trail led not to Southall, Bradford or Leicester but to India, Pakistan and Morocco. It was visions of the exotic rather than the day-to-day reality of Asian people that attracted attention. The romantic vision did not, however, prevent the spread of tales about 'thuggery', 'thievery', 'idleness' and 'disease' in the less 'civilised' parts of the world and not a few intrepid wanderers were glad to return to the security of this 'green and pleasant land'.

However, the 'revolt of middle-class youth' was in many ways seen as more threatening than the activities of working-class youth. Although the 'Paki-bashing' and 'queer-bashing' of the skinheads – who were forced apart from Black youth by their own racism and Black youths' resistance to it – reinforced by the image of violent working-class youth, the development of the 'counter culture' seemed to show just how far the rot had set in (Clarke *et al.* 1976). It was not just that they 'turned on, dropped out and slept around'. The sight of the student population – the 'chosen ones' – sitting-in, occupying buildings and demonstrating on the streets not only about things that directly concerned them (teaching, grants, and so on) but also taking part in extra-parliamentary activity over wider issues such as the war in Vietnam, proved to be profoundly disturbing. In the context of the first signs of economic crisis in Britain and against the backdrop of campus battles between students and the police in the USA, insurrection in Paris and riots in Berlin in 1968, the 'moral panics' about youth, fed into other anxieties about the 'rise in violent crime', political violence and industrial conflict to produce a composite picture of an increasingly violent Britain (Hall *et al.*, 1979).

Race in class

The problems of Black youth were, at this stage, almost exclusively identified in relation to school. It was here that the 'wide-grinning piccaninnies' would be socialised into the English way of doing things. In the era of assimilation which preceded the era of repatriation, school was the place in which the distinctiveness of Black youth was first recognised and defined as a problem.

As with the idea that racial prejudice would die with the older white generation, so here it was felt that the 'alien' cultures of Black people would die out with the 'first generation immigrants'. The course of 'misunderstandings' which created racial problems would have withered away, Black youth would be assimilated, and the 'race problem' would disappear. But the incipient culturalism in this type of argument gave a misleading picture. By locating the problem simply at the level of culture, theorists underestimated the extent to which racist practices were embedded in the social structures of British society. The *'laissez-faire'* racist practices which in the era of the 'colour bar' had located Black workers in particular occupations and which forced them to take up residence in particular parts of town meant that as a predominantly *young* Black population began to send its children to school in the same neighbourhood, the school also became a site of racist agitation. Just as the invitation to Black people to come and work here had entailed no strategy for housing development or urban renewal, so also there had been no thought about modernising or re-equipping old inner-city schools. These were the schools to which Black children, alongside the White children whose families had been left behind in the move to new estates and new towns (P. Cohen, 1972) were sent. Furthermore, as later research was to demonstrate (Coard, 1971), Black children were subjected to an education system which was ethnocentric where it wasn't racist.

This was the situation in which White residents' and parents' associations, armed with their common sense about the inferiority of Black people and encouraged by the fact that the government *did* seem to be influenced by the lobbying of their 'kith and kin' on the immigration issue, turned their attention to the numbers of Black children attending *their* schools. The Blacks, they argued, were 'holding our children back'. At the same time the Commonwealth Immigrants' Advisory Council, taking the 'culturally homogenous nation' as its point of departure, was warning that 'a national [education] system cannot be expected to perpetuate the different values of immigrant groups', thereby giving credence to the 'fears' of white parents. It was with the re-election of a Labour government, however, that *'laissez-faire'* racism was finally laid to rest and *state* intervention began in earnest. Pledged to repeal the Commonwealth Immigration Act in opposition, the Labour party renewed the provisions of the Act once in government and in their White Paper of 1965, proposed to restrict immigration even further. The rationale for this was encapsulated in Roy Hattersley's justly infamous remark: 'Without integration, limitation is inexcusable; without limitation, integration is impossible'. In practical terms, the Home Office's White Paper (HMSO, 1965) had already acceded to racist demands by instituting a quota system for Black pupils. The justification for this paralleled the arguments for immigration control. The more Black pupils there were in a school, the less the chances of their integration, and the greater the 'hostility' of White parents who 'feared' that Black pupils were lowering standards. At this point the debate about the education of Black children gravitated around the 'problems' they posed in terms of their numbers, their 'intelligence' and their cultures, particularly their languages (Carby, 1980).

A number of studies appeared throughout the 1960s which theorised common-sense notions of 'low standards' and pushed the concern with how Black cultures constrained assimilation to its logical limits. The 'fact' that Black pupils scored lower on ethnocentric educational tests was taken as proof of their educational and intellectual inferiority. This 'poor performance' was, in turn, linked to the family and cultural background of the pupils. 'The whole pattern of a culture', argued the National Foundation for Educational Research (NFER) (NFER, 1966), 'determines the educational and vocational potential and combines to reduce effective intelligence.' In order to 'raise the level' of Black pupils' performance, then, it would be necessary to intervene and disrupt the reproduction of their different and 'backward' cultures. The language of the home, which allowed Black pupils to exclude the teacher from their conversations, was constructed by the theorists as *the* major sign of the pupils' 'culturally induced backwardness' (NFER, 1966) and became the principal site upon which intervention was to take place. The acquisition of Standard English, which had always been presented as an essential part of the educational process, was further theorised in the case of Black pupils as being necessary for their successful assimilation. It was made clear, however, that the learning of Standard English by Black pupils should not be conducted in the same way as English pupils learned French or German. Afro-Caribbean creoles, in particular, were singled out as 'immature' and 'inadequate for expressing the complexities of present day life' (see Carby, 1980). As such they actively interfered with intellectual development and educational progress. These languages, therefore, should not survive the assimilation process and as if to drive the point home, theorists went to the trouble of cataloguing the deficiencies of the 'immigrant' language systems. These theories helped to shape the consensus across the traditional British political spectrum about what the problem was and together with the ideas about the 'nation' which Harold Wilson's Government had tried to mobilise (Hall *et al.*, 1979) made it difficult for those who did not agree with Enoch Powell's solution, to challenge his ideas in any meaningful way. By conceding the importance of 'numbers' and 'culture', they were sharing the assumptions of Powellism even if Powellism was more honestly racist. Moreover, the tendency to theorise, rather than dismantle, racist common sense and to locate the 'problem' in the households of Black people – where their cultures are reproduced – has remained a persistent feature of accounts and analyses of 'race relations'. It unites theorists of the Right, Left and Centre on this issue, where their politics on other matters divides them (Lawrence, 1982).

If those who were 'sympathetic' to Black people were often at a loss as to how to tackle racism and challenge its Powellite manifestations, Black people were less daunted by the scale of the task. Black parents in Haringey and Southall began to organise against the 'bussing and banding' of their children and their campaigns were important in the Department of Education and Science's (DES) later decision to reverse its policy on quotas. The brief existence of a Black Power movement in Britain was also important. Because it took account of the ways in which Black people were organising themselves, it created a climate in which local campaigns around specific issues could be fed into the broader debate about the whole edifice of racism and how Black people could begin to combat it. It was here, for example, that Black parents' criticisms began to be transformed into a more thorough-going critique of the education system. One outcome of this was the demand for Black studies to be included in the school curriculum, although the way in which these demands were framed – in terms of 'absences' in the curriculum rather than in terms of the social relations of schooling – allowed them to become incorporated into arguments for multicultural teaching. The pro-blem here was that multiculturalism tended to be thought about as a form of compensatory education which would address Black pupils' supposed home or cultural handicaps and identity problems by giving them a 'positive image' (Jeffcoate, 1979). As such it was an extension of existing theories and policies designed to compensate for deprivations of White working-class pupils' backgrounds. Thus, compensatory theory's failure to address the relations of power which subordinated the White working class were merely compounded in the case of Black pupils.

For Black pupils, the 'handicaps' that needed to be overcome consisted of coping with racist insults; defending themselves from attacks by their White peers; and coming to understand the subtle and shadowy racism which permeated relationships with teachers and which implied tacit support for the racism of White kids. Resistance to this state of affairs and to the more general boredom and routine of schooling – which White pupils also suffered – was first recognised by teachers in the behaviour of Afro-Caribbean pupils, and was rationalised more often than not as the recalcitrance of 'disruptive pupils'. This merely cemented their feelings about the low potential of Afro-Caribbean children, feelings which seemed to be confirmed by the testimony of the 'experts'. Afro-Caribbean youth who were defined early on as 'difficult' or as 'slow learners' were dumped in schools for the 'educationally subnormal', and those who escaped this fate stood a reasonable chance of ending up in bottom streams of the secondary moderns or comprehensives (Coard, 1971). At this point pupils in the lower streams, aware of their likely destinies in terms of 'shitwork' or 'no work', ceased to see any point in schooling. In some schools compromise went out of the window and whole classes became virtually impossible to teach or to discipline (Dhondy, 1978).

The fact that this resistance appeared most intensely within the lower streams has made it easy for theorists of the Left to dismiss it as the behaviour of an ignorant lumpen or 'marginal' element. Those who think otherwise are merely being romantic. Stephen Burt puts it this way:

> Dhondy places great emphasis on resistance in school – including 'black failure' seen as 'black rejection' of school – leading to wider black consciousness . . . but he is wrong to equate 'messing about' with organized resistance; this is no 'crisis of schooling', it is the exacerbation of subjugation through *ignorance of the dominating culture.* (Burt, 1982) [Our emphasis.]

This is indicative of the thinking of the Labour Left, which is unable to view Black people in any terms other than as 'thoughtless victims' in need of a good dose of 'bourgeois education'. This, it is felt, will show them the correct path for struggle. The point is that Farukh Dhondy does not actually equate 'messing about' *in itself* with organised resistance. Although Willis has shown that 'larking about' can be more meaningful than Burt allows, the sheer scale of the activity to which Dhondy refers should be enough to warn us that we are witnessing something which is qualitatively different from the resistance of Willis's 'lads'. Stephen Humphries' (1981) historical account of the working-class experience of schooling in the first half of the twentieth century, is helpful here. For he demonstrates that school-based resistance ('messing about', truancy, subverting lessons, school strikes, and so on), was at that time intimately connected with the struggles of the working-class communities from which the pupils came. While Dhondy does not provide the same detail as Humphries, he is arguing that similar connections are important for Black youth today. As he rightly says, 'the education of black youth starts and continues within the communities of which they are still a part' (Dhondy, 1974). The school strike and demonstration in support of the Brockwell Park 3 in 1973, organised by students of the school and attended by upwards of 1000 pupils, is one vivid example of youth's recognition of the connections. It was made all the more poignant by the fact that the students, unlike some of the Black communities' 'leadership', refused to make any distinctions between unemployed youth, young workers and school pupils (see *Race Today*, June 1974). The local campaigns in support of Rastafarian youths refused entry to school until they had cut off their locks, and the closure of schools and colleges in south London during the Black People's Day of Action (March 1981) in protest over the nature of the police investigation of the New Cross fire, provide other examples.

We would argue that it is a mistake to reduce the resistance of Black youth to the 'messing about' of a few pupils in the lower streams. The breadth of it is signalled nor merely in hostility to racist teachers and the disruption of lessons, nor even in the support for school strikes, but in the widespread adoption and transformation of Caribbean creoles, the very languages that the schools had attempted to undermine. For older youth in the 1950s and early 1960s, creole simply was their language. This would also have been true for some Afro-Caribbean pupils at school while others learned phrases from parents and older brothers and sisters and used it as much for recreation as with any serious subversive intent. However, throughout the 1960s, regional variations of creole began to be established as the principal way they spoke to each other. In many ways speaking creole became a 'sign' of being Black. This process was reproduced in the schools, where the denigration of it as 'poor speech' or 'bad English' served only to underline its importance. The tendency has been for theorists to date this process from the popularisation of Rastafari and to view the years before as years in which Afro-Caribbean youth suffered from 'crises of identity' and floundered about in a kind of 'limbo' somewhere between the Black and White worlds (Cashmore, 1979; Pryce, 1979; Cashmore and Troyna, 1982). Because the history of the transformation of creole and the struggles it signifies remain hidden in these accounts, the significance of the Rasta intervention is also misunderstood. It becomes an idiosyncratic path out of 'limbo'. The problems here are compounded by the insistence on treating Rastafari as though it were only about subscribing to a few dogmatic tenets and sporting the symbols of 'dread', rather than beginning from its mass character within the Black communities.

Other theorists, while recognising the existence of a linguistic community, anchored in Rasta concepts, see its significance purely in terms of the 'misunderstandings' it can cause between teacher and pupil. In this view creole languages are presented as cultural retentions with little or no relevance for struggle. Events in the classroom, however, tend to undermine this view. The sketch written and performed by a group of school-age Black girls and filmed by London Weekend Television for one of its early Minorities Unit programmes ('*Babylon*', November 1979) provides one small example of the ways in which Afro-Caribbean youth are able to use creole to challenge the teacher's racist assumptions and to express solidarity with each other. The sketch began with one of the girls being asked by a White teacher to read a passage out loud. The girl complied by reading it perfectly correctly but with an 'accent'. The teacher objected to this 'poor' performance, at which point there was brief disagreement about the merits of the girl's reading. Eventually, the girl said in 'broad' creole to the class words to the effect that 'if she doesn't like it she knows what she can do'. Other girls showed their support for her by replying in equally 'broad' creole. A conversation began between them about the arrogance of the teacher's assumptions. By this time, of course, the teacher had lost control of the class and was reduced to making disparaging remarks about the girls' 'kissing their teeth', apparently oblivious of the fact that she had already been dismissed by them. What the girls were portraying is not simple 'misunderstanding' but cultural conflict. In some schools, teachers have moved to circumvent this conflict by allowing a 'space' for creole. Afro-Caribbean pupils are encouraged to bring their language into drama classes or to share with the teacher and the rest of the class in English lessons and in some instances this has been successful. But incidents like the one reported by Jeffcoate (1979), in which after one of these interrogations one of his pupils wrote on the classroom blackboard, 'Sir is nosey about Black people's language'; suggests that these are at best short-term strategies.

These resistances may not yet amount to a 'crisis of schooling' but it is clear that it is taxing the ingenuity of teachers and education departments. While the resistance of the boys can at least be dealt with by male teachers 'man to man' as it were, and the more combative individuals, both boys and girls, can be despatched to the 'sin-bins', the collective resistance of the girls has proved much more difficult to cope with. At least one headmistress has felt threatened enough to call for the assistance of the police (Clapton Park School, 1974). When the police arrived, fighting broke out between them and the girls, after which four girls were arrested, charged and convicted for 'assault' on the police. But generally, as we saw above, the resistance takes a different form, although even here teachers in some schools view groups of Black girls with apprehension. As Janey Wallis, 'a white teacher in a mixed, inner-city comprehensive school', told *Spare Rib* in October 1980:

> The Black girls in my school tend to form themselves in groups – for friendship and for security. The White pupils don't appear to find these groups threatening, but certainly many of the teachers do. It's not talked about though. You discover teachers avoiding break duty in certain areas of the school . . .

We have already said that the resistance of Black youth in school is linked to political struggles which mobilise their communities more broadly. Foremost among these has been the pattern of conflict between Black communities and the police. This is central to our concerns here too. In the context of crisis and the development of more authoritarian criminal justice and welfare policies, this issue has constituted a bridge between the political traditions and concerns of the Black communities and those of their White neighbours.

Though a minority of those arrested in the riots of July 1981 were Black, a majority of them were under twenty years old. Extensive White participation was masked by the 'racialisation' of these events, but having discredited that racial explanation, we must still see the riots as the end product of a longer struggle around police abuse in Black, working-class communities the length and breath of Britain. The multi-racial character of the rioting is but one small illustration of the relation between Black and White youth which crisis conditions have fostered. No discussion of racism and anti-racism in Britain is complete without consideration as to its background.

Racism, anti-racism and riots

The way in which the riots of the summer of 1981 were presented in the media had the inevitable effect of lumping together anger born of different grievances and imposing a uniformity on struggles with disparate local meanings. These were synchronised by the way in which 'rioting' became possible during those two weeks in July. But how was this synchronisation possible?

Most commentators share the view that, with the possible exception of events in Southall, intra-class conflict along racial lines was not a feature of the disturbances. Consequently, whatever the riots were, they were not race riots in the 1958 sense. We have already argued that for a while the idea that the violence resided merely in the fact of youth and the degeneration of familial relations in the 'riot torn' areas of Britain was dominant.

This view retreated in the face of the subsequent racialisation of the events. Yet, in recognition of a germ of truth which this initial explanation contains, we wish to return to it as the basis of our examination of race and racism in the cultural politics of working-class youth today. Common experience of youth had something to do with it. A hint of the complexities of how young people live out the contradiction between race and class is provided by the way that the political struggles of Black youth of Afro-Caribbean descent have gradually become meaningful for other groups of young people. After the riot in Bristol 1980, skinheads in Birmingham's city centre taunted the police who sought to move them on with a chant of 'Bristol, Bristol'; and young Asians in Coventry in May 1981 baited the police with a chorus of 'Brixton, Brixton'. By July, the chant was heard wherever young people fought the police. However trivial this may appear, it points to the resonance of one struggle for another and therefore to the possibility of common purpose which was to reveal itself in July 1981, concentrated by particular experiences of a youth and class culture increasingly circumscribed by the weight of political and economic crisis. This ought to be a reminder that young people in the heart of the cities do in many significant respects share a culture. It is assembled from many different elements, and incorporates recognisable fragments from previous struggles and traditions of resistance previously separated by thousands of miles as well as the Imperial gulf between master and slave. In many areas the culture and politics of working-class youth exhibits a seamless and organic fusion of Black and White sensibilities. Recognising this should not be read as a suggestion that racism has become obsolete in the processes by which this unique fusion has been sustained. Racism, albeit in new forms as the crisis deepens, remains to proscribe participation in some forms of this youth culture. It threatens this fragile unity and challenges every step in the logic of cultural processes which promise to reduce the mystique of race and nation to scarcely more than cobwebs on the coffin of the British Commonwealth.

After the Falklands episode, it may appear that this burial is premature, and there can be little doubt that the nationalist fervour generated in the South Atlantic cements the notion of a racially exclusive and biologically-based national culture in opposition to experience of Black-defined pluralism at the two-tone grassroots of the inner city. But, it must also be said that the potential remains to curtail severely the credibility of racist reasoning among the young. In saying this, nothing can be taken for granted, particularly as this task has to be recognised as a distinct problem rather than viewed as an appendage of the struggle against youth unemployment.

The scale of the crisis itself imposes new limits on the plausibility of racist explanations of decline in the quality of life, but positive outcomes in the struggle against racism among young people also become less likely when every day the Right are allowed to monopolise this field of struggle.

There has been very little interest in either young people's racism or the specific qualities of the anti-racist work which has disrupted and even banished it. Here the Left share the dominant view of youthful 'folk devils' as symbolic of political problems rather than as political actors in their own right. It is tempting to conclude that the Left seizes on the issue of youth and racism for two reasons. First, because the skinheads' image confirms common-sense perceptions of them as violent', and second, because the task of examining, let alone contesting, racism elsewhere in society has become too huge to contemplate.

The sinews of nationalism run very deep into the body of labour ideology. Though seldom attempted, the painful exercise of trying to remove them could do little more than confirm the left's own marginality, and the precariousness of genuine internationalism in British political life. To varying degrees, left initiatives against the Common Market, and in favour of the Alternative Economic Strategy and the Campaign for Nuclear Disarmament have all made explicit appeals to nationalist and, we would argue, racist sentiments. The left theorists who argue that patriotism and nationalism must be wrested from the Right seem unable to see that the contemporary manifestations of these ideologies cannot be emptied of a racist meaning. What is more, a 'European' identity does not provide a challenge to the racial strands in British nationalism, but emphasises them. The key to this intellectual sleight of hand is the false separation of racism and nationalism. In this, racism becomes a moral question, wholly distinct from the aspirations and fears of 'free-born Britons' whose snow-white heritage in the declining urban areas includes the very nationalism which will resuscitate the left if only they can break Mrs Thatcher's monopoly of it. Parallel to this, racism among youth is interpreted as an 'anti-social' tendency which, like glue-sniffing and street crime, will be eradicated by socialist policy and ideologies of community responsibility.

There is no uniform racism which has taken root among all young people. It is, therefore, necessary to begin to differentiate the popular nationalism/racism which 'makes Britain Great Again', from more authoritarian forms which are potentially in contradiction with those ideologies which emanate from young people themselves. These currents overlap, but they are rarely in complete alignment. Like the racist ideologies which have their origins in the concerns and practices of organised Right-wing groups, they are stamped by crisis conditions, yet racisms are never homogenous, and the contradictions between them, in particular the different ways they represent and explain different groups within the Black population, are very important indeed. At the moment, it appears that the viability of local, multiracial cultures based around shared experiences of youth and class depends very heavily on the relations between Asians and West Indians. This is not least because the coherence of a racist culture falls where there is unity between Afro-Caribbeans and the Asians. The out-and-out 'alien' characteristics of the latter group are the object of a 'purer' hatred (often centred on a view of them as a hard-working, if deceitful, petit-bourgeoisie) which is absent from the racist view of West Indians for whom the 'bastardised' elements of Englishness visible in their culture secure an image of child-like figures posing no real *economic* threat. A further complexity arises where young racist Whites maintain an interest in West Indian culture, as, for example, in their affection for reggae music. This group are in a highly contradictory position where any alliance between Asians and Afro-Caribbeans fuelled by a mutual definitions of themselves as 'Black' limits the extent of White borrowing from the more attractive West Indian culture and recreational pursuits. The possibility of alliances between Black youth should be no surprise. The harmony of interests and political understanding between different groups in the Black communities is not confined to young people. Yet the cultural continuity in youth culture and the simple fact of young people's segregation in school allow this relationship to become more readily visible among youth. It is remarkable, then, how imagery of youth is frequently central to pessimistic presentations of the relations between West Indians and Asians.

These accounts draw on a common-sense racism that stereotypes Afro-Caribbean youth as violent criminals and all Asian people as the personification of victimage. In opposition to ideas like these, organised political groups in both communities strive to construct a definition of 'Black' which can encompass diverse political traditions and personal experiences. Such a definition affords a considerable political advantage to the communities *as a whole*. The fact of its existence, albeit uneven, ought to prevent simple-minded typologies of the July 1981 events along the facile 'racial' lines suggested by some writers on the left:

> The Southall riot began as a fight between skinheads and Asian youths. Anger swiftly shifted to the police, but because they were protecting the skinheads in a way they have rarely protected Asian communities – the implicit Asian demand was for more not less policing of their streets. (Frith, 1981).

This passage is important for a number of reasons. It typifies an avowedly anti-racist understanding of race and class which is all too popular on the left and it has been written in apparently blissful ignorance of previous events in Southall. In both 1976 and 1979 young Asians had revealed the sophistication of their capacity for defensive self-organisation against state institutions. The author here is not only denying this particular history of struggle – class struggle – by reducing it to a 'fight' between young people, he is also overemphasising youth by presenting it as an ahistorical factor unaffected by the cultural and political patterns which make 'racial' groups appear distinct.

The difficulties which arise where the concepts of 'Black' and 'youth' come together have their roots as much in problems with the notion of youth as over 'race'. Left and Right alike are unable to conceptualise 'youth' as other than a transitory phase between school and eventual work, rooted in the classroom rather than the changing relations of social reproduction linked to the division of labour. Social groups such as youth or women or Blacks whose consciousness and organisation are formed outside the workplace have traditionally been viewed with suspicion and even hostility by the fractions of the workers' movement organised at the point of production.

However, the political importance of young people's struggles has grown as the imagery of 'rebellious youth' has attained prominence in the language and politics of Law and Order. This derives both from the powerful symbolic threat which confident youth 'subcultures' pose to their respectable 'elders and betters' and from growing day-to-day difficulties in the policing of young people's cultural institutions as well as their use of public space (the street, parks, and so on). The governmental responses to economic crisis have transformed 'youth' into a stage of extended dependancy stretching the gulf between childhood and the adult- hood which arrives with the first wage packet. Young people's response to this development has brought the social movement of youth – Black *and* White, into a range of conflicts with state agencies, yet these are seldom seen as legitimately political or taken on their own terms. In addition to the pathology of Black families referred to above, it has been quite extraordinary to watch the reappearance of moralistic and pathological categories in much discussion of White youth. This brings about a convergence in which both Left and Right, though they may disagree over the causes of the malady, share a perception of its symptoms and the most appropriate solution: more Law and Order:

> A police presence is a rational defence for working class and bourgeois, black and white alike, against the unforeseeable expression of contemporary youth cultural nihilism. (Taylor, 1981)

However, where this nihilism/cynicism is discussed in detail its racist components tend to be presented as the symptom of other ills rather than a dynamic and important problem in their own right. This can mean that recognising them and combating young people's racism as a distinct area of political work is viewed as a distraction from real struggle or political activity. In this model, racist sentiments will evaporate either in a 'deeper', 'structural' grasp of the 'current situation' or in some experience of work. This approach possesses no appreciation of how ideas about class are shaped by racial segmentation, nor of how socialistic rhetoric, for example, 'British jobs for British workers' has taken root in youth-orientated Right-wing propaganda. The corollary of this is the Left's tendency to mourn in moralistic fashion the non- appearance of sustained anti-racist policies without troubling to examine the mass anti-racist mobilisations of the late 1970s, and it is to these we must now turn.

'There ain't no black in the Union Jack'

The Anti-Nazi League and Rock Against Racism (RAR) gave expression to the feelings of young people who had seen the inadequacy of racist explanation. They revealed for all to see the implicit politics of youth cultures which were defined by and often copied from Black forms and traditions. The heyday of RAR was also the hour of punk rock and this too created scope for the development of new kinds of opposition and new ways of organising. These factors combined to allow new ways of being political. Punk was specially important in that its demystification of pop culture and ideology spilled over into criticism of broader social relations. The do-it-yourself enthusiasm for playing and producing music which animated the early issues of 'fanzines' such as *Sniffin Glue* had the additional effect of reaffirming the creative power of its readership not only as individuals but also *as a group*. Punks rendered the coded, complex relation of mod and skinhead cultures to Black cultural forms at last open and explicit. Their distinctive use of the language and symbols of Rastafari in turn created the potential for RAR to intervene and make a conversation which had once been elliptical and covert, but now was loud, clear and indicative of a cultural and political process which forced an awareness of race on the most mainstream of young people. The success of RAR in reconciling the antagonistic styles of groups within White youth culture is important not only because the range of musical and stylistic tastes assembled under its banners points to the impact of Black culture on the least flamboyant currents in working-class youth culture, but also because the sheer scale of the project belied any narrow or sectarian (in subcultural terms) base. Rock Against Racism staged 200 concerts in its first year of operation.

Some will be tempted to look back on the RAR period and explain its demise in the failure of its organisers and activists to develop a real politics from the 'pop' version which they marketed with such skill and perception. This would be a great mistake, for though the demise of RAR can be traced in part to the orientation of its activists, it had little to do with the limitations of their cultural politics. Much of the Left in both its trade union and its revolutionary incarnations was suspicious, cynical and indifferent to the growth of RAR. A Workers' Revolutionary Party paper *Newsline* headline read 'No Politics At The Carnival', whilst the Revolutionary Communist Group and the Workers' Socialist League both issued leaflets which attacked the whole project, arguing instead for 'workers' self-defence' as the answer to racist violence. These would be a crucial link between the struggles of the Black communities and the other 'domestic' issue in which British nationalism distorted the potential of the working-class movement – the war in Northern Ireland. For the International Marxist Group, Tariq Ali argued that RAR could be a staging post *en route* to a more sophisticated and complete political consciousness:

> Lots of people will come along for Rock Against Racism today and see that it should be Rock Against the Stock Exchange tomorrow. (Ali, 1978)

These positions share the reluctance to accept that experience of racism and hatred of racist ideas could provide a point from which valid political consciousness might develop. At best, the parliamentary Left tended to view RAR as the acceptable face of youthful high jinks; at worst it represented the sinister fruit of ultra-Leftist manipulations of the young. Almost all Left writers advanced the view that many of those who had attended RAR events had not gone to register their opposition to racism or Fascism. Ultra-Leftists argued that RAR produced, 'Fun music with no political connections beyond the private affiliations of the musicians' (SR 3.6.78). A chorus of professional revolutionaries more sympathetic to the cause insisted that RAR had to be 'consolidated as an organisation' and proceeded to attempt to impose an organisational structure which had no relation to RAR's constituency or to the culture which had attracted them. A branch structure with delegates, conferences and cadres was, quite simply, inappropriate to the loose, intermittent and necessarily local nature of RAR work. Though RAR preceded the Anti-Nazi League (ANL), mutual connections with the Socialist Workers' Party (SWP) meant that they drew many activists from the same source. The ANL gradually came to dominate public perception of popular anti-racist politics. First, because the SWP elements in the RAR coalition began to put their energies into a project that was more obviously political in the traditional sense; and second, because the major anti-Fascist demonstrations of the 1977–78 period hit the headlines. The dominance of the ANL, punctuated by a steady stream of RAR concerts and jointly-organised carnivals, changed the tempo and the key of anti-racist politics. Young people were still a major constituent but the switch to anti-Nazism began to target older people. It signified a decisive shift towards a broader orientation. 'Rocking against racism' allowed scope for youth to rail against 'Labour Party Capitalist Britain', but being 'anti-Nazi' located the political problem of British racism almost exclusively in the activities of a small, though dangerous, band of lunatics. Though they were more than usually visible in the 1977–1979 period, and regardless of whether it would have been possible for them to make serious inroads into the traditional allegiance of working-class voters, they were only a small part of the problems which had fired the RAR youth. *Temporary Hoarding*, the RAR paper, expressed young people's anger in its account of Martin Webster's lone promenade through Thameside. They were inflamed by the way his solitary, flag-bearing walk escorted by hundreds of police expressed a relationship between 'Fascism' and the state institutions they knew to be oppressive. On the other hand, ANL propaganda made much of the fact that Britons who had given their lives in the struggles against Hitler were being mocked by his latterday disciples. The Nazi pasts of John Tyndal, Martin Webster and their like, disqualified them from use of the Union Jack. The ANL argued that anti-racist work was as important in the factory as it was on the street. Yet, for many youth, consigned to street corners by the downturn in the nation's economic life, issues of police harassment and malpractice were central to RAR's appeal. It was in the street that they were able to connect their personal experience with a wider understanding of racism and to see how racial oppression related to their own experience of repression. The police, regulating the boundary between childhood and maturity, remain at the heart of youth cultures' political development. They were certainly no less vicious under the watchful eye of a Labour Home Secretary than they had been previously. Through reggae, the Rastafarian discourse of 'equal rights and justice' provided a political analysis of 'police and thieves' for young Whites. They too were increasingly drawn into conflict with the law and its officers as crisis conditions began to dictate a police policy in which the state of youth itself was sufficient to provoke suspicion of criminal intent.

Merlyn Rees's reign at the Home Office can also be used to illustrate a second problem: the simple fact of a Labour Government. This period saw Labour's elusive socialism further diluted by their lack of an overall parliamentary majority and its remoteness contrasted sharply with the vitality and relevance of RAR's political culture. Socialism was identified almost exclusively with the James Callaghan – Merlyn Rees – Dennis Healey axis who monopolised it, and promised nothing to young people whose political choices were unfogged by expectations of any alternative Labour could provide. In this climate, a dynamic anti-racism, made urgent by an upsurge in 'Fascist' violence and by the excesses of nationalist fervour which were a feature of the Royal Jubilee celebrations, represented a creative, pleasurable and human challenge to what RAR called 'Krisis Time 1977'. Hebdige (1979) has correctly argued that the punk movement involved the creation of a White ethnicity in which the cultural forms of Rastafarianism were a central reference point, specifying in particular a fervent assault on the nation's symbols of Britishness. The punks' attack on the icons of British nationalism, particularly the Queen's face and the Union Jack, is relevant to an understanding not just of 'style', but also of popular anti-racism. Their dissociation from the nation needs to be located in this process too. We have already suggested that the particular character of British nationalism (even in its Left-wing varieties) has always inclined in the direction of racist logic. With this in mind, it is unsurprising that the Punk's attack on the symbols and ideologies of the nation (as they appeared at the height of the Royal Jubilee celebrations at their most patrician, remote, and sodden with upper-class connotations), could have paved the way to an organised political rejection of the whole racist culture which formed them. This is even less surprising if we recall that the murderous realities of Great Britain had been brought home to many by coverage of Fascist-inspired brutality in the East End. *Temporary Hoarding* described the mood of its readers:

Everyone wants stickers, everyone wants badges, everyone wants posters, everyone wants T-shirts, everyone wants to tell us their experiences, their fave local band, their ideas about how to fight racism, about their bigoted families, about mates beaten up, about anger and frustration about their town, about racism in their street, their block of flats, about fear . . . helplessness. (*Temporary Hoarding*, no. 4, 1977)

To impose the elimination of Nazis as a priority on this complex political consciousness was a miscalculation. The narrower definition of racism as a Fascist product, matched by a hasty broadening of the constituency who would support the campaign against it, drew on the momentum of RAR, punk and anti-Jubilee sentiment. However, this change imposed a shorter life and more limited aims on the overall movement. The 'Nazis' were certainly isolated and eliminated at the polls, but this was as much a result of press representation of their confrontations with the anti-Fascists and the inner-city Blacks whose communities had played host to their patriotic demonstrations, as it was of ANL propaganda. Problems for future anti-racist work were created by the exclusive association of racism with 'Nazi' activities. However frequently the Nazis are 'kicked out', the populist and resilient nature of British racism means that most racist Britons do not recognise themselves as Nazis or identify their ideas as being related to those of Hitler. Emphasising the 'Nazi' character of their politics may have defeated them by reviving the hatred of foreigners which saw us through the darkest hours of the Second World War. Yet this same sentiment would disable the movement on the day the racists shrugged off accusations of Nazism and started to present themselves as true British patriots. RAR might not have been so successful if it had been named 'Rock Against Royalty', 'Rock Against Patriotism' or 'Rock Against the Nation', but in its early stages those were the contradictions upon which it grew. At its worst, the anti-Nazi perspective, laden with all the political baggage of failed Left-wing movements, counterposed the consciousness of youth, like that of women or Blacks, against the authentic class consciousness of real workers who would defeat real Fascists on the shopfloor. The switch to sectoral mini-organisations: School Kids Against Nazis, Teachers Against Nazis, and so on, fractured a fragile unity created by a shared cultural opposition to nationalism, Fascist violence and police harassment, all of which RAR had identified as symptoms of the crisis.

Racists and youth movements

The election of a Conservative government on a racist law-and-order ticket did not rejuvenate anti-racist fervour and since then the anti-racist youth movement, with few honourable and notable exceptions, has ceased to function. The RAR episode has been forgotten, or seen as not really political. The real political struggles which sprang up on the border of Thatcherism and corporatism would consist of the 'right to work', trade union issues and, later, the Campaign for Nuclear Disarmament (CND). Part of the early spirit of RAR had been opposition to work; at least to the boring, dispiriting forms of youth labour.

In confirmation of the fact that the Left has nothing to offer young people, the issues of race in schools and multi-cultural education have become a substitute feature of Left thinking on youth and racism. Yet the political lessons of RAR have not been lost on racist and nationalist Right-wing groups. The National Socialists have their own tradition of work with youth which must also be taken into account, and their youth-orientated publications reveal an impressive ability to relate to and express the needs of powerless White boys on their own front lines in the alleys of 'slump city'. In contrast to their Left counterparts, which are riddled with abstract prescriptions for the maladies of the crisis, the pages of *Sussex Front, South London News, Bulldog* and *Young Nationalist* are remarkable for the extent to which they are local, immediate and exciting. They are also violent, macho and virulently racist, but there is a rich irony here – not just in the lessons they have learned from RAR, but also in their use of the discourse of 'truth, rights and justice' which is the cornerstone of Black youth culture. Of course, the 'Fascists' invent concepts and images where 'White' cannot simply substitute for 'Black', as where they construct a White Power ideology to answer the Black Power they fear in the playground and the dole queue. Thus, echoing Bob Marley, *Bulldog* tells its readers that the hour has come for them to stand up and fight for their rights: 'black and white unite and fight' becomes 'white youth unite and fight' (Bulldog, 7 May 1978). This process amounts to more than 'Fascists' merely borrowing the rhetoric of Rastafari and moulding it to their own ends: *they have been forced to adopt the language and symbols of Black political tradition as the price of doing successful work with young Whites.* Unlike the post-RAR Left, they are prepared to acknowledge the distinctive content of young people's political concerns and to make that content the basis of their appeal to youth. Rather than seeing youth and their political cultures as transitory phases on the way to more complete or substantial 'adult' beliefs, they are (as did RAR) taking that culture as they find it and adapting their propaganda accordingly. One example of this is the way conflict between the police and young people is handled in their youth-orientated papers. Though the usual 'Fascist' stance echoes governmental preoccupation with 'Law and Order', these papers recognise conflict with and harassment by the police as central to many young people's lives. They offer youth unequivocal support, in language that bears the stamp of RAR's past successes. The January 1982 edition of *Bulldog*, for example, carried a feature entitled 'Cops declare war on white youth . . . One Law for the Whites One Law for the Blacks'. The theme of Black-loving cops who 'grovel to the Blacks while they continue to pick on the Whites' is common in these publications. It represents an attempt to intervene in the struggle between young people and the police prompted by the fear that complementary struggles based on shared experiences of police harassment will draw Black and White youth closer still. Policing, which was central to the creation of anti-racism in 1977, has become part of making racism meaningful to White youth in recent years.

Conclusion

We have not looked at the place of race and racism in youth cultures because we think that racism among youth is more important than racism found elsewhere in society. In fact, we believe that examining the complex of racist and anti-racist beliefs found among young, White Britons can point towards the construction of a broader, though none the less vociferous, anti-racism than that which resulted from RAR. Though nothing can be taken for granted, there are grounds for optimism in the way that both the content and forms of White youth culture derive from Black traditions, and the young Whites are aware of this relationship. Its effects are continually felt in the fact that whether racist or anti-racist in their eventual stance, young people accept the politics of race as distinct and important.

This at least provides a starting point for attempts to provide an alternative reading of both the past and present for young people who locate themselves within a racist compass. Any new approach to history must include youth cultures themselves within its terms of reference. Equally, an alternative reading of the present crisis must exploit the fact that while young racists may sing 'there ain't no black in the Union Jack', their demands for jobs, housing and hospital care contain the seeds of disenchantment with a 'nation' that has served them so badly. The basis for developing genuine forms of anti-racist education centred on the social practices and cultural preoccupations of youth certainly exists. The task of actually building them remains. But at least we must be clear about our starting points if we are to have a chance of success.

Bibliography

Ali, T. (1978) 'Rocking Against Racism', *Leveller*, 16 June.

Barker, M. (1981) *The New Racism* (London: Junction Books).

Beetham, D. (1967) *Immigrant School Leavers and the Employment Service in Birmingham*, (London: Institute of Race Relations).

Blanch, M. (1979) 'Imperialism, Nationalism and Organized Youth' in J. Clarke, C. Critcher and R. Johnson (eds) *Working Class Culture* (London: Hutchinson).

Bourne, J. and Sivanandan, A. (1980) 'Cheerleaders and Ombudsmen: The sociology of race relations in Britain', *Race and Class*, vol. XXI, no. 4.

Brown, J. (1974) *A Theory of Police/Immigrant Relations* (Cranfield, Beds.: Cranfield Institute of Technology).

Brown, J. (1977) *Shades of Grey: Police/West Indian Relations in Handsworth* (Cranfield, Beds.: Cranfield Institute of Technology).

Burt, S. (1975) 'Race and the politics of schooling', *Socialism and Education*, vol. 9, no. 1.

Campaign Against Racism and Fascism/Southall Rights (1981) *Southall: The Birth of a Black Community* (London: IRR/Southall Rights).

Carby, H. (1980) *Multicultural Fictions*, SP no. 58 (Birmingham: Centre for Contemporary Cultural Studies).

Cashmore, E. (1979) *Rastaman*, (London: George Allen and Unwin).

Cashmore, E. and Troyna, B. (eds) (1982) *Black Youth in Crisis* (London: George Allen and Unwin).

CCCS Race and Politics Group (1982) *The Empire Strikes Back* (London: CCCS/Hutchinson).

Chambers, I. (1976) 'A Strategy For Living: Black music and white subcultures' in S. Hall and T. Jefferson (eds) *Resistance Through Rituals: Youth subcultures in post-war Britain* (London: Hutchinson).

Clarke, J., Hall, S., Jefferson, T. and Roberts, B. (1976) 'Subcultures, Cultures and Class' in S. Hall and T. Jefferson (eds) *Resistance Through Rituals* (1976).

Coard, B. (1971) *How the West-Indian Child is made Educationally Subnormal in the British School System* (London: New Beacon Books).

Cohen, P. (1972) 'Sub-Cultural Conflict and Working Class Community', *Working Papers in Cultural Studies*, no. 2 (Spring) (Birmingham: CCCS).

Cohen, S. (1980) *Folk Devils and Moral Panics: The creation of the Mods and Rockers* (Oxford: Martin Robertson).

Corrigan, P. (1979) *Schooling the Smash Street Kids* (London: Macmillan).

Denuth, C. (1978) *'Sus': A report on the Vagrancy Act 1824* (London: Runnymede Trust).

Dhondy, F. (1974) 'The Black Explosion in Schools', *Race Today*, February.

Dhondy, F. (1978) 'Teaching Young Blacks', *Race Today*, May/June.

Dodgson, P. and Stewart, D. (1981) 'Multiculturalism or Anti-Racist Teaching: A Question of Alternatives', *NAME*, vol. 9, no. 3.

Frith, S. (1981) 'Youth in the 80s: A dispossessed generation', *Marxism Today*, November.

Gilroy, P. (1982) 'Police and Thieves' and 'Steppin' out of Babylon: race, class and autonomy' in CCCS Race & Politics Group (1982) *The Empire Strikes Back*.

Griffin, C. (1982) *Cultures of Femininity: Romance Revisited*, SP no. 69, (Birmingham: CCCS).

Griffiths, J. A. G. *et al.*, *Coloured Immigrants in Britain*, (London: IRR).

Hall, S. (1978) 'Racism and Reaction', *Five Views of Multiracial Britain* (London: Commission for Racial Equality).

Hall, S., Critcher, C., Jefferson, Clarke, J. and Roberts, B. (1979) *Policing the Crisis: Mugging, The State and Law and Order*, (Macmillan: London).

Hebdige, D. (1979) *Subculture: The Meaning of Style* (London: Methuen).

Howe, D. (1973) 'Fighting Back: West Indian Youth and the Police in Notting Hill, *Race Today*, December.

Humphries, S. (1981) *Hooligans or Rebels: An Oral History of Working Class Childhood and Youth 1889–1939* (Oxford: Basil Blackwell).

Hunte, J. (1965) *Nigger Hunting in England* (London: WISC).

Jeffcoate, R. (1979) *Positive Image, Towards a Multiracial Curriculum* (London: Writers and Readers Publishing Co-operative).

Jefferson, T. (1973) *The Teds: A political resurrection*, SP no. 22, (Birmingham: CCCS).

John, G. (1970) *Race and the Inner City* (London: Runnymede Trust).

John, G. (1981) *In The Service Of Black Youth: A Study of the Political Culture of Youth and Community Work with Black People in English Cities*, (Leicester: National Association of Youth Clubs).

Lawrence, E. (1982) 'The roots of racism' and 'Sociology and Black Pathology' in CCCS Race and Politics Group (1982).

McRobbie, A. and Garber, J. (1976) 'Girls and Subcultures: An exploration' in S. Hall and T. Jefferson (eds) *Resistance Through Rituals* (London: CCCS/Hutchinson).

McRobbie, A. (1978) *Jackie: An Ideology of Adolescent Femininity*, SP no. 53 (CCCS, Birmingham: CCCS).

McRobbie, A. (1980) 'Settling Accounts with Subcultures', *Screen Education*, Spring.

Mungham, G. and Pearson, G. (1976) *Working Class Youth Culture* (London: Routledge and Kegan Paul).

National Foundation for Educational Research (NFER) (1966) *Coloured Immigrant Children; A Survey of Research Studies and Literature on their Educational Problems and Potential in Britain* (London: NFER).

Parmar, P. (1981) 'Young Asian Women: A critique of the pathological approach', *NAME*, vol. 9, no. 3.

Parmar, P. (1982) 'Gender, Race and Class: Asian women in resistance' in CCCS Race and Politics Group (1982).

Peach, C. (1968) *West Indian Migration to Britain* (Oxford: Oxford University Press and Institute of Race Relations).

Pryce, K. (1979) *Endless Pressure* (Harmondsworth: Penguin).

Rex, J. and Moore, R. (1968) *Race, Community and Conflict: A study of Sparkbrook*, (Oxford: Oxford University Press and Institute of Race Relations).

Sivanandan, A. (1976) *Race, Class and the State: The Black Experience in Britain*, (Race and Class pamphlet) no. 1.

Sivanandan, A. (1981/2) 'From resistance to rebellion: Asian and Afro-Caribbean struggles in Britain', *Race & Class*, vol. xxiii, nos 2/3.

Taylor, I. (1981) 'Law and Order' in Benn, T. *Arguments for Socialism*, (London: Macmillan).

Willis, P. (1979) *Profane Culture* (London: Routledge and Kegan Paul).

Willis, P. (1978) *Learning to Labour: how working class kids get working class jobs* (Saxon House: Hants).

Young, J. and Lea, J. (1982) 'Urban Violence and Political Marginalisation', *Critical Social Policy*, no. 3.

3

Institutionalised Racism: Policies of Marginalisation in Education and Training

John Solomos

Introduction

The question of 'Black youth', and more specifically the position of young Blacks in the labour market and in relation to the police, has become one of the central issues in the development of race relations policies over the last decade. Numerous government reports, media reports and academic studies have looked at specific aspects of the experience of being young, Black and marginal in contemporary Britain (John, 1981; Troyna and Smith, 1983). Moreover, the riots of 1980 and 1981 served to highlight and give a measure of the depth of socio-economic marginalisation, the web of police harassment, and anger, which make up the everyday reality of young Blacks in and out of the labour market (CCCS, 1982; Benyon, 1984).

Recent dramatics notwithstanding, however, the issues of unemployment, police harassment and the lack of adequate political response have been important issues within the Black communities since the late 1960s, if not before (John, 1970; Hall *et al.* 1978). The common-sense view of the origins of these problems seems to be that they are a fairly recent phenomenon, with the implication that they will gradually disappear once policy-makers have understood what is happening and produced adequate policy responses. Such a view, however, runs counter to the actual history of the Black youth question since the 1960s, and fails to explain why the various policy initiatives pursued by governments since then have been relatively unsuccessful, if not in many cases counterproductive. It also fails to question the assumptions on which government policies have been based, and to expose whether and how they have helped construct the crisis which confronts young Blacks.

This chapter will begin by analysing, albeit schematically and briefly, the changing assumptions and practices which have shaped, guided and reproduced state policies in relation to young Black people. It will then look at three areas of state response in more detail – education; youth unemployment and training; and law and order. On the basis of these analytical sections an attempt will be made to show how the possibility of changing current policy priorities will remain restricted unless a thorough questioning of the assumptions of past policies is worked through. Although there are many aspects of the 'Black youth question' which this chapter will not cover, for example, the complex ways in which young Blacks have themselves responded to state policies,[1] the overall objective will be to show how and why state policies towards Black youth have become part of the problem rather than provided the solution. In addition, the concluding section will look at the question of how to develop an alternative approach, which emphasises the role of racism in the present juncture and the problems that this poses for a radical anti-racist political strategy.

Socio-political ideologies and Black youth

From the late 1960s onwards there were two dominant images in official thinking about the 'second generation' or the 'Black youth question': (a) the image of the second generation as a 'social time bomb'; and (b) the social construction of young Blacks as suffering from a 'complex of disabilities' deriving from their own background and their lack of integration into the wider society.

The first image has been a recurrent theme since the late 1960s, and has gained a sharper focus since the 1980–81 riots.[2] Writing in the aftermath of the riots in America, A. H. Halsey captured the meaning of this image when he argued that the central question about the second generation was, 'Will they revolt?' (Halsey, 1970). More substantially, a number of official and semi-official documents took up the 'social time bomb' theme and used it to emphasise the need for state intervention in order to defuse the danger of an explosion (Department of Education and Science (DES), 1967; Select Committee on Race Relations and Immigration (SCRRI), 1969; John, 1981).

If anything, the 'social deprivation' theme has been even more central to official thinking on this question. Beginning with the 1969 Select Committee report on *The Problems of Coloured School Leavers*, with its emphasis on the 'complex of disabilities' suffered by young Black people, subsequent reports have linked the experience of living in deprived inner-city areas to that of being a member of a disadvantaged community (Solomos, 1983). In a number of reports produced by government departments, parliamentary committees and official agencies it is precisely this notion of disadvantage that has gained wider acceptance, although it is linked implicitly at least to other notions about 'unrealistic aspirations', 'psychological maladjustment', 'cultural conflict', 'language disabilities', 'weak family units' and 'cycles of deprivation'.[3]

Both of these dominant images have been translated into different, and sometimes contradictory, policy initiatives; ranging from social democratic programmes aimed at compensating for social disadvantages to remedial programmes for 'helping' the Black communities. As has been pointed out by a number of writers, both these approaches have exhibited a tendency to focus on the weaknesses of the Black communities as the source of all problems and have implicitly assumed various inadequacies and handicaps on the part of either whole communities or specific groups within them.[4] This approach, variously called 'social pathology' or 'blaming the victim' (Lowry, 1974, Ryan, 1976), is one of the recurrent themes in institutional responses to young Blacks in British society over the last two decades. As Gus John (1981) has perceptively noted:

> The state, the police, the media and race relations experts ascribe to young blacks certain collective qualities, e.g. alienated, vicious little criminals, muggers, disenchanted, unemployed, unmarried mothers, truants, class-room wreckers, etc. The youth workers, community workers, counsellors and the rest, start with these objective qualities as given, and intervene on the basis that through their operations they could render young blacks subjectively different, and make them people to whom those objective qualifications could no longer

be applied. When this is done in collaboration with control agents themselves, as in police–community liaison schemes, or instances in which professional blacks collaborate with schools in blaming black kids for their 'failure', it is interpreted as progress towards 'good community relations'. (p. 155)

Although it could be argued that other images of young Blacks have been used by various agencies, apart from those identified by John, there are two important elements of his account which help make sense of how the various responses to 'problems' faced by Black youth can become part of the process of discrimination against them, however well-intentioned they may be.

The first, and perhaps most important, mechanism is the ascription to young Black people of certain immutable collective qualities, which are then transformed into taken-for-granted notions by policy-makers and officials working in control agencies. A good example of this type of ascription is represented by the way in which the 'second generation' theme developed during the 1960s out of rather imprecise notions about 'disadvantage', 'social handicap' and the 'threat of violence'.

The second mechanism, which in a sense grows out of the first, is the tendency on the part of the government to intervene on the basis that through their operations they could render young Blacks subjectively different. Because it is individual deviance from the norm which is defined as the problem, an inbuilt tendency exists to seek causal explanations of the problems faced by young Blacks through reference to cultural and personal inadequacies rather than in relation to the inadequacies of British society. A pathology of individuals predominates over a pathology of institutions (Dunn, 1983, Cottle, 1978).

It is on the basis of these twin assumptions that socio-political ideologies about Black youth have been constructed, albeit with some modifications (which will be noted later). What is important to note here is that the entire intervention model of programmes for young Black people rests on assumptions about inadequacies which have to be remedied. These assumptions have, in turn, been buttressed by research and reports which make a number of interlocking claims about the nature of Black culture, community structures, networks and family relations. At the same time, the emphasis on these characteristics tends to structure debate in such a way that racism as a structural phenomenon becomes only one small part of the overall race relations landscape.

It is precisely because of this bias that a number of recent studies have rejected any notion of the state's role in the management of race relations as some kind of neutral arbiter. Pointing to the often negative stereotypes of Blacks which have been fostered through political debates, they have attempted to show that political institutions themselves have played a role in amplifying certain supposed characteristics of Black youth and constructing them into common-sense images (Hall *et al.*, 1978: Hunt and Mellor, 1980). In addition, it has been argued that the language used to analyse race in official reports relies on diagnoses and assumptions which help make racism into one factor among many, and thus push the analysis in the direction of looking for solutions which aim to maintain the status quo rather than to challenge racism (Clarke *et al.*, 1974; Reeves, 1983).

It is in this context that official responses to the 'Black youth question' need to be analysed. This is an issue which has always been seen as a central element of successive governments' policies on race, and thus represents an important test for the assumptions and values which have helped shape policies on race since the early post-war period. In the rest of this chapter the goals of state interventions on this issue will be explicated and critically analysed.

From assimilation to integration

The experience of 1948–51, when the first large groups of Black settlers began to arrive in Britain, is a useful historical backdrop from which to view the roots of the so-called Black youth 'problem'. Most of these early migrants were adult workers, coming to this country in search of work, but it is interesting that one of the first 'social problems' discussed in connection with their arrival was the question of the 'second generation'. The Colonial Office was asked to report on the experience of the older Black communities in Cardiff and Liverpool, and it reported back that:

> During the past 30 years groups of Colonials have been domiciled in Great Britain. Originally they came here as seamen in the 1914–18 war. After the war, many settled down,

married and have lived here ever since. They have produced a group of citizens of mixed birth. Upon reaching working age their offsprings had little opportunity for employment, partly because of the economic depression, but more on account of racial prejudice. These family units therefore became social problems. (Colonial Office, 1948)

This same report, using language which has by now become a common theme in writings about Black youth warned that:

The future prospects of these children are not good. Few, if any, are able to remain at school beyond the age of 14, and once on the labour market they have to face the prejudice against colour. (Colonial Office, 1944–45)

Even at this early stage it was the young Blacks and their families who were singled out for attention (Joshi and Carter, 1984). Apart from some ameliorative action to persuade employers not to discriminate, the general assumption was that policy should aim at providing more youth clubs and social facilities to insure against the dangers of unemployed youngsters 'hanging around the streets'. Since Black areas were seen as presenting a threat to law and order, the fear was that a potentially volatile situation could become politically dangerous when the children of the newer migrants reached the labour market, encountered discrimination, became unemployed and drifted into crime or became alienated.

These fears were given concrete shape during the 1950s and 1960s by the growth of Black communities, and the entry of large numbers of 'second generation' children into the school system and the labour market. In addition, the first signs of Black youth counter-cultures were appearing, and by the late 1960s the question of confrontations between young Blacks and the police had become an important political issue (Humphry, 1972). From the 1950s to the mid-1960s the dominant theme in discussions of the 'second generation', and of Black workers generally, was *assimilation*. Although this concept was never clearly defined, its general meaning can be gauged from the following quotation, which comes from the 1964 report of the Commonwealth Immigrants Advisory Council:

A national system of education must aim at producing citizens in a society properly equipped to exercise rights and perform duties which are the same as other citizens. If their parents were brought up in another culture or another tradition, children should be encouraged to respect it, but a national system cannot be expected to perpetuate the different values of immigrant groups. (p. 7)

The above quotation summarises the dominant official response to Black children up to the end of the 1960s, though some elements of it still survive today. The main issues which concerned policy-makers were the numbers of Black children, and language provision. These were the themes echoed in various reports from the mid-1960s and a DES circular in 1965 defined the educational objective as 'the successful assimilation of immigrant children', a process which was seen as dependent on 'a realistic understanding of the adjustments they have to make' (DES, 1965). Because of the terms of the assimilationist problematic, the solutions to the 'problem' were largely seen in terms of interventions to ensure that Black children adjusted to the dominant cultural values. Policies of language teaching and dispersal of Black children were, therefore, pursued.

Through the 1960s the dominant idea was that policies should aim to meet the needs of 'immigrant' children and alleviate the fears of White parents about the education of their children. Such a compromise approach was seen as allowing time for assimilation to take place, and for colour differences to gradually disappear. In practice the experience of the 1960s emphasised the depth of institutional racism. According to David Milner (1975) a distinction has to be made between the official ideology of assimilation and its practice, because:

'Immigrant' children were dispersed, irrespective of whether they were immigrant or not, irrespective of whether they had language difficulties or not, including among them some West Indian children, who in contrast to what we now know, were then thought not to have language difficulties of the same order as Asians. In other words, the children were dispersed solely on the basis of colour. (p. 201)

This was because Black children, whatever the level of their educational attainment, were seen as the cause of a fall in standards in schools. The solution was, therefore, seen in terms of dispersal of Black children in order to facilitate the social process of acculturation. The main reasons advanced for keeping the children of immigrants in a minority were (a) that, it was assumed, these pupils lowered general standards; and (b) that high proportions of Black children hindered the cultural assimilation of the individual pupils (McNeal, 1971). In addition, the underlying assumption was that policies should reassure White parents that the education of their children was not being hindered by the presence of Black children:

> It will be helpful if the parents of non-immigrant children can see that practical measures have been taken to deal with the problem of schools, and that the progress of their own children is not being restricted by the undue preoccupation of the teaching staff with linguistic and other problems of immigrant children. (DES, 1965)

The experience of Southall and other London boroughs, where White parents groups complained vociferously about the 'swamping' of schools by Asian and West Indian children, strengthened the logic of the dispersal policy at a national level (McNeal, 1971). At the local level the common-sense assumptions held by local government officials and teachers, even when they opposed dispersal, tended to be based on the argument that high numbers of Black children led to a fall in standards.

Underlying the concern with linguistic and cultural provisions, and the dispersal policies, was the notion that if only the children of immigrants could be transformed into 'English children' the process of assimilation would somehow become irreversible. By the late 1960s, however, there seemed to be little hope that such an evolutionist policy framework could succeed. Evidence from areas such as Cardiff and Liverpool, where many Black children were second- or third-generation, questioned the central assumptions on which the assimilation perspective was based (Rose *et al.*, 1969). At a broader political level, race relations legislation seemed to undermine the idea that 'a national system cannot be expected to perpetuate the different values of immigrant groups'.

Precisely because assimilation was not working, policy-makers began to advocate a more active role for the state in securing an 'equal' participation by immigrants at all levels of society. The rationale of this new approach was the notion of *pluralist integration*, which began to take shape in the late 1960s (Abbott, 1971).

Special needs and special treatment

> If we fail to give the coloured school-leavers of the future full, fair, and equal opportunities on entering adult life we are unlikely to succeed in any other sector of race relations. (SCRRI, 1969, p. 6)

The above quotation, from the Select Committee on Race Relations and Immigration's report entitled *The Problems of Coloured School Leavers*, encapsulates the shift from the culturalist bias of policies in the 1960s to the more institutional approach of the 1970s. By the late 1960s a growing amount of evidence had shown that Black youth were being subjected to institutionalised racism at a number of levels – at school, in the labour market, with the police, in the courts, and so on. Black political organisations and pressure groups were beginning to protest about the harassment of youth in many Black communities and the failure of the educational system to help them achieve the same qualifications as their White counterparts (Coard, 1971). The assimilationist and culturalist perspectives did not appear to be able to explain why Black youth in areas such as Liverpool suffered from the same disadvantages as the newcomers. The outcome of these pressures was the articulation of a critique of assimilation, and the erection in its place of a new model of policy interventions based on a loose notion of *pluralist integration* and a normative conception of *equality of opportunity*.

This new approach can be traced back to the mid-1960s, although it was formally codified in the context of the 1969 report of the SCRRI. One of the first formulations was provided by Roy Jenkins (1966), when he spoke of his understanding of 'integration':

> Integration is perhaps a loose word. I do not regard it as meaning the loss, by immigrants, of their own characteristics

and culture. I do not think that we need in this country a 'melting pot', which will turn everybody out in a common mould, as one of a series of carbon copies of someone's misplaced vision of the stereotyped Englishman. I define integration, therefore, not as flattening process of assimilation but as equal opportunity, accompanied by cultural diversity, in an atmosphere of mutual tolerance.

This strategy was only one side of the coin, since it was accompanied by a further institutionalisation of restrictions in immigration and stricter controls on the Black workers already settled here (Lea, 1980). But it helped to create an atmosphere in which policy-makers could shift their attention from 'assimilation' to 'integration' – with the promise that the latter strategy would bring about the 'good race relations' which the first had failed to produce.

The logic of the move away from assimilation to integration has to be seen in terms of the growing recognition that language and cultural differences alone could not explain the educational and employment difficulties faced by young Blacks, whether West Indian or Asian. Previous explanations were not discarded as such, they were integrated into a broader notion of 'complex disabilities'. In its evidence to the Select Committee, the Community Relations Commission argued that the disadvantages of young Blacks arose from a 'complex of disabilities to which social deprivation, deficiencies in education, psychological stress and racial prejudice all contribute . . . it is the impact of this complex of disabilities as a whole which puts the young coloured people in general at a disadvantage compared with other school leavers when they face making a start in their careers and adult life' (SCRRI, 1969, p. 15). The final report took up this theme in a section called 'Special Problems Need Special Treatment'. Basing its argument largely on Jenkins' definition of equal opportunity, the Committee reported that for young Blacks this did not 'flourish naturally in the crowded central areas of our towns and cities. Many of them have special problems, whether because of their upbringing in another country or from discrimination, that handicaps them from entering adult life. White school leavers do not suffer the same handicaps' (SCRRI, 1969, p. 31). The new approach of 'special treatment' which it suggested was rationalised in these terms:

Equality of opportunity does not always mean treating everyone in exactly the same way. All people are not equal. Special problems need special treatment. We apply this principle in many areas. Economically depressed areas at home and overseas get financial assistance. Backward school children are given special attention. Physically handicapped people are given special assistance in both education and employment. This principle should be equally applied to the problems of immigrants and especially to those of coloured school leavers. In so far as they are handicapped in competing with other school leavers, then special assistance is needed to give them equal opportunity. However, it must be recognised that such special assistance must be provided fairly with due regard to the needs of the indigenous population, some of whom are also in need of special assistance. Recognition of this point is essential if we are to ensure good race relations. (SCRRI, 1969, p. 31)

The report then went on to recommend that both central and local government departments become more concerned with the interests of young Black people, particularly in urban areas where the problems were already acute. It thus provided a paradigm for state intervention in relation to Black youth which, in certain respects, remains unchallenged to this day.

Two main features characterise this paradigm. First, a seemingly progressive notion of the need for special assistance to Black youth to overcome 'their' handicaps. Second, a pathological view of the family background, community life and culture of Black children. Both these elements coexist in practice, since the focus on 'special needs' and 'special treatment' helps locate 'problems' within the person rather than in society. It is a short step from this to the notion that minority cultures are deficient in relation to the dominant culture, and that they need to be remedied through the intervention of the state. As has been discussed elsewhere (Solomos, 1983) it seems clear that remedial programmes in race relations more generally have been grounded on a social pathology base, which assumes the inadequacy of black culture and family life.

Forms of state intervention

It is important, then, to understand that the notions upon which the state has reacted to the 'problems' of Black youth rest on assumptions which take it for granted that the causal mechanisms explaining their disadvantages can be understood essentially as personal, communal and cultural. Racism, in this model, is only relevant in explaining some of the more extreme forms of discrimination from which young Blacks are supposed to suffer. This process of problem definition and policy intervention can be illustrated with reference to education, youth unemployment, issues of law and order, and in the context of official responses to the 1980–81 urban disturbances. It is to these examples that we now turn for substantiation of the propositions outlined above.

The educational system and Black children

The new 'pluralist' approach to integration was first developed in the educational system from the late 1960s onwards. A number of reports by official bodies and by Black political groups had singled out education as an area where urgent action was necessary, to meet the special needs of Black children and to overcome the opposition of White parents to the entry of Black children into schools. In these early stages, therefore, the role of the state was seen largely in terms of action to change attitudes to race within the school system (Carby, 1982). The new integrationist perspective, however, differed from the early assimilationist arguments in emphasis rather than content. Rather than locating the whole 'problem' in relation to Black children it was now implied that society as a whole needed a greater understanding of race:

> White people in the host community should try to understand coloured people and immigrants, and coloured immigrants should try to understand the problems of the host people. But the main obligation for improving race relations rests with the indigenous people in this country, if only because they are by far the majority. The central problem of race relations in Britain today is that of colour. Difficulties arise from people's attitudes towards colour. Here again is an educational challenge. (SCRRI, 1969, p. 20)

In addition to the 'educational challenge' of changing society's attitude towards colour, it was implied that the schools themselves could perform a useful role in changing the attitudes of White and Black children by providing more teaching about different religions, cultures, and customs. It is from these early shifts that the multicultural education movement of the 1970s grew into a fully-fledged response to the presence of Black children in schools (Troyna, 1982). As is clear from the above quotation, however, this response contained within it two sometimes conflicting elements.

The first was the recognition that the special needs of Black children had to be given more priority than hitherto. These needs were seen largely in terms of language, culture, family backgrounds and identity. The second element was the acceptance that black children suffered from discrimination on the basis of colour. This second question, however, has tended to play only a minor part in official discussions of education, and most central and local state agencies have chosen to concentrate on special arrangements to meet the 'needs' of ethnic minority pupils. But how have these needs been defined? What assumptions have been made in formulating policy options?

Two major assumptions were made by the pluralists in the way they defined the needs of Black children. First, it was accepted that Black children would not be assimilated in a linear fashion, and that for some time to come they were likely to retain specific characteristics which had to be allowed for. The fourth report of the Select Committee on Race Relations and Immigration was on education, and one of its main conclusions was that:

> The presence of fairly large numbers of immigrant children in this country makes special demands on many local education authorities. The children themselves must have special help if they are to compete on equal terms in a technologically-advanced, multi-racial society. They will continue to come here for many years, a large number of them ill-educated, most of them illiterate in English. Even many of those born here, of all ethnic groups, will be handicapped by language difficulties, family backgrounds and different cultures. (SCRRI, 1973, p. 53)

Second, it was assumed that if racialism was educated away

then equal opportunity would begin to flourish. In addition, the development of a more culturally diverse curriculum in the schools was seen as a launching pad for efforts to achieve a more racially harmonious society. Education was seen as central to producing such a situation because it was a process through which every individual had to pass. Within the broad ideological terms of multiculturalism the objective was to produce more understanding of racial issues in the wider society through the reform of the educational system.

Against the background of fears about the political implications of the alienation of Black children from the dominant culture and political institutions, the extension of the curriculum to include other cultures was also seen by policy-makers as a way of keeping the lid on the pressures arising from Black community groups and the children themselves for more 'relevant' teaching. It was a means of incorporating the teaching of 'black studies' within the schools, but at the same time depoliticising its content. In relation to pressures from the West Indian community to reform the education system in order to meet the special problems of Black children, the Home Office (1978) recommended that:

> For the curriculum to have meaning and relevance now in our schools, its content, emphasis and the values and assumptions contained must reflect the wide range of cultures, histories and lifestyles in our multi-racial society. The more informed teachers become about a wider range of cultures and communities and the more possible it is for all pupils to see their values reflected in the concerns of schools, the less likely is the alienation from schools and indigenous society experienced by some minority group pupils. (p. 6)

A number of subsequent official and academic reports have developed this response further in relation to specific local and national issues, but they still retain the basic assumption that cultural pluralism is the only adequate response to the specific needs of pupils of different ethnic origins. This is why among the numerous celebrations of the theory of multicultural education we find little discussion of the social relations of power within which minority and majority cultures exist, or the wider determinants of the educational needs and attainments of Black children. The emphasis is on what an ideal multi-racial society should look like, and not why it has so palpably failed to emerge.

To summarise the argument so far: we have argued that in relation to education the pluralist model involved an incorporation of the assimilationist arguments within a more sophisticated concept of complex disabilities, or 'specific difficulties arising from linguistic, cultural, religions and historical differences'. This introduced an emphasis on policies aimed at providing 'special treatment' to compensate for home and cultural backgrounds:

> We must compensate for these difficulties if such pupils are to be given the same range of opportunity and choice as indigenous pupils. Consequently in areas of minority group settlement local education authorities, schools and teachers are involved in responding to the specific needs of pupils of different ethnic origins. (quoted in John, 1981, p. 6)

In terms of policy this response, despite all the talk about 'special needs', has certain similarities to the old assimilationist framework. It identifies the special needs as a 'handicap' from which Black children have to be extricated, and therefore places the onus of adaptation on the children themselves. In addition, even when discrimination or racism are seen as a problem, it is not the social conditions and political relations in urban areas that reproduce racism which are put under scrutiny, but the attitudes and behaviour of Black children.

This bias towards policies that attempt to ameliorate the position of Black children and control their responses is not a mere accident. Recent research on the implementation of multicultural education has shown that it has been applied largely in those education authorities with high and medium concentrations of Black pupils, since authorities with low numbers of ethnic minorities assume that teaching about a multicultural society is not a matter for them. The practice of the pluralist approach, therefore, has little to do with the promise of providing a more adequate response to the problems facing Black children in schools or helping to overcome racist attitudes in society as a whole. It can best be seen as a contradictory attempt to keep the responses of Black children and their parents to institutional racism in schools under control. It offers token changes in educational practices, but does not question the overall structures of racism within which schools function, or the reproduction of racially specific attainments through the school system. The limited application of multiculturalism is not a mere function of inadequate policies or weak guidance by government. It is a reflection of the common-sense and policy notion that Black pupils are the target group which policies should aim at, since it is their 'deficiencies' and 'problems' that have to be overcome. Even when clothed in progressive language, this view tends to support the notion that it is West Indian or Asian children who cause problems for schools and not vice versa.

The recent debates about multiculturalism have tended to question this central assumption, and inevitably official thinking has had to take account of such criticisms. The Rampton Report entitled *West Indian Children in Our Schools* concluded that 'in the eyes of many West Indians the major cause of their children's underachievement is racism and its effects in schools and society' (DES, 1981, p. 12). Its main recommendation was, however, to extend the teaching of multicultural curriculum to all schools, and it did not examine the question of racism in society as a whole. By limiting its focus on the schools this report could therefore accept that racism was a problem, and at the same time fail to allow this to question the notion that multiculturalism was an adequate solution the problems faced by Black pupils. In the context of the youth unemployment crisis, however, it is not going to be easy for the existing state agencies to control the responses of Black youth. At the local level many Black community groups are very active in the areas of education and youth unemployment, and this has put the existing mechanisms of control under strain. This is why a narrow policy framework focused on schools is now proving inadequate, and new policies are being developed in relation to young Blacks outside school. The new paradigm of state intervention, developed since the mid-1970s, involves strong linkages between multiculturalism in schools and special provisions for the growing numbers of unemployed young Blacks who are seen as drifting beyond the control of statutory agencies.

In addition, the period since the late 1970s had witnessed the flowering of a new model of multiculturalism, namely anti-racist education (Green, 1982). Premised in part upon a critique of notions of cultural deficit and pathology (Williams, 1981) the anti-racist model attempts to break new ground in the race and education debate by making racism the central issue, as opposed to the general tendency in the multiculturalist model to emphasise culture and the role of personal variables. The direct impact of this approach on policy remains variable. While some local authorities have adopted 'anti-racist' statements, this does not mean that what they actually do in practice is much different from the kind of multicultural initiatives that were prevalent through the 1970s.

Training and the transition from school to work

So far we have concentrated on the general characteristics of state interventions in education. Since the mid-1970s, however, the main focus of the state's role has shifted to the labour market, or more precisely to the growing ranks of young unemployed Blacks. This is partly the result of growing concern about the political effects of high levels of youth unemployment, but it is also connected with the realisation that Black youth are more vulnerable to unemployment than comparable sections of White youth. In the late 1960s and early 1970s a number of studies showed that the so called 'second generation', far from becoming more 'integrated', were being marginalised in economic and social terms. A national survey of Black school leavers, set up at the recommendation of the 1969 Select Committee report, showed how pervasive racial discrimination was in terms of the transition from school to work.[5] The growth of unemployment nationally during the 1970s has also had a more pronounced impact on Black youth, particularly in areas such as London and Birmingham, but also in other centres such as Manchester and Liverpool.

The cumulative impact of this evidence has helped to construct a common-sense and policy view of Black youth unemployment as a 'problem'. An early statement of this view is a report published by the Community Relations Commission in 1974 called *Unemployment and Homelessness*:

The evidence leads to the conclusion that unemployment among young black people is substantially higher than among their white contemporaries; that it is connected with homelessness; that each represents a social problem; that the interaction between the two makes the problem more acute. Unemployment may lead to homelessness and vice versa. When combined they create a vicious circle which it is difficult to break. Individuals who find themselves in this situation – unemployed or homeless, or both – unable to fulfil their aspirations legitimately, may be tempted to resort to unlawful means. (CRC, 1974, p. 23)

Within the context of fears about 'race riots' and a growth of 'Black crime' these views were able to gain wide currency. Sweeping assertions about Black youth, which often were no more than ideological reworkings of common-sense ideas, became widely accepted among policy-makers and practitioners. As the unemployment figures for young Blacks in Brixton, Hackney, Handsworth, Moss Side and Liverpool began to reach 'crisis proportions' in 1978–79, a report by the Commission for Racial Equality (CRE) described the problem in the following manner:

The black youngsters we are describing are an alienated generation and, unless we do something positive, this alienated generation will become a progressively stronger racial alienation. By this we mean that it cannot be supposed that this is a temporary experience, a phase these young people go through. It must be making a permanent mark on them in such a way that it is hard to imagine them ever settling down satisfactorily in the inner cities which they generally inhabit . . . The fact that the vast majority of those who immigrated have, to a greater or lesser degree, managed to integrate, to assimilate, must not blind us to the fact than an increasing number of black people, who have been exposed to all the integrating services of our society from birth, seem to be moving naturally into a style of life which is positively alienated. It even starts to evolve its own justification for alienation (CRE, 1979, quoted in John, 1981, pp. 151–2).

Alongside this fear of where 'positive alienation' may lead, there have grown doubts about whether the existing institutions can manage the crisis situation facing Black youth. After all, if the 'integrating services' have failed to prevent discontent, let alone provide equal opportunities for Black children, what hope does the future hold for the pluralist model of 'equal opportunity, accompanied by cultural diversity, in an atmosphere of mutual tolerance'?

The contradictory nature of the transition from school to work has long been known, through both government and academic research. The pervasiveness of racist practices in relation to recruitment practices, allocation to jobs, promotion and redundancy has been shown over and over again. The urgency of the reaction to the growth of Black unemployment cannot, therefore, be understood merely as an attempt to overcome institutional racism in the labour market. The state's response has to be contextualised against the background of the massive growth in unemployment since the mid-1970s and the growing resistance by Black communities to their economic marginalisation.

One aspect of this response has been a self-proclaimed acceptance that the reality of 'equal opportunity' has proved fundamentally different from the promise. Within the logic of this approach can be included the CRE and other arms of the race relations industry, which see the economic and political marginalisation of Black youth as the outcome of a lack of political will for action. The other aspect of the state's response, however, takes as its starting point the 'alienation' and 'disaffection' which Black youngsters are supposed to be afflicted by, and translates them into a potential political threat to the social fabric of society.

This second aspect is the dominant approach adopted by the Home Office, some elements of the CRE, and other official bodies. Its necessary corollary is that the way to overcome such a 'threat' to society is through a combination of piecemeal social engineering and a refinement of the forces of law and order.

It is a short step from such an analysis of the issues to the construction of the classical 'culture of poverty', and other pathological explanations such as the 'cycle of deprivation'. For policy-makers, such phrases become a form of shorthand, a method of fixing the question of Black youth within a specific form of discourse which produces its own solutions to 'the problems'. The real question of how the institutions and social relations of the dominant society allocate Black youth to marginal socio-economic positions, thus becomes into one of how they are becoming 'alienated' or 'over-aspiring'. There is an inherent tendency in a racist society like Britain to construct essentially pathological and racialist explanations of the 'problems' facing Black youth by 'blaming the victim'. Recent accounts of unemployment among Black youth are an example of how this inversion takes place.

A recent report by the Select Committee on Race Relations and Immigration notes that, whatever their qualifications and skills, young West Indians are more likely to be unemployed or to occupy the least skilled jobs. It then notes that increasing awareness of such realities may lead them 'to reject with some bitterness the way of thinking and way of life both of the mainstream society and of their parents, and to find that this leaves them with nowhere to go' (SCRRI 1981, p. liv). Both the CRE and the Manpower Services Commission (MSC), which have taken their lead from such research, have concentrated their attention on those groups of Black youth which they define as 'alienated' or 'at-risk' in order to prevent them from getting involved in criminal activities or riots. The two classic statements of this position are the joint MSC/CRE report called *Ethnic Minorities and the Special Programmes for the Unemployed* (1979) and the CRE's *Youth in Multi-Racial Society* (1980). Both these reports express a deep concern about the dangers of young Blacks 'hanging about' on the streets with nothing to do and suggest a number of ameliorative measures to give them something to do. On the wider issues of combating the chronic unemployment among young Blacks they have little or nothing to add, except in calling for a further extension of the government's youth unemployment schemes to include their special needs. The joint CRE/MSC report limited its focus almost exclusively to the 'disaffected young people from ethnic minority communities who are losing touch with the statutory services and who are therefore in danger of remaining unemployed for long periods of time' (MSC/CRE 1979, p. 11). This is not an accident. This is the group which state agencies were unable to control through normal channels, and policy-makers were constantly attempting to develop new agencies that could more adequately deal with them.

These agencies include the youth unemployment programmes, such as those run by the Manpower Services Commission, and extensions of the legal–police apparatuses. We shall discuss the second element in the next section, but here a few remarks are necessary about the relation of Black youth to the MSC programmes.

MSC training programmes are universal and aim to provide young unemployed people with training in order to ease their transition from school to work. They therefore make no special provisions for young Black people as such, although a number of MSC policy documents (particularly since 1981) allude to the 'special needs' of youth from ethnic minorities. In practice, however, a number of attempts have been made by the MSC, often in conjunction with the CRE, to sponsor local schemes which aim at providing training for those groups of Black youth which are seen as liable remain unemployed for some time or to cause trouble. During the last two years it has also begun appointing liaison officers in the main areas of Black settlement, whose express purpose is to increase contact between the MSC and black community groups. Evidence is also beginning to emerge that unemployed black youngsters are concentrated on certain MSC programmes, especially those which operate according to ameliorative and remedial criteria (Stares *et al.* 1982, Cross *et al.* 1983). This is not surprising, given the classification of large sections of Black youth as 'alienated', and therefore in need of training to socialise them into the dominant cultural institutions and values.

As the reality of long-term black unemployment takes shape, it is likely that the role of 'training' programmes such as the Youth Training Scheme will become a more-or-less permanent feature of the transition of Black youth from school to work. The logic of recent moves to extend provisions for ethnic minorities in this field points in that direction. The perception of Black youth unemployment as a 'problem', and more generally its location as one of the sources of 'race riots' will inevitably lead to a rethinking of wider relations of control and authority. This rethinking cannot be viewed apart from the policies discussed above, since the ways in which pathological explanations of the social conditions which produce the 'alienated' Black youngsters have been constructed over the last decade are likely to shape future interventions. The strengthening of repressive measures against Black youth over the last few years is a good example of how this process works.

The breakdown of law and order

You may remember that at the beginning of the 1970s. A. H. Halsey argued that the most obvious question to ask about the Black British was, 'Will they revolt?' Although the numerous government reports on race relations since then have not addressed the issue in such a stark fashion, Halsey's question has certainly been an underlying theme in many of them (CCCS Race and Politics Group, 1982). A report by the Commission for Racial Equality in 1980 articulated this approach, albeit from an *ad hoc* perspective:

> There is no definite insurance policy against further occurrences like the events in St Paul's. However, such events are a confirmation of the reality underlying the warnings, too long ignored by policy makers, which have been given by race relations organisations. Bristol should be seen as a barometer of the situation throughout Britain today. If it is still ignored, there will be stormy weather ahead. (CRE, 1980, p. 8)

A committee of experts from a number of European countries admitted frankly that 'in many cases special measures for young people [are] also a way of protecting society against the dangers of idle and restless youngsters who could cause riots and voice strong criticisms of government and society' (International Labour Organisation (ILO), 1978, p. 25). The historical connections between the themes of 'idleness', 'restlessness' and race are by now well known enough not to need further comment. What we want to show here are the ways in which the economic and social marginalisation of Black youth has been understood as a law and order 'problem', and their impact on government policies.

By the time Halsey had posed his question, the experience of race riots in the United States was clearly weighing heavily in the minds of policy-makers, who were beginning to ask the question, 'Will it happen here?' In the same year as Halsey's article, however, a study of Handsworth by Gus John (John, 1970) showed that relations between the police and Black communities were rapidly deteriorating. Numerous complaints were being voiced about police harassment, harsh treatment of Blacks when arrested and a tendency by the police to see all forms of subcultural activity among Blacks as somehow criminal. At the same time the police were beginning to construct their own ideologies about the role of crime in Black communities, particularly among the young. At the level of some Black communities the intervention of the police became a pervasive everyday occurrence. These pressures increased as a result of the 'mugging scare' of the early 1970s, and successive moral panics about the law and order problems in areas of high Black settlement (Humphry, 1972; Hall *et al.*, 1978).

Two processes were at work in this field throughout the 1970s. First, there was an attempt to construct links between material relations such as unemployment, bad housing and social deprivation with lawlessness and criminality. Second, the police and other state agencies were beginning to identify specific groups of Black youth who were 'at risk', and who, therefore, required special attention. At the beginning of the 1970s these youths tended to be the 'muggers', but increasingly it was those youths who were classified as Rastafarian or 'at risk' who were singled out. These two processes are significant because they involve a combination of common-sense and policy assumptions which have guided official thinking on police/Black relations and a number of other central issues. It is, therefore, important to trace the shaping of these assumptions historically.

Through the 1960s the relations between Black communities and the police were still seen largely in environmental terms, with bad housing and inadequate social facilities appearing to be the cause of friction. By implication, the solutions proposed were mainly in terms of a reassertion of the primacy of law and order, and ameliorative measures such as recruiting ethnic minority policemen, community relations training and 'greater understanding'. With the intensification of the employment crisis facing Black youth, however, and their growing rejection of the dominant values of work, there was a tendency for the police to define 'problem groups' among the Black population who presented a danger to the maintenance of law and order – mainly the young Blacks and 'criminalised' sections of the Black population. The image of large sections of West Indian youth as 'unemployed and totally disillusioned with society' has been mentioned already in relation to the role of state interventions in the labour market and during the early 1970s this image was strengthened by the pervasive concern of the police to enforce new forms of control over young

Blacks. The rationale for this new approach was that 'extremism' among the young could take on a more politicised form and weaken the buffering institutions which the central and local state had attempted to establish in the Black communities. In 1976, the Metropolitan Police were moved to warn that the task of policing a multi-racial society was putting the existing police procedures under stress:

> There has been a growth in the tendency for members of London's West Indian communities to combine against the police by interfering with police officers who are affecting the arrest of a black person or who are in some other way enforcing the law in situations which involve black people. In the last twelve months forty such incidents have been recorded; each carries with it the potential for large scale disorder . . . experience indicates that they are more likely to occur during the summer months and that conflict invariably is with young West Indians. (Metropolitan Police, 1976)

Around these everyday confrontations with the police, and the more collective struggles of the late 1970s, there grew up the mythology of associating Black communities with 'criminality'. They were seen increasingly as 'breeding grounds' of discontent, since it became part of common sense that in a situation of multiple disabilities, weak family backgrounds and 'alienation from White society', Black youth would inevitably drift into 'unlawful means'. Such views were strengthened by quasi-academic research which attempted to construct an explanation of the 'criminalisation' of Black youth. John Brown's (1977) study of Handsworth is a good example of this approach. It saw Black youth, and to some extent Black communities as a whole, as being composed of a small 'criminalised sub-culture' and a mass of hard-working and law-abiding citizens. The second was under threat from the first, and the police had to act in order to maintain law and order.

Such views, which essentially see Black youth as a law-and-order 'problem', congeal around pathological labels of 'alienation' and 'cultural conflict' in order to legitimise the solutions which they propose. In practice this means that the state intervenes not in order to transform the socio-economic conditions which reproduce Black youth as marginalised, but to deal with the symptoms of their discontent. Over the last decade this has meant that whatever the abstract protestations of goodwill in the field of police/Black relations the state has intervened more to meet newly-created insecurities or potential conflicts than fundamentally to transform the overall situation. The main concern has been to develop better policies of control, while still taking for granted the need to depoliticise Black youth and prevent them from rioting.

The pervasiveness of this concern with preventing or better controlling the problem 'next time' has supported pathological explanations of the 'restlessness' of young Blacks, which leave unasked questions about racism in the police force, racial attacks on Black youth and the development of racist practices within other state agencies. The concern with controlling the actions of Black youth is evident in the following quotation, which is referring to the 'alienated' young Blacks:

A special form of independent, political, religious and cultural thinking is evolving which attempts to define the separateness of the group. Faced with this growth within our society, what measures can we recommend to integrate it in such a way that the quality of life of these young people can be drastically improved? We cannot afford to argue that this is the sort of cultural development which is proper in a pluralistic society and that we should assist the group to realise its separateness. For this development, however understandable, actually offers these young people little hope in our society. They are set on a track which can only lead to permanent unemployment and permanent estrangement from the indigenous population. It can only pose the sort of problem for our society for which we have no solutions other than firm control. (CRE, 1979, quoted in John, 1981, pp. 151–2)

The image is of an alien growth 'within our society' which needs to be treated quickly if it is to be stopped from getting out of control, but nowhere in this document, or in numerous other official studies, is the question of alienation and estrangement treated seriously. Rather, these terms become a metaphor for legitimising the failure of existing policies, by situating marginalisation within the individual, and group attitudes of young Blacks themselves. Through this process Black youth are pathologised via their association with the 'criminalised sub-cultures' and the 'cultures of deprivation' that are thought to sustain them.

The 1980–81 'riots'

The response to the street riots in Bristol, Brixton, Southall and Toxteth during 1980 and 1981 provides a clear example of how this pathologisation works. A number of internal government reports during the early 1970s had warned that violence could be one outcome if there was no improvement in the socio-economic position of Black communities. The most influential was the 'Think Tank' report of 1974 which stated that: 'There are uncomfortable parallels between the situation of Britain's coloured population and that of the Catholics in Northern Ireland. For 50 years British Governments condoned discrimination and deprivation in Ulster, and in the end Ulster blew up in their face. We believe that not only for reasons of social justice but also to preserve social stability and order in the longer term more should be done with the problems of race relations in this country' (Runnymede Trust Bulletin, December 1977). Such warnings, however, were interpreted as either exaggerated or as implying that more money poured into inner-city areas was the way to prevent race riots. When policies failed to work, and particularly when the first signs of mass resistance by Black youth appeared, policy-makers had to construct explanations for such 'dysfunctions'. And these have emphasised the problematic nature of Black households, which are seen as having failed to adapt to new realities. This is how the riots during 1980 and 1981 have been seen by both the police and by government. In Liverpool the Chief Constable responded to the July 1981 riots by asking:

What in the name of goodness are these young people doing on the streets indulging in this behaviour at that time of night? Is there no discipline that can be brought to bear on these young people? Are the parents not interested in the futures of these young people? (*The Guardian*, 8 July 1981)

Admittedly, the government's response was somewhat broader, including promises of help to depressed areas and measures to deal with youth unemployment (State Research Bulletin, 1981;

Benyon, 1984). Nevertheless, at the level of common-sense and the mass media's presentation of the riots, the resonant themes were those of 'young hotheads', 'alienated Blacks', 'agitators' and 'criminalised youth'. The issue of racist attacks and police harassment was either underplayed or blamed on a small minority of racists.

By explaining the riots in terms of the actions of 'alienated' Black youth the state has attempted to place the blame on the conditions which produce alienation, and to seek solutions through new agencies whose purpose is to establish contact with this section of Black youngsters. In so doing it fails to analyse the basis of racially exclusive practices within its own structures. The setting up of new agencies to deal with the 'special problems' of Black youth thus becomes a way of shunting important structural questions on to a political siding. As the experience of 1980 and 1981 has shown, the law and order issue is one way in which this tactic is being used to prevent any deep questioning of the roots of racism in British society as a whole, by locating Black youth as *the* dysfunctional element in good race relations. In this sense the current position of Black youth cannot be viewed as an isolated issue, since it will provide the paradigm through which the state will attempt to manage race relations as a whole.

Although it is difficult to gauge the full impact of the 'riots' on policies at this stage, there is at least some preliminary evidence to suggest that the short-term effect may be more at the level of ideology than of actual changes in the broad orientation of policy. The debate about Black youth in the aftermath of the 1980–81 riots signalled some criticisms of pathology models, but subsequent policies have done little to displace the common-sense view that at least a major factor in explaining high levels of Black youth unemployment are their own cultural and social deficiencies. There is still a strong body of official opinion which sees higher levels of unemployment as being caused by young Black people's attitudes to work, language difficulties, educational disadvantage and the double disadvantage of being concentrated in deprived inner-city areas. This has produced a contradictory mixture within official thinking about minority youth: on the one hand it continues to see them as a problem category because of their supposed cultural deficiencies, and on the other it sees its role as one of compensating for broader social disadvantages resulting from the position of Blacks as a deprived minority in British society.

Writing about the events in Bristol, Brixton, Liverpool and numerous other urban areas during 1980 and 1981, the MSC's Corporate Plan for 1982–86 contained the following interpretation:

> Last year saw an explosion of unrest and violence in some of our inner cities which has focused public attention on the problems of these areas, and, in particular, those of the ethnic minority groups who are concentrated in them. The ethnic minorities in these areas suffer a double employment disadvantage: registered unemployment among ethnic minority groups is particularly high, and the unemployment and social problems of many inner city areas are also acute. This represents one of the most difficult challenges in the field of social, economic, environmental and employment policy, and the programme of development for Merseyside announced by the Secretary of State for the Environment indicates the range of problems and remedies under consideration. (MSC, 1982a)

It then goes on to outline the ways in which the MSC was responding to this challenge, and in the process summarises its own philosophy of the 'problem':

> Our approach has been based on the view that over a wide area of employment the problems of ethnic minority groups in inner cities and elsewhere are similar in kind, though often much more acute in degree, to those of the labour force generally . . . Through our planning system we try to concentrate our services on areas where labour market needs are greatest and where they can be most effective, and ethnic minorities in inner cities benefit from this. (MSC, 1982a, paras 5.20 and 5.21)

The logic of this approach fits in quite well with the thinking of the MSC as a whole about 'special client groups': the disabled, ex-offenders, young girls and the educationally disadvantaged (MSC, 1982b).

Another element of the post-riots response to Black youth unemployment is the development of co-operation between the

MSC and the CRE in drafting an equal opportunity strategy for the new Youth Training Scheme, and encouraging public and private employing organisations to take on board more positive action initiatives to help young unemployed Blacks. During 1982–1983 the CRE produced a statement on equal opportunity and YTS, and a broader document on equal opportunity and positive action (CRE, 1983a and 1983b). By January 1983 the MSC itself had adopted a statement on equal opportunity which stated:

> The YTS will . . . be open to all young people within the range of eligibility regardless of race, religion, sex or disability. The scheme will need to comply with legislation forbidding discrimination, but more than that it should provide special help for disadvantaged groups. (quoted in CRE, 1983b)

Beyond that the MSC has introduced monitoring by racial and ethnic group within its schemes, and supported a number of research projects on the special needs of minority youth.

Quite apart from these public consequences, however, there seems to be another consequence of the 1981 'riots' which is much more difficult to quantify. The stress on the part played by Black youth in street violence reinforced the pre-existing stereotype of young Blacks as a subculture of criminality and renewed the concern with 'riot prevention' which had been a theme of public debate from the 1960s onwards. In the aftermath of July 1981 the fear that unemployment among young Blacks could lead to street violence became an important influence on police thinking and it also came to be accepted as a major rationale for more government actions. It no longer seemed inopportune to view youth unemployment as a highly political issue, since even neo-conservative ideologists accepted the need to provide greater support for the unemployed in order to reduce the likelihood of violent confrontations on the streets (Mungham, 1982; Croft and Beresford, 1983).

By reinforcing the mythology which links Black youth with crime and social unrest the 'riots' may have, in fact, strengthened the image that Black youth needs discipline and direction to prevent it becoming marginalised from society as a whole. As a consequence of this there are two slightly separate issues which have to be looked at in an analysis of the policy impact of the

1981 'riots'. First, the direct impact on actual policy outcomes in the period since the 'riots'. At this level the more interventionist stance since 1981 has meant that more resources have been directed at young Blacks as a social category. Nevertheless, we cannot simply read into this increase in resources an actual improvement in the position of young Blacks in the labour market. This seems to be borne out by the persistence of relatively high levels of unemployment and the high numbers of young Blacks on training schemes (Anwar, 1982; Bedeman and Courtenay, 1983).

The second issue to be analysed is the ideological interpretation and definition of the 'riots'. Pearson (1983) has argued that the image of the 'hooligan' has performed the function of mobilising respectable fears about youth, and metaphorically about society as a whole. The 'riots' represent an extreme example of this process, because they concretised fears about a number of 'problems' around the theme of street violence and the breakdown of law and order. Moreover their representation on the media made them into a national issue, and also one which was about politics as well as policy. It is this political aspect which cannot be pinned down to policy outputs, but which is perhaps the most important aspect of the ideological aftermath of 1981. Perhaps a good measure of this ideological confusion can be gauged from the *Financial Times* account of the events in Brixton:

> Last weekend's riots can be interpreted either as the growing pains of a society gradually moving towards racial integration or as the omen that racial tension will eventually tear society apart, particularly when it is exacerbated by a high level of unemployment among the young. Which of these interpretations eventually prove correct may depend in large measure on what people are not prepared to believe. For there is plenty in Brixton to suggest that a genuinely multi-racial society is achievable. But racial insecurity, partly fostered by the deliberate actions of successive governments, can all too easily destroy the cohesion on which all societies must base their system of preserving society and order. (18 April 1981)

Such statements were reproduced many times during July 1981 (see Tumber 1982), particularly in relation to youth unemployment and law and order. They are a measure of the uncertainty and destabilisation caused by the image of young Blacks as alienated, socially marginalised and prone to violent political action. The long-term consequences of these images remain to be seen, but in the short term they seem likely to strengthen a 'problem orientated' approach to young Blacks.

What kind of alternative?

In the current conjuncture there are various choices open to the state, local authorities, the police and other agencies in responding to the struggles in which Black youth are engaged in many urban areas. These include the ameliorative, control and repressive options discussed above. In practice, concrete types of state intervention are likely to include a combination of all these elements (Benyon, 1984). As was argued above, however, the exact weight attached to each element is bound to be the outcome of complex processes of resistance, negotiation and accommodation. Black youth, whether in schools, YTS projects, or in their communities, are not simply the objects of state actions. They are also collective social actors, and their everyday actions often have the effect of questioning the legitimacy of the role of specific state agencies. The role of the police since 1981 and particularly the experience of community policing strategies, is a case in point (Gilroy, 1982; Cowell *et al.*, 1982). Young blacks, and the Black communities as a whole, have shown themselves to be capable of making their own political demands and challenging the definition of their cultures and values as the source of racial problems.

The likely course of state interventions will, at least partially, be influenced by these everyday struggles. What, however, are the chances of new initiatives against institutionalised racism having a significant impact on policy initiatives as a whole? Clearly, in terms of the balance of political forces today the most likely channel for such a strategy would be the Labour Party, and particularly its Left wing. Although it should be noted that much of the Labour Party's thinking on race is still dominated by various versions of Ray Jenkins' 'equality of opportunity' arguments and the acceptance of the need for immigration controls, it has of recent years attempted to take a more active stance on these issues. Its response to the 1980 Nationality Bill is one example of this trend, as was its response to the 1981 riots. Despite these initiatives, the view of 'race' dominant in the Labour Party's discourse is severely limited. A lengthy manifesto issued by the Left wing of the party provides an illustration of this point. After commenting on the experience of immigration controls, the role of the police, the plight of Black youth and the growth of racist attacks, its main positive recommendation is that:

A future Labour government should consult with women's organisations and representatives of racial minorities to consider what policies of 'positive discrimination' might have to offer in the short run. (Cripps *et al.*, 1981, p. 210)

The term 'positive discrimination' is implicitly a critique of Jenkins original formulation, but the writers of the manifesto still hold on to a more radical version of normative 'equality of opportunity'. It is also of interest that although it is entitled, 'A Radical Strategy for Britain's Future', it devotes only four pages out of two hundred to race-related issues.

The official position of the Labour Party gives even more cause for concern. In the aftermath of the July 1981 riots its main response was to call for more jobs, increased aid to the inner-city areas, and greater public control over the police (Hansard, 6 July 1981 and 9 July 1981). This was in response to the Conservative Government's attempts to explain the riots through the role of 'outside agitators', urban deprivation and the 'alienation' of the young. By explaining the riots as the outcome of the neo-Conservative economic strategy of the Thatcher Government, the Labour Party in effect argued that the 'solution' lay in pursuing more expansionist economic policies, and more positive action to overcome urban deprivation. But this approach has severe limitations in terms of explaining why it is that Black youth has been the main target of police harassment, or why they have been most severely affected by economic and social marginalisation. As Hazel Carby (1980) has argued, discourses about social disadvantages, whether of the Left or the Right, can have the effect of 'subsuming inherent contradictions and conflicting economic and political interests between racial, sexual or class groupings' (p. 64). The consequences of such subsumption within the Left in Britain, have been a failure to allow for the autonomous struggles of women, Blacks or other social groups that do not have strong representation in traditional political institutions (Gilroy, 1982). In addition, the assumption has been that paternalistic reform strategies could 'help' minority communities become more integrated with the wider society.

The ambiguous nature of these assumptions was exemplified during the July 1981 riots by the Labour Party's emphasis on the role of social deprivation in causing the disturbances, while showing little insight as to how these social conditions could be overcome. By prioritising social deprivation as an explanation of the riots, Roy Hattersley argued that it was possible to think of solutions short of hard policing. But he, along with other Labour politicians, showed little or no inclination to listen to the voice of those who took part in the riots and who experienced police practices and racism as the central issues.

Unless the voices of those not represented through established political channels are allowed to be heard, there seems little chance of building new and innovative responses to the problems faced by young Blacks in British society. The assumption that reform policies imposed from the top down can be such an alternative has not been substantiated by the experience of policies over the last two decades.

Any long-term strategy for fighting the effects of institutionalised racialism must attempt to combine the already developed struggles of Black communities with anti-racist mobilisation in all areas of state activity. Otherwise there is always the danger of committing the same mistakes as existing equal opportunity policies which have in effect attempted to equate the unequal. In relation to Black youth the structural roots of their marginalisation lie so deep that both ameliorative and social control strategies are likely to prove contradictory. If this is the case there will be new pressures from the law and order lobby for more repression, and the early signs of this have already appeared.[6] A simple 'economic' strategy of rejuvenating the inner cities is bound to collapse under the weight of its own contradictions if it does not tackle the reality of the racial, class and political and cultural forms of marginalisation which work against Black youth. A sustained political response to processes which produce the marginalisation of racial minorities must start with a reorganisation of power relations at all levels of

British society and build upon the autonomous organisations set up by Black communities.

The experience of the last three decades shows that this will not be achieved on the basis of policies which aim to insure against social disorder by patching up the existing order of things or by increasing the 'understanding' of race. In a society which is so deeply racist, the overcoming of racism will only come about through long and hard struggles at all levels, both within and outside institutions. Short of this general transformation of racist practices and institutions, it is only possible to imagine short-term and contradictory 'solutions'.

Conclusions

The central argument of this chapter is straightforward: it is that the form and content of policy intervention in this area has tended to ignore the direct and indirect impact of racism on Black youth's educational and employment chances and to interpret evidence of underachievement and unemployment as the result of disabilities and handicaps originating from within the Black communities – in other words, as the outcome of the weaknesses or inadequacies of Black family life and culture.

As a result, present policies have at best proved to be contradictory, to have had only a marginal impact on the problems they are supposed to deal with, and at worst ignored the real issues and helped to construct mythologies about the 'problems' faced by young Blacks. For example, it seems to be quite clear that initiatives aimed at providing 'training' for young Blacks and therefore increasing their 'employability' can have little or no impact on the supply side of job creation since this depends on the broader economic and political priorities which underlie government expenditure and employment policies. But the emphasis on training can have quite an important ideological effect, in that it helps construct the image that job training can actually solve unemployment, and that those who are unemployed lack necessary skills.

These criticisms of present policies may seem to overstate the case somewhat, since it does seem clear that some of the recent initiatives (particularly the Youth Training Scheme) have taken the issue of racism more seriously. While this is undoubtedly true, the evidence necessary to support any claim that these initiatives will have a substantial impact on levels of Black youth unemployment remains thin on the ground, particularly in the context of the recessionary policies being pursued by the Thatcher Government. Apart from some immediate help provided during 1981–82 in the aftermath of the riots, there is little evidence of a substantial allocation of resources to help Black youth in the worst hit areas.

The role of Black political action is likely to be crucial if there is going to be a concerted effort to overcome the limits of present policies. Recent debates in the Black press would seem to indicate that education and youth unemployment are becoming central issues within the Black communities, leading to both local and national pressures on state agencies to 'stop paying lip-service to equality and accept that Britain is a racist society and start to deal with the problem honestly'.[7] Because of these pressures the issue of Black youth will remain near the top of the race agenda during the next few years, and is likely to arouse political and policy interest from both within and outside the Black communities. In this context, an anti-racist response could play an important role in sensitising the political debate to the social relations which have helped marginalise Black youth, and which are generally ignored, or put at the bottom of the policy agenda linked to official explanations of the 'problem' of Black youth.

This chapter has attempted to show that an important starting point in all this must be the questioning of assumptions which do little more than 'blame the victim' (Ryan, 1976), and a critical analysis of the effectiveness of policies in tackling the central issue of racism and its institutional expressions. The message I have attempted to convey in this chapter is that fundamental changes in institutionalised racism are unlikely to come about unless we understand the complex ways in which it works in British society, and the role that state policies have played in reproducing mythologies and common-sense images of 'race'.

Notes and References

This chapter is based on research carried out at the ESRC Research Unit on Ethnic Relations between 1980–83. The opinions expressed here are, however, my own, and do not in any way reflect those of the ESRC or of my colleagues at the Unit. I gratefully acknowledge the comments of Philip Cohen and Richard Jenkins which helped me to rewrite the chapter. A detailed historical analysis of the issues covered in this chapter can be found in my *Black Youth, Racism and the State* (Cambridge University Press, 1988).

1. On this point see the rest of this volume, along with John (1981), Carby (1982) and recent issues of *Race Today*.
2. A fuller discussion of how this change has come about is beyond the scope of this chapter, though some comments about the events of 1980–81 will be made in the concluding sections. But see the detailed analysis of the events in Bristol in April 1980 by Joshua *et al.* (1983).
3. A critical analysis of the origins and influence of these notions on recent policy developments can be found in Solomos (1983).
4. This line of analysis has been pursued by Lawrence (1982) and Gutzmore (1984).
5. This study has still not been published in full, but a careful analysis of some findings can be found in Dex, 1982.
6. A concise and critical analysis of the law and order lobby and its impact since 1981 can be found in Sim, 1982.
7. *West Indian World*, 11 April 1984.

Bibliography

Abbott, S. (ed.) (1971) *Prevention of Racial Discrimination in Britain* (London: Oxford University Press).

Anwar, M. (1982) *Young People and the Job Market: A Survey* (London: Commission for Racial Equality).

Bedeman, T. and Courtenay, G. (1983) *One in Three: The Second National Survey of Young People on YOP*, Research and Development Series no. 13 (Sheffield: Manpower Services Commission).

Benyon, J. (ed.) (1984) *Scarman and After* (Oxford: Pergamon Press).

Brown, J. (1977) *Shades of Grey: A Report on Police – West Indian Relations in Handsworth* (Cranfield, Beds.: Cranfield Institute of Technology).

Carby, H. (1980) 'Multi-Culture', *Screen Education*, no. 34, pp. 62–70.

Carby, H. (1982) 'Schooling in Babylon' in CCCS Race and Politics Group (1982).

Centre for Contemporary Cultural Studies (CCCS).

CCCS Race and Politics Group (1982) *The Empire Strikes Back: Race and Racism in 70s Britain* (London: Hutchinson).

Clarke, J., Critcher, C., Jefferson, T. and Lambert, J. (1974) 'The Selection of Evidence and the Avoidance of Racialism: A Critique of the Parliamentary Select Committee on Race Relations and Immigration' *New Community*, vol. 3, no. 3, pp. 172–92.

Coard, B. (1971) *How the West Indian Child is Made Educationally Subnormal in the British School System* (London: Beacon).

Colonial Office (1948) *Working Party on the Employment of Surplus Colonial Labour in the United Kingdom*, Co 1006/2 (London: Public Records Office).

Colonial Office (1944–45) *Report of Investigation into Conditions of the Coloured Colonial Men in a Stepney Area*, Co 876/39 (London: Public Records Office).

Commission for Racial Equality (CRE) (1980) *Youth in Multi-Racial Society* (London: CRE).

Commission for Racial Equality (CRE) (1980) *Ethnic Minority Youth Unemployment* (London: CRE).

Commission for Racial Equality (CRE) (1983a) *Equal Opportunity, Positive Action and Young People* (London: CRE).

Commission for Racial Equality (CRE) (1983b) *Equal Opportunity and the Youth Training Scheme* (London: CRE).

Commonwealth Immigrants Advisory Council (1964) *Second Report* (London: HMSO).

Community Relations Commission (CRC) (1974) *Unemployment and Homelessness* (London: CRC).

Cottle, T. (1978) *Black Testimony: The Voice of Britain's West Indians* (London: Wildwood House).

Cowell, D., (eds) (1982) *Policing the Riots* (London: Junction Books).

Cripps, F. *et al.* (1981) *Manifesto: A Radical Strategy for Britain's Future* (London: Pan).

Croft, S. and Beresford, P. (1983) 'Power, Politics and the Youth Training Scheme', *Youth and Policy*, Vol. 2, no. 1, pp. 1–4.

Cross, M., Edmonds, J. and Sargeant, R. (1983) *Ethnic Minorities: Their Experience on YOP* (Sheffield: Manpower Services Commission).

Department of Education and Science (DES) (1965) *The Education of Immigrants*, Circular 7/65 (London: DES).

Department of Education and Science (DES) (1967) *Immigrants and the Youth Service* (London: DES).

Department of Education and Science (DES) (1981) *West Indian Children in Our Schools*, Cmnd 8273 (London: HMSO).

Dex, S. (1982) *Black and White School-Leavers: The First Five Years of Work*, Research Paper no. 33 (London: Department of Employment).

Dunn, D. (1983) 'Black Youth, the Youth Training Scheme and the Choice at 16', *Multiracial Education*, vol. 11, no. 3, pp. 7–22.

Gilroy, P. (1982) 'Police and Thieves' in CCCS Race and Politics Group (1982).

Green, A. (1982) 'In Defence of Anti-Racist Teaching: A reply to recent critiques of multicultural education', *Multiracial Education*, vol. 10, no. 2, pp. 18–35.

Gutzmore, C. (1984) 'Capital, "Black Youth" and Crime', *Race and Class*, vol. 25, no. 2, pp. 13–30.

Hall, S., Critcher, C., Jefferson, T., Clarke, J. and Roberts, B. (1978) *Policing the Crisis* (London: Macmillan).

Halsey, A. H. (1970) 'Race Relations: The Lines to Think On', *New Society*, 10 March, pp. 472–4.

Home Affairs Committee, Sub-Committee on Race Relations and Immigration (1981) *Racial Disadvantage* (London: HMSO).

Home Office (1978) *The West Indian Community* (London: HMSO).

Humphry, D. (1972) *Police Power and Black People* (London: Panther).

Hunt, G. and Mellor, J. (1980) 'Afro-Caribbean Youth: Racism and Unemployment' in M. Cole and B. Skelton (eds) *Blind Alley* (Ormskirk, Lancs.: Hesketh).

International Labour Organisation (ILO) (1978) *Youth Unemployment in Industrial Market Economy Societies* (Geneva: ILO).

Jenkins, R. (1966) 'Speech to National Committee for Commonwealth Immigrants', 23 May.

John, G. (1970) *Race in the Inner City: A Report from Handsworth* (London: Runnymede Trust).

John, G. (1981) *In the Service of Black Youth* (London: National Association of Youth Clubs).

Joshi, S. and Carter, B. (1984) 'The Role of Labour in the Creation of a Racist Britain', *Race and Class*, vol. 25, no. 3, pp. 53–70.

Joshua, H., Wallace, T. and Booth, H. (1983) *To Ride the Storm: the 1980 Bristol 'Riot' and the State* (London: Heinemann).

Lambert, J. (1970) *Crime, Police and Race Relations* (London: Oxford University Press).

Lawrence, E. (1982) 'Just Plain Common Sense: the 'roots' of racism', in CCCS Race and Politics Group (1982).

Lea, J. (1980) 'The Contradictions of the Sixties Race Relations Legislation' in National Deviancy Conference, *Permissiveness and Control* (London: Macmillan).

Lowry, R. P. (1974) *Social Problems* (Lexington, Maryland: D. C. Heath).

Manpower Services Commission (MSC) (1982a) *Corporate Plan 1982–86*, (London: MSC).

Manpower Services Commission (MSC) (1982b) *Memorandum on Special Client Groups*, unpublished Paper (London: MSC Special Programmes Division).

Manpower Services Commission and Commission for Racial Equality (1979) *Ethnic Minorities and the Special Programmes for the Unemployed*, (London: MSC and CRE).

McNeal, J. (1971) 'Education', in S. Abbott (ed.) *The Prevention of Racial Discrimination in Britain* (London: Oxford University Press).

Metropolitan Police (1976) 'Evidence to Select Committee on Race Relations and Immigration', (London: Metropolitan Police).

Milner, D. (1975) *Children and Race* (Harmondsworth: Penguin).

Mungham, G. (1982) 'Workless Youth as a Moral Panic' in T. L. Rees and P. Atkinson (eds) *Youth Unemployment and State Intervention*, (London: Routledge and Kegan Paul).

Pearson, G. (1983) *Hooligan: A History of Respectable Fears* (London: Macmillan).

Reeves, F. (1983) *British Racial Discourse* (Cambridge: Cambridge University Press).

Rose, E. J. B. *et al.* (1969) *Colour and Citizenship: A Report on British Race Relations* (London: Oxford University Press).

Runnymede Trust (1977) *Bulletin* (December).

Ryan, W. (1976) *Blaming the Victim* (New York: Vintage Books).

Select Committee on Race Relations and Immigration (SCRRI) (1969) *The Problems of Coloured School Leavers* (London: HMSO).

194 *Institutionalised Racism*

Select Committee on Race Relations and Immigration (SCRRI) (1973) *Education* (London: HMSO).

Sim, J. (1982) 'Scarman: The Police-Attack' in *Socialist Register 1982* (London: Merlin).

Solomos, J. (1983) 'Black Youth, Unemployment and Equal Opportunity Policies', in B. Troyna and D. I. Smith (1983).

Stares, R. *et al.* (1982) *Ethnic Minorities: Their Involvement in MSC Special Programmes* (London: MSC).

State Research Bulletin (1981) 'The July Riots', *State Research Bulletin*, vol. 25, pp. 161–6.

Troyna, B. (1982) 'The Ideological and Policy Response to Black Pupils in British Schools' in A. Hartnett, (ed.) *The Social Sciences in Educational Studies* (London: Heinemann).

Troyna, B. and Smith, D. I. (eds) (1983) *Racism, School and the Labour Market* (Leicester: National Youth Bureau).

Tumber, H. (1982) *Television and the Riots* (London: British Film Institute).

Williams, J. (1981) 'Race and Schooling: Some Recent Contributions', *British Journal of the Sociology of Education*, vol. 2, no. 2, pp. 221–7.

Part III

Practices

4

Gender, Race and Power: The Challenge to Youth Work Practice

Prathibha Parmar

Young Black women are a growing and significant section of society yet their voices remain unheard and their experiences largely ignored. While challenges to the gender-and-race-blind analyses of youth have emerged in the last ten years, these have failed to see the racialised gender roles ascribed to young Black women as of any importance. This is primarily because such critiques and analyses have focused on one system of oppression to the exclusion of another. For Black women there is no such choice.

Young Black women's experiences of living in a racist society such as Britain are determined by the factors of race, gender, age, class and sexuality. It is the simultaneous operation of these oppressions which shape their experiences and contribute to their significant lack of power in society.

A relevant and valid theory for analysing the situation of young Black women has to necessarily base itself on the fact of the simultaneous nature of their exploitation and oppression. It would not be useful to dissect these different power systems and attempt to strip them away as if they formed layers of oppression, because the daily subjective and objective experiences which form the matrix of young Black women's lives are fashioned by their fusion.

Black feminist writing in the recent past, both in this country and the USA, has made significant political and theoretical contributions to our understanding of the simultaneous nature of oppressions and the limitations of political theories and practices which perpetuate notions of 'hierarchies of oppression'.

Black feminists have marked out the boundaries of their sister-hood with White women and challenged White feminist theories and practices which do not acknowledge race and class differences amongst women. The challenge of Black feminists to the continuing dominance of an imperial feminism has been extended to the various institutions and individuals that are met with in the course of daily work activities. While many inroads have been made by feminists into the youth service, where such feminist interventions have contributed to much-needed changes in a hitherto male-dominated terrain, there continues to be the tendency by many White women youth workers to marginalise the work undertaken with young Black women.

It is the aim of this chapter not only to make young Black women's experiences visible in the area of youth work with girls and young women, but also to make a theoretical contribution to integrating a Black feminist analysis of youth work practice. This will be done through a consideration of the specific situation of young Asian women in mainstream debates on the nature of the 'youth crisis' in the 1980s and the responses to it by academics and practitioners.

Invisible youth

Writings on and about the 'problems' of Black youth have been prolific in the recent past. Much intellectual and practical energy has been spent on analysing the nature of the 'youth crisis' of the 1980s. The debate and its manifestations in various disciplines of sociology and education rotates around the significance or other-wise of youth's challenges to the growth of authoritarian statism.

The riots of 1981 have, in turn, encouraged many local and national state initiatives in the form of *ad hoc* youth projects which make desperate attempts to contain the growing frustrations of unemployed Black young people, yet the experiences of young Black women are predictably absent from these debates and initiatives.

While the general invisibility of women from historical accounts of struggle have been acknowledged by many White feminists, the absence of Black women has not been seen as being of any special significance. Asian and Afro-Caribbean women's resistance to slavery and colonialism has been written out of the history books and/or rewritings by both the Left and White feminists. It is not only in historical accounts that Black women are absent or portrayed in negative and stereotyped ways, but also in contemporary media coverage of any struggles involving Black communities in Britain. The coverage of the riots of 1981 clearly showed this to be the case.

The media coverage of the riots perpetuated the image of Afro-Caribbean youth as the instigators of anti-authoritarian activities and the active participation of White working-class youth and Black young women in these acts of resistance went neatly and conveniently unnoticed.

When young Black women are visible it is in an equally negative and 'pathological' manner. While young women of Afro-Caribbean origin are seen as potentially 'at risk' through a lack of discipline and because of an uncontrollable sexuality which results in unwanted pregnancies, young Asian women are seen as either too meek and mild or as rebelling against their unreasonably backward and tradition-bound parents who insist on such 'barbaric' practices as arranged marriages.

Ultimately, the 'problems' with Asian and Afro-Caribbean young women and men are traced back to their pathological Black family: the Afro-Caribbean family is seen as being too fragmented and weak and the Asian family seems to be unhealthily strong, cohesive and controlling of its members, and it is the women of the family who are focused on as the ultimate culprits, whose inadequacies and failures as wives and mothers are responsible for the numerous 'problems' that the different welfare agencies are confronted with from their children. Afro-Caribbean women are stereotyped as matriarchs, or seen as single mothers who expose their children to a stream of different men while Asian women are construed as faithful and passive victims centring their lives around their religious rituals, family and home.

Asian women are identified as failures because of their lack of English and their refusal to integrate by adopting English eating, dressing and speaking habits is seen as the cause of the problems their children experience.

On another level, the Asian family is both condemned for its repressive togetherness and praised for a stability which all would like to emulate. The apparent stability and close-knit nature of the Asian family is often used to deprecate the Afro-Caribbean family – a double standard of representation which is a potential source of disunity amongst the different Black communities.

Sociological literature on 'race relations' has been instrumental in adding 'scientific' objectivity to common-sense notions of Asian passivity and Afro-Caribbean aggressiveness. A critical review of the literature has been done elsewhere,[1] but suffice to say here that the concepts of identity crisis, cultural conflict, language and communication problems are some of the key constructs within which the pathology of the Asian family is developed and embodied. In this context the arranged marriage system has been focused on as central to the oppression of young Asian women. It is not only 'race relations' literature which has grabbed this particular cultural tradition – the media has also had its fair share of 'newsworthiness' by citing sensational individual cases of Asian girls running away from home. The state too has not been slow in picking up on these instances to justify racist and sexist immigration laws as working to protect 'innocent' Asian girls who are victims of 'backward' and 'tradition-bound' parents forcing them against their will into unwanted marriages.

Against such reasoning, what many have argued and continue to argue is that Asian women do not want the state to act on their behalf, nor do they want liberal social workers, teachers or community workers to act as would-be protectors, liberators or saviours. Asian women have been struggling, and continue to struggle, around these issues within and outside their communities on their own terms and in their own culturally specific ways.

The danger of such common-sense images of arranged marriage continuing to dominate official perceptions of the Asian family is that this will systematically distort the delivery of public services and resources to a particular group in society, namely, young Asian women.

The following section offers a detailed look at the experiences of Asian girls and young women within educational and recreational institutions. The arguments are based on the findings of a three-year action research project[2] which aimed to identify and meet the needs of young Asian women.

Working with Asian young women

Asian young women have too often been wrongly stereotyped as meek, mild and docile people. This 'common-sense' racist thinking has implications for the way in which many of them are denied access to educational and recreational resources as well as contributing to their experiences of racism in schools. So, for example, when one young Asian woman wanted to go on to higher education, her teacher's response was, 'What's the point in giving you any advice. Stop dreaming and be realistic. You are probably going to be married off anyway, so don't waste time on educating yourself'. Here, the racist stereotype that the White teacher believed, that all young Asian women are victims of forced arranged marriages, is not uncommon. Such views result in many young Asian women being denied adequate careers counselling, and being prevented from going on school trips and taking part in other school activities. Our work with Asian girls and young women has challenged existing myths and stereotypes about them and our findings indicate the direction in which future work with Asian girls needs to develop.

Our primary role was that of youth workers working specifically with Asian girls and from the outset we both experienced problems with the ways in which professional individuals and agencies perceived us. The majority of the 'caring/helping' agencies and individuals in schools and colleges saw us as social workers/counsellors who would help them to sort out their problems with 'their' Asian girls.

On introducing ourselves to individuals in many educational and social welfare agencies it immediately became apparent from the overall response that young Asian women were identified as a problem group for whom strict parental restrictions and demands were seen as the main cause of problems. We were repeatedly asked questions such as, 'What do you think could be done to change the parents' attitudes?'; 'It's terrible the way their parents don't understand the poor things!'; 'I think it's the parents who are responsible for their unrealistic aspirations', and so on *ad nauseam*.

This deep-rooted and pervasive pathologising of Asian cultures and Asian family structures was the biggest obstacle in our attempts to develop youth work activities with Asian girls.[3] The general climate when we began our work was one where many agencies did not recognise the need to develop youth work with Asian girls, while others, whose thoughts were confined within the stereotyped framework of 'culture conflicts' and 'generation gaps', believed that in a couple of decades all 'problems' would be solved as the second generation became assimilated into British society and there was, therefore, little point in doing anything in the present.

The emphasis of our work with Asian girls is, and always has been, to facilitate the positive development of cultural, racial and sexual consciousness through activities in a relaxed, non-threatening and non-intimidating atmosphere. In separate Asian girls' groups there is no fear of being sneered at or having to take a secondary role so as not to attract attention because of being 'different'. Despite the fact that girls are often from different cultural backgrounds there are common experiences, perceptions and situations which create a strong, uniting bond amongst them. However, the girls are still subjected to name-calling and jeering taunts from White youth of both sexes because they choose to form an all-Asian girls' group. We, in turn, as workers, have to struggle against the resistance of teachers and youth workers towards separate provision. Even in situations where they are sympathetic we have to take care that we are not being used as an excuse for non-action in this area by White teachers or youth workers and that our work is not used to cover up for their gaps and shortcomings.

We made contact initially with girls and young women through many different channels, such as community and religious organisations, Youth Training Schemes, neighbourhood groups, schools and colleges. While each channel had its own positive and negative features, we could not say that any one channel was the 'correct' one – it was the method of work rather than the channel which determined the success of each group.

Girls' groups in schools

Through descriptions of our experiences of initiating Asian girls' groups in schools we want to highlight the ways in which Asian girls' experiences at school reflect the general racism prevalent in society today. The negative 'common-sense' notions of Asian girls that White society generally has are to be found in some White teachers' attitudes towards them, and in the actions of White students in either ignoring them, or throwing racist abuse, or attempting to beat them up.

Schools were a formal means of gaining access to Asian girls and contact was usually made with the heads of schools which had been identified as having a substantial number of Asian pupils. We had varied responses from the head teachers and teachers with whom we had made contact. In some cases we were given the brush-off by heads who said they had 'no problems' with Asian girls in their schools, while others insisted we should come into school as 'counsellors' and hold 'surgeries'.

The final decisions regarding which schools we should choose to initiate groups in depended on the reception we received from the school authorities and on the attitudes of the teachers towards our work. Some schools welcomed our approach not so much because they understood why this was necessary but more out of their need to be seen as practising 'progressive multi-cultural policies'. One college only accepted us after they realised that they would be gaining an extra, unpaid member of staff, as a result of timetabling the Asian girls' group as part of a General Studies class.

When the groups met at lunchtime or after school hours, they were affected by the school environment in a negative way. We often had to meet in classrooms, which didn't help to break down the traditional teacher/pupil relationship. We were also sometimes seen as part of a school-initiated project and we had to work hard at creating an informal and non-authoritarian relationship with the girls. Meeting at lunchtimes often meant being disturbed and having racist abuse shouted at us by White students. In one case a group of White boys threw pellets made of rubber bands at us when we met. Although we complained to the school authorities about this, nothing was done to reprimand the boys concerned or to find the group alternative accommodation.

Other problems we experienced include the non-acceptance of the groups by some teachers and other school staff such as cleaners, who resented our presence outside school hours. Some of the groups we worked with were not accepted by the school unless teachers were involved, and many of the young Asian women were not able to relax in their presence. One of the major problems we had was from hostile teachers who accused us of being 'racist' because we held separate Asian girls' groups. A lot of our time and effort was spent on 'educating' teachers and other workers about the need to organise separately, the racist implications of their curriculum, and so on, so that our work had the space to develop with as little hindrance as possible from teachers' ignorance, misunderstanding and racism. We rejected the common approach to work with Asian girls which identified them as a problem group. Most projects set up to look at the special needs of Asian girls have been premised on the fact that this section of the Black community is increasingly becoming a problem for their parents, their schools, and for White society generally.

Girls' work in youth clubs

Work with Asian girls is always seen as being 'problem-centred'. We are expected to help girls with their supposedly innumerable problems at home and as long as we don't mention the fact that very often the problems Asian girls have are nothing to do with their families, but more to do with the racism they experience at school from teachers and pupils alike, then peace will reign. Even when we do persist in challenging the idea that the source of the problem is not Asian cultural habits, but the institutional racism of British society, which prevents Asian girls having an equal share of the provisions that exist, our Youth Service colleagues turn a blind eye.

If we link work with Black youth, and Asian girls in particular, to the history of the Youth Service's attitudes *vis-à-vis* work with girls generally, there are many similarities. It is the white male worker who is always seen to be the so-called provider at the club and instigator of activities, that is, the controller. It is he who determines the level, if any, of decision-making that young people are involved in. He encourages the girls to remain 'invisible' or at most peripheral to the activities of the youth club. In fact, 'girls'' are seen as an alternative activity for the boys, an activity fostered by the youth workers' attitudes. A youth worker was heard to say that he did not encourage Asian boys to come to his club because it was unfair to the White boys who could not 'have' any of 'their' (the Asian boys) girls, while the Asian boys could mix with White girls. The racism and sexism so blatant in this attitude needs no elaboration.

Reactions to girls' work initiatives such as girls-only evenings at clubs are seen as a threat to the White male ego, as are initiatives by Black youth. One of us was told by a youth officer that she hoped she would be around to see that the idea of a girls' night had failed. Both girls and Black youth are demanding equality of opportunity with the majority of people who frequent youth clubs, that is, White boys. As they are seen to be a strong group with a collective consciousness concerning their own situation and status within the wider society, they inevitably threaten the status of existing structures.

Youth work with Asian girls is seen by the Youth Service as supplementary social education for youth at risk, and therefore not necessarily the responsibility of the Youth Service. In one of our areas we were made aware of a particular case where the Youth Service sacked an Asian woman worker because, it was claimed, she disrupted the smooth running of the Service's bureaucracy by changing the time of the girls' club so that more girls were able to come. She was informed that she ought to be doing this work in a voluntary capacity in her own time. The fact that the Asian girls' club had to take place after school hours instead of on a Saturday morning because of the girls' involvement in family activities at the weekend was not accepted. This Asian worker was attempting to practice a family-centred approach which meant having the families' approval of the timing and place for the group. Because the Youth Service did not understand that the group could not exist without the parents' approval, they did not support the worker and the group had to close down temporarily. Subsequently, funds were obtained from the CRE and the education department to restart the group. This exemplifies the way in which certain Youth Services departments are refusing to take responsibility for work with Asian girls. This is because they refuse to see that work with Asian girls cannot be developed in isolation from their families and communities.

So, if our work doesn't fit in with the standard evening youth club times, and instead we want groups to meet in the early evening, that is, after school or during the lunch break at school, then we are not doing youth work but social work or counselling and, therefore, the Youth Service wants no responsibility for it.

However, having a disco on three nights a week seems to constitute youth work in some Youth Service clubs. It seems that while all agencies working with Black youth, especially in the Youth Service, make youth fit into existing provision, their real needs will not be met. It is only when more young people themselves make their demands heard that many feel their needs will finally be met: national and local government call these cries 'riots'.

For Asian girls and young women, being a section of the Black community and being female has a double disadvantage. The Youth Service must begin to change not only its ethnocentric approach but also its gender bias if it is to adequately meet the needs of Asian girls.

Why separate provision is needed for Asian girls

Having explored the concept and practices of the youth service and its provision, it is quite clear that the existing structure and functioning of the Youth Service is not suited to meeting the needs of Asian girls. There are a number of reasons, therefore, why it is necessary to direct and organise youth work activities with and for Asian girls and young women separately from White girls and boys.

First, separate provision is required because of the 'special' needs that Asian girls have: needs which are different from those of male Asian youth and White male and female youth. These needs arise primarily from their position as determined by their race, age, class and gender. It is the way in which their identities and experiences are influenced by these structural factors that determine their access to various resources and facilities not only within the Youth Service but also more widely in society. So the specific needs of Asian girls are primarily not about whether they have facilities to play table tennis or football, or to go canoeing, but it must be assured that facilities suitable to their needs *are* made available outside the conventional youth clubs environment in which the activities are dominated by White boys and girls. There is also a need for a more fundamental concern about how the Youth Service and other institutions can ensure that they, the Asian girls, have an equal share of the youth work provision. To do this the Youth Service needs to encourage and recognise more innovative types of youth work such as, for example, girls meeting at each other's homes to do group activities. One way of legitimising this style of detached youth work would be to channel resources for workers and activities to develop work in this area. This shows how an institution should change, and not how a specific client group should change, in order to fit in with existing structures and provisions. Separate groups and clubs for Asian girls can provide, in the short term at least, a redressing and more equal distribution of resources and facilities for the recreational and social educational needs of Asian girls.

General leisure and recreational facilities are geared towards meeting the needs of White male youth, thus excluding other sections of youth in society. Because the Youth Service is not free from the racism of other institutions in society, it is clear that racist attitudes and structures which are prevalent in such areas as education and social services are also present in the Youth Service. Asian girls-only groups provide an atmosphere free from threat and intimidation from White youth, making it possible to facilitate the development of a positive cultural, racial and sexual identity. Such groups provide the space and opportunity for the girls to meet in a comfortable and tension-free environment, giving girls and young women the opportunity of acquiring skills necessary to cope with the consequences of the racism they face daily, skills they are not taught or given a chance to develop by the institutions they pass through, such as schools, colleges and employment schemes. By virtue of being together, with a shared heritage, there is no fear on their part that they will be looked down upon or that their conversations about their favourite Indian film star, the latest Asian film or song, and so on will have to be carried out surreptitiously in case the English girls and/or boys mock them. So, although the activities, the programme and the content of our face-to-face work may or may not be that different from work with White girls, it is the methods of work with which these activities are carried out that is crucial.

The term 'youth club' occasionally has unacceptable connotations for Asian parents. Clubs are seen to be places where there is smoking, drinking, gambling and dancing and also places where girls and boys mix freely with each other. Although it was found through our contact with parents that sometimes this was the reason for their reluctance to send their daughters to youth clubs, there was another crucial reason which is not acknowledged and this was their fear that their daughters may be victims of attacks on the streets – not only sexual attacks but also racial ones. There has been a rise in the number of street attacks on Asian people and there is a legitimate fear amongst the Asian communities that they are a target for these acts of racist violence. Therefore, the precautions the Asian parents take in not allowing their daughters to venture too far away from their homes in the evenings are necessary precautions determined by real fears. In a situation where Asian parents see hostile forces attempting to alienate their children from them and their cultural traditions it is important to allay their fears. Our findings show that it is essential for parents to be consulted and their trust to be gained. If Asian parents feel that their authority is being questioned and their cultural values are being challenged by unsympathetic outsiders, they are justified in being suspicious of anyone who wants to involve their daughters in activities outside the home. Legitimate activities on premises approved of by parents and organised by women they have come to know and trust have been proved to be acceptable.

Who should do the work?

We believe that there is a fundamental necessity for Asian women to do youth work with Asian girls and young women. There are several reasons for this: initially it is because we share similar linguistic, cultural, religious and social backgrounds; and we are also affected by the racism prevalent in our daily encounters and therefore understand exactly what these experiences feel like.

It is because of this dual experience of belonging to minority groups and the resulting racism that we are better able to understand the girls' experiences. We, too, are caught in the evolutionary processes of political, social and cultural changes taking place within the Black communities and therefore have a much better grasp of 'conflict' as individuals. More importantly, communication between us and the parents is not patronising; we do not, like most White workers, make judgements concerning the norms and values upheld by the girls and their families. This, of course, determines the quality of the relationship that the worker and the family can built up. Being Asian, we see the lifestyles of the girls as valid and we do not hold the typical Western view of Asian family life as being oppressive to girls and young women.

In conclusion, we would emphasise that work with Asian girls and young women requires a different approach, method and conceptualisation of youth work practice. There needs to be acceptance, without having to continuously justify the validity of youth work with young Asian women which is not necessarily club-based. Funding for work with Asian girls must not depend on the extent to which it is problem-centred and crisis-orientated. A variety of different projects such as organising festivals, residential courses, adventure weekends, holiday schemes, day trips, and so on, should be encouraged by provision of adequate funds by the Youth Service. Too often, Asian girls, like other young Black women are totally ignored while funding for work with girls goes to White girls and funding for work with Black youth goes to Black young men. There needs to be greater awareness by the educational and recreational institutions of the need for separate provisions for work with young Asian women. This is the only way forward for Asian young women to develop a confidence and consciousness as young Black women in British society.

Conclusion

The findings outlined above seriously and systematically undermine the theoretical and politically established forms and practices in this field. A serious implication of these findings is the need to re-evaluate existing forms of training for youth work practitioners.

The challenge of anti-racist and anti-sexist youth work practices cannot be ignored. Feminist youth workers' interventions in the field have a sharply focused on the experiences of groups of young women hitherto ignored: work with young Black women, young lesbians, and disabled young women are areas where many of the 'norms' in youth work practice and training have been questioned.

A consideration of the multiple oppressions operating in society not only challenges the assumptions upon which much of the available Youth Service is based but also necessitates a look at the 'crisis' conditions under which the Youth Service is attempting to survive.

Youth work practice cannot be carried out in a vacuum and what is being demanded is the recognition that the oppressive power systems that operate in wider society also operate within the Youth Service itself. Training is an essential part of the service and the reluctance to integrate issues of race, gender and sexuality into the overall framework of youth workers' training courses has serious consequences not only for youth workers but also for the youth they are supposed to be reaching.

In the long run, if these issues are not taken up and serious attempts made to change the fundamental premise and ethos of youth work theory and practice, the youth service will remain irrelevant to the changing needs of young people in society. Ultimately, its inflexibility and inability to change can only be interpreted as its unwillingness to make the space for radical interventions, thus aligning itself with the state's attempts to control and manipulate young people's anger and resistance.

Notes and References

1. See CCCS Race and Politics Group (1982) *The Empire Strikes Back: Race and Racism in 70's Britain* (London: Hutchinson).
2. The research project was carried out jointly with Nadira Mirza and the next section was written jointly with her and first published in *GEN*, Women and Education Group, no. 1, July 1983.
3. See Parmar, (P.) (1981) 'Young Asian Women: A Critique of the Pathological Approach', *Multi-Racial Education*, vol. 9, no.3.

5

The Journey Back

Tuku Mukherjee

This article has been written in close collaboration with Balraj
Purewal. We belong to different generations; our starting points
have been different, and to outsiders we might appear to have
little in common except the colour of our skin; but in our responses
to racism, in our view of Southall and its youth movement we find
ourselves on the same ground – the ground of our culture and our
community, a shared *political* colour.

I qualified as a mature teacher at Avery Hill College in 1969.
At the time there were hundreds of other experienced teachers
from the Indian subcontinent sweating out their aspirations on
factory floors. Yet I was told I had 'made it'; I had been offered
the opportunity to escape from the scrap heap of working in a
bottling factory in east London – I was a recognised teacher with
a DES (Department of Education and Science) number. Yet even
then I realised that a Black man only made it on White society's
terms. My new teacher friends argued that I should project the
right image, act as an ambassador and work for 'harmony and
understanding' in areas where 'immigrants' had not yet settled.
My experience of teacher training college had been one of profound
shock. Not the 'culture shock' that sociologists tell us we are
suffering from, but a sense of disappointment and outrage that
this sanctuary of White liberal culture, with its proclaimed values
of tolerance and humanity, should have been so profoundly racist.
It was a more subtle racism than the insults and humiliations I had
encountered as I roamed from low paid job to low paid job; it
was a racism of silent collusion and polite denial; very English,
very middle-class. What was painful about the experience was the
recognition that the liberal racism of the education system was

211

actually more of a threat to my identity than the popular racism of the shop floor.

Yet to have grown up as an Indian and a Bengali Hindu was already to be equipped with the knowledge that the external view imposed on us by others and the inner meaning of our lives are two different things. Our personal development is marked into ceremonial stages of a spiritual journey accompanied by the continuous lullaby of 'Aum.'[1] It teaches us a compassionate but critical view of life which does not allow external events and institutions to interfere with our fundamental commitments and goals. To remain faithful to these inner strengths of our culture is to have the power to resist even the most insidious forms of racism. Indeed, the experience of victimisation and oppression can actually liberate us from the external position of isolation and marginality to which we are officially condemned. As Shivaji[2] suggests, it can set us on the road back to 'our conscience and our collectives'. Already, before I had left college, I had decided to begin that journey: I decided I would teach in Southall, because Southall was, and still is, a home from home to me. And there I met Balraj.

Balraj never had to make that journey, or undergo its emotional upheavals. He had always been a part of the collective, at home in its linguistic, cultural and social space, which has been carved out of the cold, decaying heartlands of industrial Britain. His early experiences were of racism in its most brutal physical form. As a kid he faced threats day in, day out, inside and out of school, while teachers stood by and watched. The experience toughened him, strengthened his roots, enabled him to teach me, his 'elder', how to face up to my race and class location. For those of us who have 'made it' can never escape the reality of colour, however hard we try to pretend we are other.

But the reality of Southall is not just the reality of colour. We are not just an undifferentiated patch of brown or black on the 'multi-ethnic' maps which the race relations industry spends so much time and money drawing up. Our solidarities are based on a common struggle against racism in which the dynamics of caste still remain central. The dominant group in Southall are Jats: the Jat leadership has organised the political, economic and religious life of the community for over four decades, yet within this, there is both a horizontal and vertical chain of communication; every group in Southall, and there are nine, has retained its distinctive linguistic and cultural affiliations. These autonomous spaces are linked into a whole network of shared activities, yet at the same time each of the minority groups has free and equal access to the resources of the Jat power structure. The ways in which caste relations are changing under the impact of the British race and class system are complex, but they are working in the direction of a more open system of power sharing within the community, rather than simply consolidating Jat hegemony. This indeed is one of the conditions that made the emergence of the Southall youth movement possible. But that is to anticipate. My journey back to the collective began much earlier, with my first experience as a teacher in local state schools.

Receiving racism in the classroom

For my first teaching post I was inevitably appointed to a reception class in a secondary modern school. I say *inevitably* because as an 'immigrant teacher' I was regarded as having nothing to offer except a 'race-cast' role teaching English as a second language (ESL) to immigrant pupils. Before starting the job I visited dozens of reception classes and found to my horror that the position of 'immigrant pupils' was identical to that of their parents in the labour market – at the bottom of the scrap heap. The classes were educational ghettoes based on colour. The pupils were reduced to mere shadows; silent and withdrawn, they communicated only a sense of rejection and hopelessness. One such pupil wrote, 'In this school there is a Reception Class. It is for those who come from other countries and do not know much English. I felt very sad and lonely in the class. I do not take any subject except English. It is boring to stay in the same room studying the same subject all the time.'

The cultural assassination of the Black child took place as soon as he or she arrived at the school gates. Implicitly or explicitly the child was instructed to leave his or her identity at home 'where it belonged' in exchange for a segregated existence as a fourth-rate pupil. As one headmaster put it to me, without being aware of any contradiction, 'These children are with us socially, but kept apart in normal schooling'.

The emphasis on the inculcation of Standard English and its

grammars of literacy as a central aim of the school's 'civilising mission' provided much of the rationale for this cultural racism, just as it had previously been used to discriminate against White working-class children. But the fact is that despite all the resources that have been poured into ESL, it has failed to achieve its stated objectives. The reasons are not hard to find. Research has shown that a threshold knowledge of the mother tongue is an essential precondition of any second language acquisition. Black childrens' experience of rejection, the denial of identity, the fetishism of English literacy, have all served to mobilise their resistance against the dominant language, and against those who teach it.

As an 'immigrant teacher' I cannot honestly remember a day free from polite confrontation with the liberal racism of my colleagues in the staffroom. My requests to have pupils transferred out of reception classes and back into mainstream schooling were always turned down by the heads of departments with a smile and the offer of a cup of tea. But nor can I remember a day when I didn't have to accompany the children to the bus stop to protect them against the constant threat of physical attacks. As they entered or left the school these children all too clearly wore a colour-coded badge which spelt out the indelible message: 'We come as outsiders, we remain outsiders, and we will go back as outsiders'.[3]

ESL teaching was, and still is, premised on an assimilationist model: its declared aim is to 'wean' the Black child from its home environment. Note the use of the term 'wean'. It is meant to suggest a natural process of human development rather than what is really taking place – the imposition of an unnatural development which distorts the Black child's cultural identity.

The strategy of educational assimilation was first spelt out by Lord Boyle; a liberal of high principles, he gave institutional racism a 'human face' – the face of the 'problem Black pupil'; in a notorious circular he wrote:

> As the proportion of immigrant children increases, the problem will become more difficult to solve, and the chance of assimilation more remote . . . up to a fifth of immigrant children in any group fit in with reasonable ease . . . but if the proportion goes over one third . . . serious strains emerge. It is therefore desirable that the catchment areas of schools should,

whenever possible, be arranged to avoid concentrations of immigrant children.

Where this proves impracticable simply because schools serve an area which is largely occupied by immigrants, every effort should be made to disperse the immigrant children round a greater number of schools.

He went on to suggest that the process of assimilation and absorption:

Can be helped if the parents of non-immigrant children can see that practical measures have been taken to deal with the problems in the schools and the progress of their [own] children is not being restricted by undue preoccupation of the teaching staff with the linguistic and other difficulties of immigrant children.[4]

'Boyle's law' of dispersal created the ideological framework of most subsequent educational policy and practice. Within it the 'immigrant child' is constructed as the 'enemy within': to be civilised, corrected and controlled. In this way the 'problem Black child' becomes both the cause and effect of racist schooling. The measures which have been taken to deal with the Black presence in schools have alienated Black pupils to the point where they move into open revolt against the system, reaffirming everything which is denied about their culture and community in the classroom. But in the eyes of White teachers this only serves to confirm 'Boyle's law', in locating the problem 'in' the Black child. It is a self-fulfilling prophecy, but one whose dynamics are exclusively located in the apparatus of racism itself.

Just as the debate about the 'special problems' of the 'inner-city child' served to deflect attention from the way class inequalities are reproduced in British society, so the debate about the delinquent or educationally subnormal (ESN) Black child served to deflect the teaching profession from examining its own racist attitudes and practices. Here is a classic example of liberal deflection at work, from a headteacher's memorandum concerning the 'race relations' in her school in Acton:

At present the sense of grievance doesn't get past angry

outbursts – the black adult leadership is not present, at least in Acton, to organise and channel the pupils hunger, curiosity and aggression in positive ways. Consequently, a lot of steam is let off in aggressive behaviour at school, showy, proudful confrontation with members of staff who they feel are unsympathetic. Obviously necessary, though negative, when there are no positive ways of expressing your self-identity.

She goes on to suggest:

I would have thought that liaison with the right kind of WI [West Indian] adult and parents is essential – and often their colonial mentality is a terrifying and depressing stumbling block for their children.

Here the 'problem' is not just located in the Black child, but in the Black parent as well. By implication a whole pathology of the Afro-Caribbean family is invoked, as is a culture conflict model of relations between the generations. As a result, the issue of White racism, whether institutional or personal is never confronted. For to do so would involve exploding the self-image of the white teacher as a caring professional treating all pupils equally 'irrespective of class, colour or creed'.

Yet the simple fact is, it is just not possible for White teachers to escape the effect of their own ethnocentric upbringing and education, any more than they can escape the wider legacies of racism. What they learn, however, are subtle techniques for dissociating themselves from the real 'enemy within'. Racism is somehow always 'out there' in the National Front, or in White pupils, but never, never in themselves, or in the structures of schooling.

Recently the teaching profession has looked towards the confused concept of multi-cultural education as offering a way out of their frozen predicament. For a minority this represents a genuine attempt to confront the depth of their involvement in reproducing racism. But for many more it is simply another educational bandwagon to climb on to, to safeguard jobs or promotion in these increasingly hard times. For others it is a meaningless third-rate concept which does nothing to get at the roots of the problem. Is it any coincidence that multi-cultural programmes are concentrated in schools with a large Black presence? I have never heard of any such programme being developed in all-White schools, or in the Conservative shires. 'No Blacks – no problem' still seems to be the assumption, yet it is precisely in these schools and these areas where racism is most 'respectably' entrenched. And is it any coincidence that the new 'positive' image of Asian or Afro-Caribbean life which multi-culturalism is supposed to project, presents a picture of us frozen in the colonial past, as if nothing had been changed by our struggles in Britain over the last three decades? The implicit message is that racism is a thing of the past, something to do with the bad old days of Empire, and that now we are living in more enlightened times. The liberal myth of progress is powerfully enshrined in multi-culturalism, perhaps its last refuge against 'the fire next time'.

The position of the Black teacher in all this is fraught with difficulty. Often a token presence, confined to marginal positions in the educational power structure, fighting a constant battle for survival, and in permanent danger of losing credibility in the eyes of Black youth, many teachers internalise their oppression and become 'coconuts' – brown on the outside and white inside. Very few are able to build a springboard for collective action by affiliating with their community and its young people. Yet, as I soon found out, this was indeed the only way to survive.

The youth club as an offensive weapon

In 1972 I began working at the Indian Youth Club in Southall. The club had been started in 1964 by two Asian adults, but was now 'run' by the Youth Service. I first met Balraj and his friends as members of the club and by the time I left, four years later, they were ready to take over from me as youth leaders.

The history of the club is one of structured neglect and paternalistic assistance from the Youth Service on one side; and on the other, the developing political consciousness of the membership and its eventual emergence as a new source of leadership in the community.

The only resources we had were access to a hall, two classrooms, one table tennis table and an alcoholic caretaker. To begin with the club was open twice a week, Mondays and Fridays. In fact, it would have been quite impossible to run the club at all without the wholehearted co-operation of the so called 'alienated' Black youth who used it. Music, dancing, politics and football were their main areas of interest and concern. The music and dance group pooled their own resources and staged public shows to raise money to buy proper instruments. Without the music, the Bhangra dance group, the down-to-earth humour and the political debate I don't think we could possibly have continued.

At the club, schools, teachers and their attitudes were constantly under discussion by the members. It was a revelation to realise the sharpness of their perception – they could pinpoint with precision where individual teachers stood, not only on the issue of race, but on a whole range of moral and political questions. And remember that by 'normal' standards, these young people were 'failures' and 'delinquents'. I still see a lot of them today and marvel at how so many of them have come through relatively unscathed from their experiences of discrimination and frustration. The scars are still there, but they have learnt to laugh at their oppressors; the anger is still there, but it has been given a creative political thrust. This would not have been possible without the support of the community, and more specifically that of their peers. The club itself provided a springboard for their development, nothing more and nothing less.

A further revelation was the effect of changing my role from that of teacher to youth worker. This demanded the formation of quite a different relationship with the young people based on trust, friendship and the attitude brought to running the club. The youth worker's position is based on personal authority which comes from mutual respect, whereas the teacher operates through professional dictate backed by the power of the state.

It is perhaps significant, then, that although both my assistant and the club chairman were White, this did not occasion any resentment amongst the membership. There is no doubt that initially both these individuals were very apprehensive, as White people usually are on Black territory, yet within weeks their fears had been dissolved, and they often ran the Club in my absence without any confrontation or 'trouble'. In one club discussion my assistant actually voiced his amazement at the degree of acceptance, given the disillusionment of our membership with White teachers. One of our members gently pointed out to him that his initial fear was intrinsic to himself, and his culture, not to the real environment of Southall.

In fact, we rarely had White visitors, and the few that did come were inevitably accompanied by a Black person to show him or her around. In all my years as a youth leader in Southall, I never had one White teacher drop in for a chat or to offer help, but I feel that this was only the personal aspect of a more official policy of structured indifference and neglect by the youth service. We were desperate for funds, and the fact was that in an area of 30 000 Asians, we were the *only* place for young people to meet. It seemed we had a legitimate claim on public funds, and I wrote to Mr A. D. Mathews, Immigrant Adviser, in the following terms:

> The Indian Youth Club is open only twice a week and the equipment available is limited because of finance and lack of storage facilities. I doubt, if we could have kept the Club open without financial assistance of the Indian Workers' Association . . . At this time the community in Southall is facing a critical period with the Youth. Resources have been poured into the schools but there has been little provision for the children out of school hours or after school leaving age. What we in fact need is a permanent site for the Youth Club with a full time leader and much greater resources . . . There are two areas, which I see as particular pressure points . . . drinking is becoming an increasing problem among the youth, the result of frustration in schools, work and social life. There is also severe friction between the Police and the young.

The response was an agreement to waive letting charges. No offer of a capital grant for equipment was ever forthcoming. You may well ask why we should pay a letting charge in the first instance. Why should the local state, in a relatively rich borough like Ealing, charge the community for the use of such facilities? Why, for example, should we pay thousands of pounds to hire classrooms in which to learn our own mother tongue? It is a clear case of double taxation and indicates in my view, the way the argument about scarce resources supports practices of youth provision which institutionalise racism.

Throughout the 1970s the debate about youth facilities in Southall (or rather the lack of them) continued, on and off the street. Political parties came and went with their manifestoes aiming at nothing more than Black votes. Staff from local schools regularly went away for weekend conferences to discuss 'Boyle's law', and what to do about the 'problem Black child'. Yet in their midst, on the streets of Southall a new leadership was emerging, and a new Black community was being born. Just as Amritsa became a cradle of freedom fighters as a result of the Jaliwana Bagh massacre, so in Southall, it was the murder of Gurdip Singh Chaggar on 4 June 1976 which triggered off the Sikh 'marcha'[5] against White racism and the National Front (NF). The youth of Southall were once more in the front line of all the struggles of all the 'wretched of the earth'.

The Southall Youth Movement

The death of Chaggar was not only a great tragedy for all those who knew him, it also brought home to everyone in the community the brutal reality of racism, and the futility of hoping that 'time' or 'reason' would diminish its effects. It crystallised too the political chasm that had grown up between the elders and the younger generation, between a strategy of negotiation and one of open revolt. As a collective wave of anger swept our youth on to the streets, the issue for those among the elders who retained any credibility, was not how to diffuse or contain it, but how it could be organised politically in a way that did not lead to an immediate escalation of both police and NF violence against us.

In fact, it was the young people themselves who solved the problem. They realised that any immediate physical counter-attacks would only provoke reprisals against isolated individuals in the community. They discovered for themselves the old slogan 'don't mourn, organise', and they discovered it in practice. The founding of the Southall Youth Movement was the result of a deliberate decision to build upon the ashes of Chaggar: a single death lead to a collective rebirth.

Almost overnight, before it had had a chance to consider its first move, the SYM was inundated with liberal promises of help, socialist expressions of solidarity and ingratiating advances from the mass media. All these agencies which had for so many years ignored the situation in Southall, were now suddenly falling over

backwards to get their feet in the SYM door. Yes, they all came –
the Community Relations Council, the local authorities, the so-
called 'experts'. Anything and everything was promised, but still
nothing was delivered.

The emergence of SYM revealed all too clearly the marginality
and impotence of the liberal institutions, both Black and White,
created by the state to act as buffer organisations. They set
out to neutralise the leadership of the revolt by softening our
demands, to make them more acceptable to funding agencies such
as the Community Relations Commission and the Commission
for Racial Equality; and they set themselves up as spokesmen
and women of the movement to the 'outside world' (for example,
the media and the government), building their little empires while
installing the dynamics of dependancy in the heart of SYM. Over
the years their main objectives have been to retain control of the
situation, and to emerge as negotiators between 'youth revolt' and
White agencies of control. The National Association of Asian
Youth and the CRC, were prime examples of the apparatus created
by the state, to house a class of political middle-men and to
sabotage the aspirations of youth by activating the policy of 'divide
and rule'. The CRC, then headed by The Honourable Mark
Bonham Carter, totally colluded, implicitly and explicitly, with
this policy. We quote from correspondence to support our theory
of duplicity: following a meeting between Mark Bonham Carter
and the young people of Southall in June 1976, help was promised
and H. S. Gill, then President of SYM, wrote to the Chairman of
the CRC on 27 October 1976 to this effect:

> Although most local community organisations have refused to
> recognise the need of Asian young people for a long time, they
> appear to be more interested in maintaining the status quo or
> would like to control the resources which might be available for
> youth provision in this area.

He went on to request funds, 'to set up a project, independent of
community organisations . . . it is anticipated that over a period
of time, youth would be able to define their needs and carry out
research into the problems, thus taking positive action'. The CRC's
collusion with the Home Office becomes agonisingly clear when

we consider Mary Lyons' response of 19 October 1977 – a year later, and not to Gill but to Ravi Jain, of the National Association of Indian Youth (NAIY), about the application of Southall Youth Movement:

> As you know, an application addressed to the Self-Help fund by SYM in the CRC's lifetime was turned down by the CRC and later by CRE because the project did not meet the criteria for funding from that scheme. If and when a Self-Help fund is made available for projects with young people of Asian origin then the SYM would be eligible for consideration, but there is no indication as yet that the Home Office will establish such a fund.

The letter is remarkable in that it states categorically the Home Office policy to divide and rule between 'Black' and 'Asians', to stage-manage a battle for resources between different organisations in the community, a kind of *de facto* 'two nations' policy towards ethnic groups. The Southall Youth Movement learnt with bitterness, but no false regret, that their initiative was their own. It was up to them to transform their needs into reality. Perhaps it is fortunate that they learnt this lesson so early on, because out of that recognition came the desire and the will to develop their own expertise, organisational skills and political awareness. As Balraj put it, 'In a multi-racist society, we have nothing to lose. We have taken on board the fact that we are under seige, and our only security is our understanding and acknowledgement of what it means to be Black. Any other position would be a pathological escape from realism.'

The SYM has succeeded in getting the young together, in constructing a collective identity, and has learnt how to deal with powerful organisations without being co-opted or developing the fatal dependency syndrome. The 'hooligans' of 1976 have come a long way and are the protectors of the whole community today: they are no longer asking for handouts, they are making positive demands. In the process the political distance between the elders and the young has closed and that is precisely why the 'old guard' refused to condemn SYM when its rank and file took to the streets and burnt out the Hamborough Tavern in July 1981 as retaliation against the territorial encroachment of NF skinheads.

It is hardly surprising that the street has been appropriated by our youth and transformed into a political institution. It is for them at once the privileged space of confrontation with racism, and of a relative autonomy within their own community from which they can defend its very existence. There have, of course, been young people who have stayed away from the street, and SYM. We admit frankly that at present both are male-dominated, but this is something that will, in time, change. More seriously, there are those who could provide leadership but who stay away because they believe that their educational attainments will offer them a way out. They have achieved their 'O' and 'A' Levels but learn that they are Blacks a little too late. Their sense of dislocation is often directly bound up with the fact that they did not have the institution of the street to teach them their real place in British society. Yet even here, many are beginning to make the long journey back to their collective, as their onward and upward thrust comes up against a stone wall of White rejection despite their acceptable appearances, fluency of speech and academic qualifications.

SYM's greatest asset is partly its financial independence but more sharply its policy of exclusion of 'middle men or women' of whatever colour, so that the central issue of combating racism remains at the core of its thinking. In the process, it has blown the myth that the Asians are timid, passive and unable to react to racist confrontation. The membership, as we see them, are not caught up 'between cultures' as so many writers, both Black and White, would like us to believe. This became abundantly clear to us when we ran a series of seminars with members in 1982, on relevant issues such as Black consciousness, 'between cultures' and the concept of a Sikh school in Southall. The age range of those attending was between fourteen and thirty. They clearly acknowledged that they were Black – Black was their *political* colour – the colour of the oppressed; and that it represented the experience and structural position of Black people in Britain. On the second question, they were firmly convinced that they were not caught between cultures. They knew they were Sikhs – what they didn't know clearly was what Sikhism is about. They maintained that people, who were caught 'between cultures' were those who had gone through a process of denial of their own culture and identity, and had faced total rejection bhy the dominant culture.

There is no doubt that in Southall *de facto* political power has shifted towards the young. Their dilemma is what, apart from a culture of revolt, they are going to transmit to their children. They know where they are and where they have come from, but they still need to know the content of the history they carry on their backs. In fact, the experience of SYM is likely to be historicised by its own struggles. For in the wider context, Southall has emerged as not just another Black community but as the sacred centre of the Khalsa Sikh. A historical legacy of struggle rooted in the plains of the Punjab and in the Sikh psyche is being reclaimed as the birthright of a new generation. As Balraj said to me in 1971 – prophetically, in the light of what was to follow: 'I'm a Jat. I reckon the amount of racial violence I've seen in school nobody will ever realise in their lifetime. And as I'm a Jat Sikh I feel we must learn how to organise, how to survive and even more important how to retaliate.'

I am optimistic that the new alignments in the power structure of Southall will strengthen our resistance against all the racist forces which Thatcherism has co-ordinated against us. The reasons for Britain's decline are complex, but at the heart of them is the refusal to recognise the consequences of Empire and its decline. As Martin Wiener has put it, 'a society which had overinvested in an Empire, and surrounded itself with the increasingly shabby remnants of its inheritance, could not bring itself, at a moment of crisis, to surrender its memories or alter the antique pattern of its life.[6] Until White people learn to change the antique patterns of race discrimination which still govern their society, the uprisings of Black youth will continue to interrupt their historical daydream. The message of our youth to these people speaks through their actions: we are the future. Change because you have to, not because of us.

Notes and references

1. 'Aum' means 'consciousness' in Sanskrit.
2. 'Shivaji' is a prefix used to denote respect and affection.
3. See my article in *New Society* 4 April 1974.
4. Department of Education and Science (DES) *The Education of Immigrants*, Circular 7/65 to local authorities, June 1965.

5. 'Marcha' in Punjabi means fight and resistance.
6. See M. Wiener (1981), *English Culture and the Decline of the Industrial Spirit* (Cambridge University Press).

6

Southall Youth: An Old-Fashioned Story

Harwant S. Bains

My intention is to give an inside view of a particular community called Southall, famous to outsiders for its tandooris, its saris, its multi-cultural organisations and its riots. I have lived here all my life. All my life is rooted here. Not much in the way of detachment. The only method of this piece is based on trying to understand that experience.

I have been told many times, by elders who should know better, that there are certain things about the Black communities which we must conceal, that must not be talked about, because to reveal them would be to fuel the fires of racism and state oppression. We must close ranks at whatever cost.

But what we keep hidden from 'Whitey' we also conceal from ourselves. These facts about *ourselves* must be faced. Consciousness cannot be raised on the basis of ignorance. We cannot divorce our reality from the way we ourselves represent it, and neither can we be allowed to be governed by the reactions of White society. Whatever is there to be seen must also be said, something realised more than two decades ago, by Frantz Fanon, amongst others. For we are *not yet* in the true conditions of solidarity and struggle. Instead, a mythology has been created, a mythology of militancy with which few Black people can identify because it strikes no chord in their everyday experience.

So my aim here is to confront the facts as I see them about Southall, its youth and its politics. I will look at some of the basic elements involved in growing up in Southall – the practical ideology of the parents, the function of State schooling, the forms of community – and try to assess some of the factors of continuity and change.

The vast majority of Asians living in Southall have their origins in the Punjab, and arrived in England over the last two decades seeking better lives amidst the 'affluent society'. The priority governing their lives was the need to 'make good', to build homes, found households, send money back to relatives. All these things represent the acquisition of status, but a status which is earned through hard work, preferably on a self-employed basis. Now, of course, these aims are far from unique to Punjabis or Asians! They have formed the core aspirations of almost every immigrant group into so-called advanced industrial nations – they are at the heart of the Great American Dream. But there is also a specifically Punjabi inflection to the work-and-status ethic, which has to be understood in historical context.

After the annexation of the Punjab, the Sikhs decided to ally themselves with their new British masters, to form something like a subaltern ruling class. The Punjab became the military and administrative centre of the Raj, and under that 'sponsorship' its economy flourished too. The Punjabi education system developed an especially close relationship with the sahib's world view. The legacy of that colonial history is still active – indeed it continues to comprise our 'birthright'. In the India of today the Punjab is still the most prosperous state, and the majority of Sikhs continue to see the fruits of their labour in terms of capital. This entrepreneurial drive, far from being hostile to Sikh nationalism, simply fuels it and gives it a politically conservative direction. The best example of this is the movement for Khalistan (a separate state for Sikhs) which peppers its chauvinistic rhetoric with the occasional attack on a Hindu temple. But it is no less present in the great emphasis given to achieving qualifications through the antiquated examination system, a system which personifies the Punjabi code of status and its association with certain bourgeois professions such as medicine or the law. As a result, every blue-blooded mother's son of any Punjabi family is viewed as a potential doctor!

Southall presents two contradictory faces. From one viewpoint it is a working-class community facing massive racial discrimination in the labour market; yet if we take a second and harder look we see a traditionalistic Punjabi community which is clinging with ever greater desperation to an outlook more reminiscent of pre-independence India than the present day. It is thus far more realistic to contextualise the labour of Southall people and the militancy which this has occasionally thrown up in terms of traditional Punjabi values of work and status than in terms of some (Western) Marxist notion of class consciousness.

For example, 'It was the Jat [tiller] caste who, in *mortal fear of becoming landless* [my italics], gambled their last and came to Britain selling land, jewellery, cattle or other family possessions, even borrowing, in order to raise the 4000 rupees needed for the journey'.

Viewed objectively, the transition was from peasantry to proletariat, but in ideological terms the change was not half as radical or nearly as clear cut. The Jats came to Britain to earn money to send home to enhance their family status. It was not so much a matter of seeking a new way of life as of finding new means of wealth to support the old one.

Paradoxically, it was their peasant work ethic (where slogging for 60 hours a week is considered quite normal), coupled with their traditional *petit bourgeois* orientation which made Punjabis so readily exploitable as a subproletariat. From the very first the new arrivals were brutally exploited by the infamous Woolfe's Rubber Company and two local bakeries.

At first – during the 1950s – it was the men who came alone to seek out work; later they were to send for their families. Inevitably, in the face of White indifference and hostility (also from the trade unions), and the fact that about 45 per cent of them spoke no English, the Punjabis stuck together, forming their own web of mutual aid and trust. By 1957, the more radical amongst them had formed the Indian Workers Association, and in 1959 the local Gurdwara threw open its doors to the faithful. During the 1950s, as the families of the male workers arrived, Asian women also began to enter the hungry job market.

Yet the experience of these men and women in the workplace does not seem to have altered their basic outlook on life. It has not, for example, led them to identify with the rest of the Black community, or the White working class, mainly because both are regarded as 'low status' in the British context. In striving for economic success, the majority of Punjabis are also seeking economic assimilation – they wish to become an integral, if subaltern, fraction of British capital. Some plough their hard-earned cash back into business investments in Southall, while many more strive to join the ranks of this local élite, for it is the successful small businessman who continues to symbolise what being in this country is all about. Others dream of returning home, building big houses and retiring in comfort, and just enough people have succeeded in doing just this to spur the rest on to redouble their efforts.

Now this economic motivation does not in itself imply a desire for *cultural* assimilation, but it does nevertheless support specific ideological effects. It is a painful fact that many of the more educated Punjabis are now strongly identifying with the White professional classes, adopting their accents, their mannerisms, even their 'liberal attitudes'. Another uncomfortable fact is that a fair skin continues to be seen as a desirable (if unrealisable) attribute by many Punjabi women. Many Punjabis harbour a fatalism about their present position in British society, and tend to take a rather cynical attitude towards political action as a means of improving it. Indeed, if the Conservative Party was not seen as being racist, large numbers of Asians would probably be paid-up members. Instead, many of the local business élite have shifted their allegiance to the Alliance as the 'natural party of the middle class'. As for the Labour Party, it has made an all-too-inactive and awkward partner for Asian aspirations.

All this places the majority of Southall people a long way away from the outlook of the 'militants'. The struggle for a 'better future' is all the less likely to be connected to challenging the status quo because it is channelled into gaining a good education for one's children. This 'educationalism' gives a powerful impetus to the more conservative forces in the community, not least amongst the youth.

Schooling

The general orientation of Punjabi culture has the most definite consequences for attitudes to state schooling in Southall amongst both parents and youth. Most parents regard their children as the means whereby the status of the entire family can be raised. And many see the success of their children at school as the key to improved family status. As we will see, many young Asians take a similarly instrumental view of education, though not always for the same reasons; indeed, academic success for some may be a way of *resisting* family pressures.

Now, of course, state schools, whether they be in Southall or anywhere else, exist primarily to reproduce existing relations of cultural domination and subordination, whether based on class, ethnicity, gender or generation. Much has been written about how this is achieved through a 'hidden curriculum', which defines what counts as legitimate knowledge in the classroom. It has been argued that the ethnocentric premises of this curriculum precipitate a conflict with the different cultural perspectives of children from immigrant communities. But in Southall schools this conflict is not even allowed to surface. We grow up knowing history, geography, chemistry, physics, English literature, just as they are known by millions of white pupils who daily go through the very same motions. If Asian pupils do not, on the whole, question all this, it is because we are denied access to alternative methodologies with which to compare these 'gospel truths'.

Free speech or thought does not arise as an issue in the majority of schools. If it is raised, if Asian pupils speak out against the school regime, the arbitrary power of teachers, the absence of the most basic democratic rights or the personal and institutional racism, they are simply defined and dealt with as a disciplinary problem, a 'disruptive influence'. Through a variety of threats and sanctions (bad reports, detentions, the cane, head of year interviews, and so on) the dissenters are marginalised and coerced into silence.

A school I worked at in Southall is a good example of how these political pressures operate. Recently the sixth form approached the headmaster with the idea for a new magazine, new in the sense that it would not be subject to vetting by the staff, even though they would be given the right to reply. The proposal was greeted by outright rejection, and no reason was given. Meanwhile, certain members of the sixth form regarded as 'political activists' were singled out for special treatment – drawn aside for 'little talks' in which it was suggested that they were jeopardising their university chances, and wasn't it more 'sensible' to concentrate on their school work and leave the running of the school to the teachers!

A similar thing happened to me a few years ago when, along with some friends, I was told that if we did not stop circulating the magazine we had started, dealing with local youth issues, we had better leave the sixth form and 'find a school better suited to our tastes'. A visit by the very popular singer, Cliff Richard, to the school caused another furore. There, in a hall packed with little brown faces from faraway places, 'our Cliff' sang gospel songs and told the godless youngsters how the only possible path to Salvation was through Jesus Christ Our Lord, Amen. The sixth formers immediately launched a protest petition, which quickly gained support, only to fizzle out just as quickly when the protestors were reminded by a few thoughtful teachers that university references were soon to be written.

The significant fact is that, in a community which is often regarded as highly politicised, student action in Southall schools is virtually non-existent. This cannot simply be put down to the repressive policy of the teachers. It has just as much to do with the absence of support from parents and the material stake which many Asian youth have in gaining academic credentials. Here there are two main groups – the so-called achievers, who dominate the top forms, are entered for 'O' Levels and usually stay on to do 'As' with sights set on university; and the triers, who don't do well in terms of academic criteria, but nevertheless stay on to collect as many 'Os' as they can muster, and then hammer away half-heartedly at their 'As' as a means of placating parents and postponing entry into the labour (boys) or marriage (girls) markets. A significant proportion of these groups are science-orientated – as reflected in the pattern of fourth-year options. Again, this is far more marked amongst the boys and reflects the enormous parental emphasis on science as a high-status career, with medicine as the pinnacle.

Not much in the way of militancy can be expected from either of these groups. They may not like the intellectual diet they are fed, but they know on which side their bread is buttered and their chief concern is passing exams. Not so the 'Divs' (slang for 'dimwit' or troublemaker). In the teachers' view the Divs exist not to be taught but to be controlled. Since they reject the academic fruits of education and prefer to spend their schooldays immersed in socialising with their friends, the Divs pose a disciplinary problem. Yet, essentially, all they are demanding is the right to be left alone; they present no direct challenge to the social and political perspectives of the school. Their involvement in street culture has made them ready recruits for Southall's community politics, but by the same token the school itself is not regarded as an important terrain of struggle.

Punjabi girls and boys are, of course, brought up with very different pressures and expectations surrounding them. Boys are expected to go out into the world, to build up family status, bring in money and support families. Consequently, their view of schooling is highly instrumental – it is just a means of earning credentials to be cashed into good jobs. Girls, in contrast, are still largely viewed in economically inactive terms. Their primary role is to maintain the household, first while with their parents and later for their husband. Girls consequently tend to view staying on at school as a means of holding some of these pressures in abeyance. Exam successes become symbols of independence, a means of establishing an existence outside the all-consuming home life. Girls are much more acutely aware of the double standards operated both within their own families and within the school. But equally their dependence on academic success as a way of sustaining some critical distance from Punjabi family ideology makes them fearful of 'burning their boats' by challenging the school regime as well.

By now some readers may be nodding their heads sagely and muttering the dreaded words 'culture conflict' under their breath. Unfortunately for them, no such thing exists. First of all I have suggested that so-called 'traditional' Punjabi education was strongly permeated by the 'values' of our 'British masters', the same class which imprinted its civilising mission on forms of state schooling for the working classes in Britain. The measurement of success in terms of examinations, and the equation of this with occupational status, is the same in both systems. What *is* different, and what has only recently lost the capacity to shock Asians, is the depth and intensity of racism in British schools. As for the conflicts which sometimes arise around arranged marriages, let me point out again that this has nothing to do with a clash between Western and Indian culture. There is a tradition of romantic love in Indian literature which pre-dates Arthurian legends and is up to every trick in Mills and Boon book! What *is* happening is that the system of arranged marriage is increasingly losing its functionality as a means of reproducing our culture and community, and this inevitably, if temporarily, creates tension between parents and children.

If young people themselves rarely experience their predicaments in terms of a conflict between the cultures of family and school, their parents and elders are much more likely to do so and they may indeed come to see the school as imposing Western values and eroding traditional ones. This is a view particularly prevalent amongst the more conservative Sikh families in Southall, and recently gave rise to an attempt by the Gurdwara to start a Khalsa school which would provide children with a better all-round education while maintaining strong discipline. The support for this project amongst potential pupils was slight; it did however, say a lot about the quality of growing distrust Asian parents have for teachers within the state system. For a long time our parents were reluctant to interfere in educational matters, believing that teachers, being professionals, should know best how to turn their children into academic successes. When this signally failed to happen, the professional status of the teachers began to be called into question. If the state school came to be seen as such a 'corrupt institution' leading Asian children away from customary paths, it was first and foremost because it was also seen as not helping them pass exams! But here again we can see a double standard in adult responses to educational discrimination. The issue of 'acculturation' is raised primarily in relation to girls' schooling – for girls are to be the 'bearers' of traditions, whereas the issue of academic failure is raised apropos boys – for they alone are supposed to need exams to prosper. Needless to say, this view has not helped Asian parents intervene effectively in educational politics!

Home truths

Contrary to the sociological stereotype of 'the Asian family', young people in Southall experience a wide variety of home situations and forms of parental pressure. This seems partly to depend on the economic position of the family. Poorer families tend to be more traditionalistic in their orientation, whereas those with a higher income and living standards seem to harbour more openly the germs of 'liberalism'. It is a fact that those parents originating from villages in the Punjab tend to be less well educated, to do less well economically in this country, and to exert the greatest pressure on children to follow the 'old ways'. Whereas the more educated parents, usually from the cities, are more willing to trade off their culture for the material benefits which they think the acceptance of their children by White society will bring to the whole family. Consequently, these parents tend to give their children more room for manoeuvre at home.

Both groups, however, share certain common assumptions and values. The first I have already discussed – the belief in a distinctive Punjabi-style work ethic. But this is also connected to a specific attitude to family consumption. The fruits of labour are status-bestowing material goods – cars, TVs, videos, furniture and stereos, for example. But these 'consumer goodies' have a symbolic function in Punjabi culture quite different from that of Western societies; for, above all, these things bring *dharma*, that is, they signify a fulfilment which is primarily spiritual, and has nothing to do with 'keeping up with the Singhs' in material terms. This also affects the way money is used within the family – it is a symbol of hard work, and thus of goodness, and for parents to give their children money is literally to give them love.

In the poorer families, however, parental love is expressed less through money gifts (for obvious reasons!) than through the transmission of a *cultural* capital, comprised of traditional customs, beliefs, clothes, and so on. The parental discipline which enforces acceptance of this legacy is thus regarded as an expression of love. The higher-income families have less need of this device; their children can afford to indulge in the trappings of European culture, in the form of hairstyles, pop records, youth fashions and so on, because this form of consumerism can still be regarded as a symbol of the parents' hard work, of family status, and ultimately of *dharma*.

Now, it is a well-known, if hotly contested, fact that in many Asian families it is the mother who is the most conservative force, the strongest supporter of traditionalism. What makes her so is not just her position in the family but also in the wider social and economic structure of Asian communities. For example, women are far more central to the community grapevine than men, and hence much more vulnerable and sensitive to public disapproval. In economic terms, women's work is far less likely to be unionised than men's, and notwithstanding some notable struggles in which Asian women have taken the leading role, they continue to be marginalised within the power structures of the community. For all these, and other reasons, mothers find it very difficult to take a stand on behalf of their daughters against the restrictions which traditionalism places upon them. Consequently, those girls who have succeeded in striking out for themselves are very few and far between.

Amongst many of my friends, both boys and girls, there is often a yearning to escape from the confines of Southall (where everyone knows everyone else's business) and to embrace the fugitive freedoms of the 'outside world'. But, of course, this 'outside' in reality consists of a racist White society which is hostile to our very existence. Thus for the majority of Southall youth the desire to break away from parental discipline is tempered by the realisation that this is likely to be construed as disowning one's inheritance. To 'leave home' under these circumstances is tantamount to being cast out of the community, to become a pariah in both Black and White society. Perhaps it's not surprising, then, that the majority play it safe and stay within the protective walls of Southall – few venture out of the area, unless it is to visit relatives in other Asian communities. It is, however, out of these defensive, insular forms that the Southall Youth Movement emerged.

Street fighting man?

On 23 April 1979, the National Front invaded Southall under the pretext of holding a meeting at the Town Hall. The ensuing riot can best be described as a spontaneous outburst of collective outrage by the citizenry of Southall directed not just against these racist thugs but against the forces of 'law and order' who were defending their right to preach Fascism on the streets.

The riots have been taken by many on the 'Black Left' as proof of a new-found radicalism within the Asian community. Unfortunately, I think that this involves a convenient misinterpretation of what actually happened.

We must first recognise that for Asians the National Front represents an organised force of violence committed to the destruction of their community through repatriation. This would, of course, mean the destruction of all their hopes, their material aspirations, all that had been so long and so arduously toiled for. To have allowed the NF to enter Southall that day would thus have been tantamount to surrendering the future of Asians in Britain. The shopkeepers decided to close their shops in protest and to stage a peaceful. sit-in on the Town Hall steps. The intervention of the state in such a brutal and overbearing manner was not expected. The dramatic and visible collusion of the British police force with a Fascist organisation was not expected. To have allowed this to happen without reacting would have been tantamount to welcoming the arrival of a police state with open arms. The youth of Southall took to the streets to make sure that this did not happen.

There was thus an alliance between a *bourgeoisie* protecting its material stake in British society and an under-class defending the territorial integrity of the community. As we will see, the terms of this alliance, as well as the organisational forces it represented, meant that the radicalising effects of the April events were minimised. However central the riots were to become to the myths of origin elaborated by the Southall Youth Movement itself, the immediate consequence was to increase the level of political involvement only amongst the minority of youth who were already politically active. The riot of July 1981, when Southall people again took to the streets to defend themselves against a racist onslaught shows a similar pattern in that it had no broader politicising effects. For example, despite the role of the police over the years, 'law and order' continues to be widely respected and upheld, and not only by the elders. Recently Southall police station held a series of open days. They were very well-attended; indeed, more people turned up to view the inside of the fortress than had attended any of the pickets of the same station organised since April 1979. Many came out of curiosity, but it was lost on no one, least of all the police, that the size of the turnout was taken to represent the degree of community support. The conservatism of Punjabi perspectives has not been overturned by the riots, or by the emergence of new organisations such as the Southall Youth Movement. The question is – why?

Co-option, confusion or con-trick?

The SYM was formed in 1976 after the muder of Gurdip Chaggar. It was essentially formed out of a coalition of local street gangs. Commonly referred to as the 'hard nuts' of Southall, they were representative of a marginal underclass quite distinct from the majority of Asian youth in the area. In fact, the relationship of the SYM to the broader community is an interesting one. They support their members against certain pressures of the parent culture – since the membership is based amongst school drop-outs, delinquents, unemployed. Yet they also maintain, or at least do not challenge, the cultural hegemony of the Punjabi work-and-status code, and the traditionalism of the elders. The way that this balancing act operates in practice is illustrated in the SYM's particular style of 'machismo'. This reproduces the patriarchal attitudes towards women to be found amongst male elders throughout the community. Any girl who tries to take an active part in the running of SYM is popularly regarded as 'loose', with the consequences that those who do try to get involved very quickly leave. When the leadership is challenged about its attitudes to women they simply reply that they were brought up that way and they are too old to change! At the same time their street culture supports the symbolic transformation of the Sikh warrior into the modern 'street-fighting man', a 'macho' pose directed as much against the passivity of the older generation as against racist skinheads and the NF.

The success of the SYM is due to what it has come to symbolise – the resistance of the Asian community to racism – rather than any ability to organise or educate local youth. The role of the SYM in the riots of 1979 and 1981 confirms this impression. These events, and the media attention they generated, enabled the SYM to establish itself with a mystique of popular grass roots appeal, and subsequently to gain major financial support from the state. Yet the actual membership of the organisation hardly grew, nor did the scope of its activities. There were almost no attempts to appeal to a wider base – for example, by relating to school students, or organising around schools issues. The interests of young women have, of course, continued to be massively ignored. As for protecting the community against racist attacks, there has been no concerted SYM action on the notorious Golflinks Estate, which harbours the greatest concentration of NF skinheads, and where Asian residents are frequently attacked. What has made Southall safe is the size and population density of the area *plus* the deterrent threat of SYM retaliation for any racist attack; yet at its boundaries the community remains vulnerable.

There are four main organisations which dominate Southall's political arena – the Indian Workers' Association (IWA), the National Association of Asian Youth (NAAY), the Ealing Community Relations Council (ECRC), and, most famously, the Southall Youth Movement (SYM). Some cynics have said that these organisations are rather better known to the media than they are to the people of Southall! Certainly their fratricidal disputes and internal wrangling can seem to many people as remote as those of the Kremlin!

Undoubtedly these conflicts have weakened the effectiveness of the organisations and alienated many young people from them. At times it looks as if the conspiracy theorists have got it right and that the state is deliberately pursuing a policy of 'divide and rule'. Consider this quote from Sir George Young:

> We've got to back the good guys, the sensible, moderate leaders of ethnic groups. If they are seen to deliver, to get financial support from central government for urban projects, then that reinforces their standing and credibility in the community. If they don't deliver, people will turn to the militants.

However, the real conflict is not between the moderates and the militants, but between rival groups of militants, each claiming to be the authentic voice of Southall's non-existent radicalised masses. It often seems that principles are up for sale in the marketplace of local politics, when those who bellow loudest or most eloquently about 'Black struggle' push themselves to the front of the queue for juicy state hand-outs, while 'all' the state asks for in return is a foot in the community's back door. In fact, the arguments are not about principles or personalities as such – they are struggles about crude power and crude cash. How has all this affected the development of Southall's community politics? Lets look at the case of the SYM.

The limitations of SYM's perspectives were in part those of its leadership and their social formation. These were the original young immigrants who had to face English racism in its most brutal and oppressive forms from the first day of their arrival in this country. This generation had real living roots in their motherland and the mother tongue and their outlook and rhetoric reflect all this. They had not experienced the subtleties of growing up in a multi-racist society and their concerns and priorities were increasingly at variance with the youth they claimed to represent.

More recently, however, the rule of the 'old guard' has been challenged. In January 1984 the old management committee of SYM was replaced *en bloc* by a newly-elected one. This election was only called because the Greater London Council (GLC) and the Commission for Racial Equality both suspended their grants pending the result of a proper democratic vote. In the event, only 250 voted out of a total membership of 900. Even this was something of a triumph, because in the previous two years membership had fallen as low as fifty. The membership drive was led by a reform group of about eight young people, including women – who previously had had no involvement with the organisation – and they argued passionately that a total overhaul of SYMs structure was now required. In particular this group campaigned for election on a platform of women's rights and greater democratic involvement. Nevertheless, those who had been closely involved with the old guard succeeded in getting themselves voted back into positions of power and the ridiculous 'presidential' structure of the movement was retained. The majority of the new committee continued to see little involvement for young Asian women or Afro-Caribbean youth within the SYM, and regard it as little more than a drop-in centre for Southall's gangs, who were indeed the very ones who had voted them back.

Nevertheless, the fact that the SYM could potentially develop into a broadly-based youth organisation was demonstrated time and again during the membership drive and subsequent election campaign, when the reform group toured schools and colleges talking to the students. But what also became clear was that it would have to be a SYM totally different in form from the one which presently exists. To understand why such changes were necessary, if unlikely, we have to look at the broader context of Southall's community politics.

The professionalisation of ethnicity

In the last decade, with the growth of central and local government funding for community groups, we have also seen the emergence of professional 'ethnics', as a new intermediary force between Black people and the state. This new élite are far from being 'Uncle Toms'; it is their vociferous claim to represent the militant demands of their community that secures them state patronage, and the fat salaries that go with it. It is no exaggeration to say that nowadays there are two communities in Southall; the first, more visible one, is created and funded by various state agencies and run by 'career militants'; the second, more hidden one, is populated by the ordinary people who live and work in the area. The first community imagines it stands in a symbiotic relation to the second – it is serving 'the people'; in fact, the relationship is largely parasitic. And it is doubled in the two-tier system which operates within the professional ethnic community itself – the upper echelon consists of Ethnic Arts Officers, Community Liaison Officers and the like employed by the local council, the CRE, or (before its dissolution in 1986) the GLC. And then below them there are the Black people who set up local organisations, often with the specific intention of obtaining funding. These two tiers are mutually dependent on each other for their survival. Thus the upper tier can only justify its existence in terms of the existence of 'grass roots organisations', while the latter in turn needs the lobbying power of the 'community bureaucrats' to gain public funding.

As an example of how this system works in practice, take the Community Liaison Officers. Their job is to find out what is going on 'in the community' (that is, community '2'), and to forge links between it and the council or government. But what do CLOs actually do? Do they knock on doors and ask people more or less at random what they think needs to be done? Of course not, that would be most unprofessional! Instead they approach the officially recognised community organisations (that is, tier 2 of the community '1') for information about the 'grass roots', and they in turn supply an account based on their own need for further funding. On receiving CLOs reports, the CRE or whoever may indeed release additional grant aid under the illusion that they are thereby strengthening the 'Black community', but, in fact, the ultimate effect is to increase divisiveness and dependency within it.

Not all community organisations rise to the state bait. A few years ago there were fewer community organisations in Southall and the majority of them were self-sufficient. With the influx of state funding the autonomy of these organisations has declined as they have grown in numbers and resources; the history of the Indian Workers' Association (IWA) is an interesting, if sad, illustration of this development.

The IWA emerged from the real grass roots; it gained support and grew because it provided some kind of voice for the voiceless. More than that, it had a definite social function; it bought the Dominion Cinema in Southall to show Indian films, and to serve as a general cultural centre. Membership of the IWA also bought reduced admission to the pictures! The Gurdwara, Mosque and Madir work along similar lines: they are independent and self-organised, they hold regular elections and their governing committees are both representative of the membership and control substantial funds. In the early years both the IWA and the Temple were self-sufficient, but while the Temple has remained self-sufficient, the IWA soon began to depend ever more heavily on outside funding – for example, from the CRE, as its support within the community has waned. The main reason for this is that the Dominion Cinema has been allowed to run down, and that successive leaderships of the IWA lost credibility with the community – it became a local standing joke that anyone who had been head of the IWA could afford to go and open a shop with the profits!

Until very recently the IWA leadership still formed part of the 'old guard'; it was they who fought to give some kind of organisational coherence to community politics in Southall. Unfortunately, they also succeeded in opening the back door to forms of state sponsorship which destroyed the very principles of autonomous organisation for which they formerly stood. Today the fruit of their pioneering work has been harvested by others – by a 'new guard'. You can find them almost on every corner, doing research, offering advice, writing pamphlets, and whereas their predecessors where for the most part factory workers or small businessmen, this new guard tend to be university graduates or students. It is not yet obligatory to have a degree to speak on the community's behalf, but what is essential is to have a mastery over the jargon of 'professional ethnicity', including the rhetoric of militancy, in order to maintain credibility with the White establishment. The old guard quite lacked these 'skills' and this largely accounts for their demise.

A way forward?

One of the worst aspects of ethnic professionalisation is the bare-fisted competitiveness it has induced amongst local organisations. The grants that are ostensibly intended to strengthen local communities are decisively weakening their organisational structures. The problem is exacerbated by the lack of common goals or consciousness to be found amongst Asian people themselves, for the social and historical reasons I have already discussed. Genuine community-based initiatives are thus very hard to get off the ground; ordinary people in Southall are justifiably suspicious: 'They're only in it for the money' is now a frequent refrain, and this cynicism and disillusionment is in itself a devisive influence.

Is there an antidote? Certainly in places like Southall, young people have a common experience – the deepening of racism in all its forms, economic, cultural and political. And we share the same material conditions: we all go to the same schools, the same temples and increasingly end up with the same training schemes outside. None of us have ever lived more than a few streets away from each other and the basis for a common strategy and common action undoubtedly exists. From my own experience I know that this potential is there, but if it is to be realised then we have to learn the bitter lessons of the past and build new types of organisation; this involves a return to the principle of economic self-sufficiency, financing activities entirely out of membership subscriptions; it means a democratically elected leadership rather than a paid staff to conduct day-to-day affairs; there is a need to broaden the scope of our appeal to embrace all sections of youth, girls as well as boys, Afro-Caribbeans as well as Asians. It can be done, if we can get the phoney militants and 'ethnic professionals' off our backs, if we can forget their rhetoric and learn instead to work *with* our community rather than *for* it, and if we can develop internal networks of communication to displace the external system of 'liaison' which the state has insinuated between us. It's all a big 'if' with a whole lot of 'buts'. But the alternative is to go on deceiving ourselves and almost anything is better than that.

7

No Heat Loss

Ansel Wong in interview with Bob Catterall

BC: Bob Catterall; AW: Ansel Wong.

BC: How would the topic of racism come up in your youth club?

AW: It comes up usually in a kind of enquiry – 'What do you do if such and such happens?' or 'Why have you got all these posters on the wall about black people? Are you against white people?' – which you know is a fishing enquiry. Then it's up to us as workers to begin to build on that and to develop the confidence and the relationships, so that the actual concerns come out. This face-to-face situation works quite well and is the bedrock of all the youth work.

It comes down to issues as to how things develop. One of the features of the work for example, was that we would have a regular notice board of press clippings and other publications featuring major events – the 1976 Carnival or after the uprisings in 1981, representing the range of newspapers from *Newsline* to the *Daily Telegraph*. They would be there on the wall with no kind of comment. It was simply to have attention drawn to them. The members would see it, read it, have a good joke, but then as they began to sit around and talk, that is where we would conveniently place ourselves somewhere on the fringes of the group and begin to intervene and participate in the conversation and discussion; as a result of that kind of action you would get a lot of issues being raised about the nature of racism in the society; and that's one way we began to deal with the issue of race.

244

It was not very structured. We tried structured discussion groups or sessions, where we would get speakers from outside and invite the young people to participate but invariably it didn't really work because they either never turned up or were passive participants. We found that the best thing is to respond to the situation as it happens there and then.

BC: How much trouble did you take with the wall displays?

AW: We had to get all the newspapers, as many of the magazines and community papers as possible and make them freely and casually available. For example, we subscribed to the *Latin American Newsletters*, and much of the information had then to be extracted and presented in both visual and literary forms that were easily comprehensible and relevant to the young. They were then put up on the wall so that people could actually get what they wanted out of it – it was a question of just having these things around all the time and people just dipping into them as and when they wanted, and then asking questions of us to clarify points and seek further information. That was good and again that came back to the question of being able to respond and to be flexible and really on the ball in relation to all the information that you have.

BC: How did you relate that to issues within the club itself?

AW: We didn't shield them from reality. They participated in all fund-raising efforts. They would see the letters that we were writing to local authorities and to funding agencies. We would take them along with us to meetings with these funding agencies so they could see how we are negotiating with the state, the problems we experience; so that when they criticise us for what they see as our indecision or our not responding quickly enough to their demands, they understand the obstacle of institutional racism, and that has been a very important lesson.

Also I think they need to develop an understanding of the way money goes very quickly. So when we obtain grant aid for equipment we involve them in the shopping for and buying of that equipment. They begin to understand that this was not a question of community 'ponces' living off their misfortune and syphoning off the money. It's a question of the money not being enough and of inflation making things worse. Invariably this prompted heated discussion on why this was so and I think that this experience is very important for them as it enables them to understand how the economic system operates.

BC: What kind of proportion of the youth are you talking about that actually were getting involved, rather than just consuming you as a nice youth refuge?

AW: Unfortunately, we got a kind of élitist reputation, where we were expected to work and get young people involved in productive pursuits and maintain a high standard of cleanliness and behaviour. There were some young people who were quite prepared just to come and see a film show and then disappear or just come and not be involved in the management, the cleaning, the structuring, the redecorating of the Centre, or in any forms of participating or understanding.

Looking back we find that there was a difference between boys and girls in levels of participation. So you would find the overwhelming majority of the girls were incredibly keen, and understood the structural and institutional forms of racism and the state, and therefore participated to a greater degree in our liaison with the authorities. The boys tended to be involved more in the physical running of the centre, the redecoration, and so on. Whether that was due to staff influence in terms of our own stereotypes of gender roles is open to debate, but that was one facet, and therefore you would find, because the centre anyhow had a bias towards women, 90 per cent of our clients were female.

BC: How many of your staff were female?

AW: The great majority were female as well – it's now 100 per cent. I think that certainly developed because we were predominantly responding to the needs of girls, and trying to redress the traditional balance. It was easier in a way to get the girls to participate. They were certainly quicker to grasp the realities of the situation, and thus they became very politicised and interested in actually making the system accountable, and in some instances were very positive in moving forward, more than staff, who were perhaps a little more hesitant.

BC: Could you give us some examples of where you think you've succeeded or failed in your work?

AW: I think the most singular failure we had was in dealing effectively with some of the youths on the fringes of the Rastafarian Movement. I think perhaps this may have been due to some very entrenched ideas held by members of staff on the political pedigree of Selassie and what he did in Ethiopia, and therefore they couldn't see eye to eye with young people prepared to venerate him. But you had to submerge a lot of those attitudes and feelings and respond to what was obviously happening within the community. Failure to do so sometimes degenerated into a direct confrontation, and I think that was not necessarily helpful, purely because many of the young Rastas saw the club as just providing resources and responding to their needs, and were therefore not putting anything into it. That posed a problem, even though we made conscious efforts to make the place available to groups. But unfortunately it was only to organised groups, so that the Ethiopian Orthodox Church, which some of the Rastas were affiliated to, had an opportunity to hold classes and to worship at the centre. As did Rasta International, which established Amhari classes. But these were organised things and we were able to get on better on that basis, an organised basis, where positive things were happening. What we were unable to respond effectively to was the 'roots man', the street man, who came in and was drifting and not affiliated to any organisations, but just had an allegiance to the idea of Rasta and was therefore not subjected to its discipline. I think we failed in developing an understanding of their particular position or in working with them to achieve their ambitions and aims, or to make them aware and conscious of some of the harsh political realities of their situation. So that was a singular failure.

BC: It sounds as though you are writing these young people off, or that's how some people would see it.

AW: No, not writing-off but defining them in terms of their life-style, in terms of their ambitions and allegiances to the society, their resistance to organised forms of struggle, their independent status; which is perhaps characteristic of their lumpen proletarian formation. And therefore our failure may have been due to the fact that we were probably trying to bring them back within an institutional form of struggle, which may not be the right thing. What they are probably doing and their forms of resistence, whether its an individual thing or not, may also be valuable, and what we were trying to do perhaps was wrong. But at the time we were seeking this elusive goal of responding to the community and bringing about some sort of consciousness and unity. That's the kind of Utopian goal most political activists think about. And we failed with that particular group, though within that failure there were opportunities for very interesting discussions and debates, however heated and however open-ended, sometimes ending in physical conflict.

BC: Can I ask you two more questions about this failure? What does this word 'lumpen' carry that's useful? And secondly, do you see anyone actually succeeding with that group?

AW: How do I see the concept of a lumpen proletariat? I think people have to accept that term for want of a different definition or a better definition for the wageless or the ones who are on the very fringes of the Black community, which itself is on the fringes of society. I think work with this group of people is important and can succeed and no doubt there will be instances of good practice around the country.

We were trying to work on particular issues in terms of fighting racism, in terms of developing consciousness and fighting sexist behaviour within the Black community. Those were target areas and therefore all our work centred around those three issues. If we had had more freedom and flexibility we might have succeeded better with the young Rastas, but our work with them was necessarily constrained by these three targets.

Certainly I would agree that Rasta is one aspect of resistance. So that the jerry curl individual or the individual who fries his or her head and boogies down to funk, whether its a funk to Jesus or funk to some notion of love, is making an assertion of his or her own identity and resistance to a lot in this society, in the same way as a Rasta who toasts with General and Clint Eastwood and has no truck with this society. So yes, in an overview of the Black community and its relationship to the state there are notions of resistance and non-incorporation, and therefore the Rasta, as other groups within the Black community, can basically be seen as a manifestation of that resistance. The independent Black churches are a similar movement. The increasing involvement of Black young people in Black British gospel is, in a sense, a kind of religious salvation from the prejudices of the established churches in this country. I certainly see Rasta as a manifestation of that resistance, but because of the anger and the intensity of their struggle it is often very difficult for youth workers to cope; because, quite rightly, Rastas have a general distrust of the state and of Black people working for the state. Youth and community workers are, whether we like it or not, gatekeepers offering social control and a baby-minding service. There will be resistance and I think it's for us to harness that resistance and develop both a caring relationship and confidence, but that will take a lot of years, a lot of time.

BC: Let's talk about one of the successes.

AW: There is a group of girls we began to work with in our local school. They were identified, this was the unfortunate case, already by the school as ones who were causing problems. We may not have necessarily agreed with that definition or that selection procedure, but nevertheless we had been given access to the school, working with this group of girls who were on the borderline of disruption, who teachers defined as being very difficult to manage. We would work with them, both in the school and at the Centre. I think we were successful in so far as we were able to open up opportunities for these young people to understand themselves as women, to find avenues for their creative energies. For example, the school was amazed at the fact that under our guidance and support this group of girls were able to develop a dramatic improvisation around some of the themes that were obviously of direct relevance to them – relationships to parents, the house and the school. This was very successful and was performed at the Centre. People were so impressed that the school asked for it to be put on as part of their programme. And these were girls who were constantly being thrown out of classes, including drama classes and dance classes, and were seen as unable to produce anything worthwhile.

Not only that, we found that by working with them we were able to get them to bring some insights into some of the curriculum changes that were happening at the school and to begin to question teachers. One remembers particularly the study of Dickens which they had taken no interest in at all; they couldn't find any relevance in Dickens to their experience in this country until we started talking to them about Victorian England and trying to demonstrate a Black aspect of Victorian England. We introduced them to a number of books, illustrations and some characters that populated the streets of London, which generated a new interest in Dickens and a new interest in social studies and social geography and they began to question and pressurise the teachers about why they weren't talking about this and why they had to get this information from a community centre.

This posed problems for the school because immediately the school saw us as being subversive, and therefore anti-teacher, and encouraging anti-social behaviour among the girls. I think it took some time to convince the school that we weren't seeking to do that, and that we were seeking to make the girls aware of some of the failures of the school and some teachers, both in terms of curriculum and methodology and the young people certainly appreciated that and began to read a lot. For example, we got down into Nigel File and Chris Powers *Black Settlers in Britain*. These were things they would not have touched before and they started to get involved by looking at a lot of those historical documents. They really enjoyed that and the school finally came round to the fact that 'yes, this could be done' and we offered our services to work with the school in developing responses. At least, providing a reading list for the teachers, which was one positive response, because the teacher was not aware herself of these things.

BC: How important for youth is reading Dickens?

AW: How we read Dickens brought a greater awareness and breadth of understanding of forms of domination in society and a Black perspective on this was very relevant because it's a question of motivation. How do you motivate young people to get into the rigours of learning and reading? That was one way of making it directly relevant to their experiences and also at the same time making them aware of the continuity of race in this country, that it's not a post-1945 phenomenon – as they are taught at school – we are looking at a long presence. I think that was important, certainly an eye-opener to them. They began to understand clearly that it is not a question of *culture* and people being ignorant about different cultures. It's a question of *how the society is structured* and how it has developed over the years; under the profit from and exploitation of the Third World.

It started developing from there and these questions began to be asked, and we had to respond. We had to also have that information ourselves, which meant the staff had to come together and think about it, and to think about how we could get across that ideological position without alienating people; so we had to clear our heads as well, our own positions. So it not only helped young people but it also helped the staff to clarify a lot of points in their own minds, and perhaps, I don't know, encouraged staff themselves to take a radical position.

BC: What political perspective and orientation are they going to need to make this not just a kind of liberal exercise in self enhancement?

AW: I think that the enhancement is important in so far as it's linked up to the question of developing a consciousness of their own position in relation to the state, in relation to other people, in relation to how power is exercised. You begin to understand that enhancement has to occur within the context of making people aware of where they stand, who exercises the power, how it affects them, the prejudice and discrimination that's brought to bear on the matter, and what kind of strategies are necessary to combat that power. You cannot talk about the historical presence of Black people in this country without looking at the forms of struggle and resistance that presence has generated, both within the community and outside the community. The forms of struggle and an analysis and assessment of that struggle, its success and failures, are important prerequisites so that one learns from that experience. So even though one talks in liberal terms of identity and developing positive notions of self, inherent in that is an evaluation of a lot of what went on.

So one is talking about developing a clarity of vision to enable a full overview of the situation and informed choices to happen. That informed choice, as far as we are concerned, has to be taken within a political context, because the presence of Black people in this country is political. The whole crisis of this society is seen through the lens of race, and therefore we are central to a lot of the understanding of the society. All youth work and community work has to be predicated on that basic assumption: that we are involved in struggle. Our presence has precipitated that struggle, has highlighted the contradictions in the society and therefore whatever we do will either enhance that struggle, further it or deny the progression of that struggle. So that is the context in which one talks about any kind of work.

I don't see youth work as just providing leisure opportunities, for table tennis and dominoes and a regular diet of reggae, because that doesn't do anything, either from the liberal position of reflecting identity and positive enhancement, or from the position of engaging in struggle. That is just baby-minding, it's cooling people off. I don't think we are in the position of cooling people off. If anything we want to be able to direct the heat in a particular way, and the most effective way, so that there is no heat loss.

8

Oi for England

Trevor Griffiths in interview with Karim Alrawi and
Harwant S. Bains

HB: Harwant Bains; TG: Trevor Griffiths; KA: Karim Alrawi.
HB: What led you to decide to write the play?
TG: I was asked by the Leeds branch of the NUT [National
Union of Teachers] to chair a meeting about racism in
education. The meeting was attended by about 140 people,
including members of the Anti-Nazi League. It quickly
became clear from what was being said that yet another
wave of Fascist recruitment was underway. What shocked
me was the way the National Front and British Movement
at this time were recruiting so successfully amongst kids in
schools, especially third- and fourth-year pupils. So when I
left the meeting I started thinking about ways of fighting
racism through the medium of a play about young people.
I started to do some research. I went round a number of
schools in Leeds, Manchester and Salford and had some
fairly intensive discussions with the pupils. Now, originally
I was going to set the play in a fifth-year detention class,
because I wanted to say something about schools as prisons.
But then things started happening on the streets, so I
reconceived the play as centring on a skinhead gang and
their relation to racialism. I originally wrote 'Oi for England'
for television, because I thought it was important to reach
a large popular audience. That production actually ran into
a lot of problems with the IBA [Independent Broadcasting
Authority], who objected to its language, and so on. They
were more concerned that people would be shocked by a

253

few swear words than by the real obscenity of racism itself. In fact, it was the politics of the play they were really opposed to – the connections it tried to make between rising unemployment and the growth of racism.

HB: What was the general response to the play?

TG: It was generally quite favourable. About 5 million people did actually get to see it. And a lot of young people liked it. That was what gave us the idea of mounting some small-scale touring productions, to transfer the play into live performances in youth clubs, community centres, and so on. It's been seen by quite large numbers of skinheads, and by the NF and BM too! The tours have been very hard, but there has been a great deal of yield at those interfaces. The whole way in which young people see the play, not as a play, but as an actual event, is very interesting. They don't give a conventional theatrical reading to the piece. I mean, they sit in their youth club maybe five feet away from one of the actors; and if he's got no lines for a little while, they'll start talking to him, 'Hey, where you from? Are you from Brixton, one of the Brixton skins?' and things like that. All sorts of strange constructions were put on what the actors were doing. One popular theory was that the actors *were* actual skinheads – 'they seen the play on TV, so they're going around doing it themselves as a way of getting on'.

The reaction of skinhead audiences generally was that the play knew quite a bit about their culture, and they respected it for that. But at the same time they thought the play was deeply wrong-headed in its central political message of 'Black and White, unite and fight'. Yet the significant thing for me was the way that, given the respect, and given the space, White skins were eager to engage with the play, and to talk about their experiences very concretely. After the performance, the actors and director would stay behind and hold a formal or informal discussion with the audience. That was a central feature of the whole exercise.

HB: One of the main objections that has been made to the play, for example by some Labour councillors who tried to ban it, was that its effect is to reinforce skinheads' image of themselves. One of them called it an 'anthem for skinheads'.

Now by your own account, the play does seem to have reinforced split perceptions. It allows skinheads to identify with it in so far as it functions as powerful representation of their culture, and then to dissociate themselves from the politics of the play in so far as this puts their racism in question. Doesn't that rather undermine the object of the whole exercise?

TG: What they find accurate about this play is that 'skins' are not stereotyped as they are in the media, or totally identified with racism, as they are often portrayed by the Left. The skinheads in the play are quite differentiated, from 'Napper' who is on the verge of psychosis, to 'Landree' who is a quietist, 'Swells' who is a hard nut, and 'Finn' who is on the verge of left politicisation. They recognise these identities within the 'skin' community. As for the effect of the play as a piece of cultural politics, it is very difficult to measure, isn't it? I've been on all three tours, and I've watched the audience response, both during the performance and in the discussion afterwards, and I've come to certain conclusions. One is that any text is open to a number of possible readings. However, in order to construct a reading of 'Oi for England' which underwrites a racist position you would have to ignore what the play is saying. When the play is actually working, charging its meaning across the stage, it does seem to give White racist kids a lot of food for thought. It challenges the rather crude preconceptions they have about Britain, and what it means to be 'British', for example. Now, in a way, I do not have any control over what goes on in the audiences' mind. All you can do is to try and initiate the beginning of a doubt.

KA: The question is, though, doubts about what. The thing that worried me about the play, as indeed the whole ANL [Anti-Nazi League] position was the simple equation of racism with Fascism. Now I can understand why tactically, at the time, this may have been useful. But it does seem to me to limit the play's relevance. The roots of racism in working-class culture run considerably deeper than the NF or BM, and are spread far wider than skinheads. Yet the play never really tried to tackle these issues.

TG: OK, let me talk a bit about the role of the Fascist character in the play. It's been criticised by some people on the Left for being so explicit, so powerful, that it swamps the anti-racist position articulated by 'Finn'. The charge is that I have given the devil all the best tunes! But how, in fact, is the Fascist construed by the other characters? He is consistently referred to as 'a nutter'. They don't say he's in the BM or the NF, they say he's a nutter. In other words, Fascism is defined as a particular kind of social behaviour that goes beyond what is considered sane in their culture. We never had cheering in a youth club for the racists speech. I think that's worth stressing – the *absence* of certain responses. The kids do *not* identify with the Fascism – though they *may* do with 'Napper', the 'skin' who hits an Asian and robs him. So here a distinction is made possible, but the connections are also explored. When the Fascist has gone, Napper attacks him, but in the course of this he says, 'I don't know where he's coming from, I don't know where he's at. I'm English and proud of it. If he's a Nazi, so am I.' At the same time, I decided to strengthen the position of 'Finn' and hence the anti-racist message itself. So I wrote 'Finn's song', which is more spoken than sung and which is done on his own at the end of the play. That should leave no doubt in anyone's mind where the play stands.

KA: I am much more concerned with the relation of racism to Thatcherism. I think Thatcherism is much more dangerous in so far as it makes racism respectable, especially in its more institutionalised forms, in a way that has made the NF and BM increasingly redundant. I know you can't do everything in a play, but there was nothing referencing these wider political contexts, the Immigration Acts, the Nationalities Bill, and so on. The play focused on the hermetic universe of these skinheads in a way which I think would enable many people to dismiss the issue of racism as marginal, or as something confined to this 'deviant minority'.

TG: My strategy in this play was to expose and then exploit the contradictions of a White working-class youth culture. The fact is that 'skins' hate police; they hate schools; they hate the state, because in some deep sense they see it as the arm of an alien power. They see that power in terms of race, not class, of course, but this is because the only ideology they have contact with in any developed way is the ideology of the NF. There is, broadly speaking, no counter-education system. The education system is led by nervous liberals, who increasingly have their backs to the wall. I do not think that much can be expected from them in terms of anti-racist initiatives. They would rather not open up that particular can of worms. Nevertheless, I think it is essential to expose the institutionalised racism in our education system, which stands so openly in contradiction with the official rhetoric of 'equality of opportunity'. My play was not about this aspect of the problem. But it can, and is, being used in some schools, by teachers who are struggling to confront directly the kind of racism that surfaces in the playground.

KA: Well, as we are talking about contradictions, I was rather surprised and disappointed that you did not make anything of the one central contradiction in skinhead culture which can be directly exposed – their fascination with Ska and Reggae, with Black music. I feel if the play had been more focused on that area, it might have been more effective in terms of the kind of nebulous cultural outcomes we've been talking about.

TG: Well, it was there, but it wasn't very foregrounded, I agree. Maybe it should have been. But let's look for a minute at what I sense is behind a lot of what has been said – a kind of disillusionment with cultural interventions of any kind, because if they are crude propaganda, then they are dismissed as just that, while if they are constructed in more open and subtle ways, then they are open to mis-, or at least multiple, interpretations. Now I think that view is really a counsel of despair. It is certainly true that if an audience's perceptions of 'Oi for England' have already been inflexibly shaped by racist discourse, then the most the play can hope to do is to present some of the ugly implications of that viewpoint. But you don't undermine a closed discourse like racism by opposing to it another, equally closed, discourse. What a writer can do is offer a preferred reading based on certain terms of engagement with what still remains open in the culture itself.

HB: Well, we do certainly have to recognise what kinds of

intervention are most effective in what situations! As far as the kind of young people you say 'Oi for England' is primarily addressed to, we have to consider what is specific about their form of racism and how it can best be combated. For example, the White 'skins' I come across seem to choose Asians to attack because they regard them as 'soft targets', in much the same way as in other context they went 'queer bashing' or 'mod bashing'. The majority of them don't have any worked-out racialist philosophy; quite the contrary. If you ask them why they do it, they say 'for a laugh' or 'for something to do'. They don't go 'Paki bashing' to make an ideological point; they don't build up a theory about racism, nor do they idealise their own practices. So challenging this kind of racism at an intellectual level, through a dramatic argument, is not going to be very effective, however much you try and sugar the pill with popular music and cultural idioms. Indeed, as you yourself point out, it seems all too likely that skinheads watching the play will be receptive precisely to its music and language in so far as it mirrors their culture, and ignore completely the argument you have tried to embed in these idioms, simply because their racism does not work at this level, and does not require arguments to justify itself. So my question is, can the practical ideologies of street racism be effectively challenged at this level? For example, if, after seeing your play, a skinhead comes up to you and says 'OK Trev, give me one good reason why I shouldn't be racist', what would you, or indeed the play, answer?

TG: I would say because it's irrational, and, ultimately, it's self-defeating. I'd argue, and I think the play argues, that unless we can build a society in which people can become fully human, then we might as well all pack it in.

HB: Well, of course, we'd all like to live in a society in which everyone was 'nice' to one another, but unfortunately the real world is not like that. Nor does reason exist in the form that you are appealing to. If only the rational and the real were same, but that is just a philosopher's daydream! You can't build an effective anti-racist practice, even and especially in the field of cultural politics, around philosopher's daydreams, or the kind of sentimental humanism you are invoking. Racism has its own, all too powerful reasons, unfortunately. It is the rationality of violence. I think it is very significant that it was only when Asian youth began to defend themselves, and fought back, that skinheads began to revise their perceptions of us and at least began to think twice before attacking our community. However, 'Oi for England' seems to me to rest on the liberal premise that it is still possible to appeal to a sense of 'common decencies' and to say to racists, 'Come on chaps, let's be reasonable about this'. Now apart from anything else, that is to appeal to a limited and highly specific form of rationality, which historically has been the preserve of White intellectual élites in Western society.

TG: I don't think the play puts across its message in that way at all. If it did, the kids would have walked out or worse. But it doesn't seem to me to be necessarily 'liberal' to try and get skinheads to stop and think *first*, before they go out 'Paki bashing', about what alternative ways of thinking and acting might be possible and open to them, which are still consistent with their sense of collective identity. Then if they leave the play and go out and attack a Black kid (something which, incidentally, has never happened while the play has been on tour), and if they get beaten up as a result, then they will have even more food for thought! I don't think the two strategies are incompatible. Rather they should complement each other. There are a number of other points I'd like to make in answer to what you've been saying: the first is, that the play's message is definitely not that skinheads are racists, and that is the problem. The problem is White society, and more specifically the society that is post-Imperial Britain. The whole society is saturated with racism, at every level. One reason for first doing the play on television was to address the problem to a nationwide audience rather than just to young people. In centring the play in certain locations within White youth culture, and exploring those contradictions, I wanted to argue that skinheads, and Paki bashing represented just a rather more extreme version of a much more general, everyday level of racist exchange, which you can see going on all over the place. So the play does attempt to locate the issue of racism more broadly than just skinheads. The second point I want to make is related to the first. At the point of production of racist violence, on the street, where these young people are located, there is a massive silence about what is going on. The fact is the press and the media generally say absolutely nothing about the countless beatings, muggings and slurrings of Black people that go on, day in, day out. All that goes unreported. That is the can of worms no one wants to open up. Because once you do, the whole liberal consensus of the race relations industry falls apart. So if a play can in some way break open the bloody official secret of street racism, then it seems to me to be worthwhile to do.

Notes on the Contributors

Karim Alrawi is a playwright who has worked extensively in community theatre. He has been writer in residence at the Theatre Royal, Stratford E15, and his play *Migrations* won him the Most Promising Playwright Award from Capital Radio.

Harwant S. Bains is a playwright and freelance writer. Southall is where he grew up, went to school and still lives. He was actively involved in the youth politics of the community, and a play, *Fighting Tight*, based on these experiences was produced recently at the Theatre Royal, Stratford E15.

Bob Catterall is Tutor in Community Resources in Education at the Centre for Urban Education Studies, and the author of *Making Sense of Cities*.

Philip Cohen is a Research Fellow at the Institute of Education in London, where he currently directs the PSEC/CME Cultural Studies project. He has written widely on various aspects of the youth question including studies of youth culture and labour, police/community relations, vocationalism, and school transitions. He is the author (with D. Robins) of *Knuckle Sandwich*.

Paul Gilroy is the author of *There Ain't No Black in the Union Jack* and a contributor to *The Empire Strikes Back*. He also writes widely in the musical press on Black culture.

Trevor Griffiths is a playwright whose plays include *The Comedians*, *Country* and *Oi for England*. He has been actively involved in left cultural politics for the past decade.

Errol Lawrence directs the Race and Housing Research Unit at the Runnymede Trust. He was a contributor to *The Empire Strikes Back*.

Tuku Mukherjee is Senior Lecturer at Southland College, London. He has developed racism awareness courses as part of in-service training in a wide variety of institutional contexts.

Pratibha Parmar is a freelance writer and works for Sheeba Publishing. Before that she was a youth worker with the Camden Girls Project, She writes on race and gender, and edited an issue of *Feminist Review* on this theme.

John Solomos is a Lecturer in Politics at Birkbeck College, London, and before that was a member of the ESRC Research Unit on Ethnic Relations at the University of Aston, Birmingham. He has researched the development of official ideologies and policies towards Black youth, and published papers on theories of race, class and the state. He edited a book entitled *Migrant Workers in Metropolitan Cities*, was a contributor to *The Empire Strikes Back* and has recently published *Racism, Black Youth and the State*.

Ansel Wong is Principal Race Equality Adviser to the London Strategic Policy Unit, and was previously Senior Race Relations Adviser to the GLC. He established a community education centre in Paddington and pioneered one of the first Black supplementary schools in Britain.